The Upper Room

Disciplines
1998

The Upper Room
Disciplines
1998

UPPER
ROOM BOOKS
NASHVILLE

The Upper Room Disciplines 1998
© 1997 by The Upper Room. All rights reserved.

No part of this book may be used or reproduced in any manner whatsoever without permission except in the case of brief quotations embodied in critical articles or reviews. For information, write: Upper Room Books, P.O. Box 189, Nashville, TN 37202-0189.

The Upper Room Web site: http://www.upperroom.org

Cover photo © Byron Jorjorian
Cover design: Jim Bateman
Interior design and layout: Nancy Cole

Revised Common Lectionary copyright © 1992 by the Consultation on Common Texts (CCT). Used with permission.

ISBN: 0-8358-0811-4
Printed in the United States of America

CONTENTS

A Prayer of Beginning 11
Jan L. Richardson

January 1–4 13
The Fullness of the Word
Cindy and David Schnasa Jacobsen

January 5–11 17
A New Year—A Renewal of Faith
Calvin D. McConnell

January 12–18 24
Healing Our Hearts
Marilyn Brown Oden

January 19–25 31
The Word That Gives Life
Jin Hee Han

January 26—February 1 38
Growing Up in Faith
Cathy Barker

February 2–8 45
When God Comes to Us!
N. Sue Van Sant Palmer

February 9–15 52
Resurrection Hope
Joyce Hollyday

February 16–22 59
Transformed by Faith
H. A. Harrington

February 23—March 1 66
The Habits of Spiritual Living
Wayne E. Oates

March 2–8 73
Trust and Obey
Mariellen Sawada

March 9–15 80
Praise God! All the Time
James R. King, Jr.

March 16–22 87
God Restores Us to Wholeness and Joy
Elaine Eberhart

March 23–29 94
Rivers in the Desert
Anne Horton

March 30—April 5 101
God Does Not Want Suffering
Carolyn Stahl Bohler

April 6–12 108
For Christ's Sake
Jan L. Richardson

April 13–19 115
The Law of Love, the Rule of Fear
Jeff Blum

April 20–26 122
Sing of God's Greatness!
Nancy Otto Boffo

April 27—May 3 129
Moving through Crises
Stephen Martyn

May 4–10 136
Tending to the Holy
Amelia Chua

May 11–17 143
God's Blessings
Janice L. Frederick-Watts

May 18–24 150
Remembering the Greatness of God
Jaydee R. Hanson

May 25–31 157
Incarnating the Spirit
Walter Wink

June 1–7 164
God's Gifts to God's People
Carol A. Wehrheim

June 8–14 171
In Relationship with God
Mary Lou Wagner

June 15–21 178
Journey toward Wholeness
Martin Thielen

June 22–28 185
Realizing God's Power
Marshall Shelley

June 29—July 5 192
Healing and Wholeness
Charles V. Bryant

July 6–12 199
Are You Listening?
Mel Johnson

July 13–19 206
Holding It All Together
Charles M. (Chuck) Olsen

July 20–26 213
God's Restoring and Abiding Love
Roela Victoria Rivera

July 27—August 2 220
Homecomings
Susan K. Wendorf

August 3–9 227
Inward and Outward Religion
Ted Campbell

August 10–16 234
To Belong to God
Norvene Vest

August 17–23 241
The Unshakable Love
Soomee Kim

August 24–30 248
Do Remember Me
James W. Kemp

August 31—September 6 255
To Whom Do You Belong?
Rebecca W. Waldrop

September 7–13 262
Lost and Found
John Indermark

September 14–20 271
When We Pray
Herbert Brokering

September 21–27 278
Dynamic Faith for Our Time
Afrie Songco Joye

September 28—October 4 285
Accountability
Woodie White

October 5–11 292
At Home with God
Aida Luz Beltrán-Gaetán

October 12–18 299
Restoring Spiritual Passion
Kathleen Stephens

October 19–25 306
Encounter with God
Timothy Jones

October 26—November 1 313
The Eternal Why
Martin E. Marty

November 2–8 320
What Does the Future Hold?
John O. Gooch

November 9–15 327
Encouragement on the Way
Ben Campbell Johnson

November 16–22 334
Christ the King
Reginald Johnson

November 23–29 341
Learning War No More
Robert Reddig

November 30—December 6 348
God's Covenant People
David M. Griebner

December 7–13 355
The Desert Shall Blossom
Ray Buckley

December 14–20 362
A Savior for You
Andy Langford

December 21–27 369
Do Not Be Afraid!
J. Philip Wogaman

December 28–31 376
All That Glitters May Not Be Gold
George Hovaness Donigian

The Revised Common Lectionary 381

A Prayer for Ending 385
Jan L. Richardson

A Prayer of Beginning

Maker of the universe, fashioner of the stars,
who dwells within time and beyond time, hear this prayer:

if I have failed to perceive you
when you have appeared
in the face of a friend,
if I have neglected to feed you
when you have come
with the hunger of a stranger,
if I have not embraced you
when you have sought me out of
a sister or brother's poverty,
if I have not laughed and played with you
when you greeted me with the delight of a child,
forgive me

Open my eyes, my hands, my arms, my heart
to know your appearing and to celebrate
the flesh-shaped mystery of Emmanuel,
God with us
Make my heart a dwelling place ready to receive you
in even the bleakest spaces,
to delight at your appearing even as the animals
who made welcome for the birth of wonder.

—Jan L. Richardson

From *Sacred Journeys: A Woman's Book of Daily Prayer* (Nashville, TN: Upper Room Books, 1995). Used by permission.

THE FULLNESS OF THE WORD

January 1–4, 1998   Cindy Schnasa Jacobsen✤
                                                     David Schnasa Jacobsen✤✤

New Year's Day

Thursday, January 1   Read Revelation 21:1-6a.

God's creative word

When we lived in Pierre, South Dakota, we used to visit a terminally ill parishioner during the last year of his life. He was dying of cancer, but he liked to kid about his upcoming funeral. "I guess you'll have the last word," he joked. Just as quickly, the response came back: "No, I won't," one of us said. "God will."

Of course, we usually consider the last word to be the last word in an argument. Not so with God. John's vision in Revelation 21 confirms that God's last word here is not about winning a verbal duel but a promise of God's fullness of presence. God's last word is not so much about *victory over* as it is about *presence with.*

Interestingly, even God's great last word receives blessing. The voice from the throne says in the Greek perfect tense, "It is done." It's as if God took that last word, the promise of presence, and stamped on its side the guarantee of satisfaction. It is done! We can live faithfully—even when God feels absent; God's eschatological promise comes wrapped in its own warranty. So with all the angels and heavenly host, we too can give thanks to God . . . for the last word.

Suggestion for meditation: **Think about how and when you have experienced God's presence or absence in your life. How have those experiences drawn you forward into faithfulness?**

✤Evangelical Lutheran Church in America clergy, pastoral counselor; Ontario, Canada.
✤✤Professor of Homiletics at Waterloo Lutheran Seminary; Ontario, Canada.

Friday, January 2   Read Ephesians 1:3-14.

The first word

"Where was I before I was born?" With such questions, children teach those of us who are parents more than a little humility. Somewhere between the mysteries of temporality and ontology stands every child's favorite philosophical conundrum: "Mommy, Daddy, where was I before I was born?"

The writer of the Letter to the Ephesians answers the query with unrivaled confidence in the form of praise (vv. 3, 14*b*). Therefore, we who have been redeemed in Christ Jesus can both ask the question and revel in its mystery in thanksgiving to God. Isn't it good to know that we are not an afterthought? God never intended that even we Gentiles, who have come late to God's salvation party, be party-crashers. We were on the invitation list all along! Or to switch metaphors: In the great family of God, we are not "accidents." We are, like giggling adopted children, a planned part of the unlikely family of God.

How do we know?—the first Word. From the very beginning God intended Christ to redeem—and Christ intended to redeem us. The spiritual gifts and blessings that shower down upon us in Christ bear witness to the fact. The seal of the Holy Spirit as the pledge of our status in Christ is not only predesigned from the start but our final destination as well: "our inheritance toward redemption." From creation on, God's first Word was, is, and will be Jesus Christ. Therefore we were, are, and always will be a glimmer in God's eye.

Prayer: **God of blessing, in Jesus Christ you have made us your own. Grant that we who have been adopted as your children in Christ may know that we are yours from the foundation of the world to your eternal praise and glory. Amen.**

Saturday, January 3   Read John 1:1-13.

The cosmic word: prologue in heaven

The great German dramatist Goethe begins his most well-known play *Faust* with a prologue in heaven. Why? Faust's temptation cannot be plausibly dramatized unless viewed in light of cosmic powers. Faust's story is never simply his own. It is cosmic in scope.

In John's Gospel, the drama of Christ begins similarly. How does John set the cosmic scene?—"In the beginning...." Just like the great creation drama, the story of Christ the Word unfolds against a cosmic backdrop. Christ here is no mere individual, not just a prophet, not even just another word. Christ is *the* Word who mysteriously was God and was with God (v. 1). Christ is no mere actor in a drama. Christ as Word belongs in creation's first act as both performer and director. The drama of God in Christ does not begin in the middle but in the beginning. That is what makes Christ the cosmic Word—from creation on.

Yet what does this "prologue in heaven" have to do with me and my redemption? Everything! The heavenly prologue reminds us that the God who redeems is the same God who created the world (contra Marcionites past and present!). That means redemption is not a means to escape this world. Hardly. With the prologue in heaven we learn that redemption is but a piece of creation. In truth, our redemption in Christ is none other than a continuation of God's creative act through Christ. That is why John so carefully spotlights creation themes like light and darkness, word and world. Christ is not just God's personal Word but God's cosmic Word of creation and redemption!

Suggestion for meditation: How cosmic is your salvation? How does it include the world God loved so much?

Sunday, January 4   Read John 1:14-18.

The Word becomes flesh

In the English language *flesh* is a substantive, down-to-earth word. If we want to move toward understanding an ethereal idea, we ask someone to "flesh it out." If a recipe calls for a piece of fruit with firm pulp, we prefer to use one that is "fleshy." When someone proves himself or herself to be genuine, we refer to them as a "flesh and blood" person. Flesh is the means by which we gauge things and people as real, substantial, down-to-earth.

Tellingly, John 1:14-18 reveals what we get when we receive the Word in the down-and-dirty life of the flesh: nothing but grace and truth! Of course, many would expect God-in-the-flesh to be full of wrath. (Have you watched some of those TV evangelists lately?) Yet, as John tells us, when God's Word becomes flesh and pitches a tent among us, it is not so much for bringing judgment—the Word becomes flesh only to get close enough to embody mercy and bathe our darkling world in the light of truth.

Does this tendency of God's Word toward fleshiness offer anything of value to us today? Definitely! For one thing, we in the church could take the cue to stop divorcing flesh and faith. Perhaps, instead of fleeing our flesh, we should head where the Word does: toward the table. There we actually share Word become flesh—with a little grace and truth on the side. And who knows? Maybe while we're there—even if only for a moment— we will embody Christ again.

Prayer: **God of incarnate love, in Jesus Christ you came among us in the flesh. Grant us such grace and truth that we might live mercifully and honestly as your people in the world. Amen.**

A NEW YEAR—A RENEWAL OF FAITH

January 5–11, 1998   **Calvin D. McConnell**✤
Monday, January 5   Read Isaiah 43:1-7.

"Fear not!" What a greeting in these opening days of the year. A new year can carry with it vague feelings of anxiety. We've just come through a full and challenging year; we know too much to be lulled into the false assumption that this new one will be a bed of roses. God's declaration to Isaiah is a hopeful one as we face the future this new year brings.

The God who created us, who calls us by name and redeems us, assures us that we do not face the unpredictable vagaries of the unknown without support. Our past life history has showed us that even though some events were difficult we always came through. Before December 31 of this year we will undoubtedly "pass through the waters . . . and through the rivers . . . and walk through fire." The prophet uses figurative language to assure us that God's compassionate concern and love for us will be sufficient for it.

We will not be overwhelmed, burned, or consumed. Why? Because God is *our* God; the Holy one of Israel is *our* Savior. Everyone who is called by the name of this ever-present, always-loving, and all-powerful God will know the companionship of the One who formed us and journeys with us.

Covenant Prayer in the Wesleyan Tradition: **"I am no longer my own, but thine . . . I freely and heartily yield all things to thy pleasure and disposal. . . . thou art mine, and I am thine. So be it. And the covenant which I have made on earth, let it be ratified in heaven." Amen.**

✤Retired bishop of The United Methodist Church, having served in the Portland and Seattle Areas; now living in Lake Oswego, Oregon.

17

Epiphany Day

Tuesday, January 6   Read Isaiah 43:8-13.

Epiphany is the second season in the church year. It extends from January 6 to Ash Wednesday (which opens the season of Lent) and is the traditional date for the magi's arriving in Bethlehem from the East to pay homage to the Christ child. The event signals the acknowledgment of Jesus as a universal savior for all humankind. The day is significant but often neglected. God's proclamation of hope through Isaiah invites those "who are blind, yet have eyes, those who are deaf, yet have ears" to gather and bear witness to the saving grace of God.

These wise magi of a race, culture, and religion other than that of Jesus willingly remodeled their religious perspective. They joined the celebration of the select few who glimpsed in that sacred and transcendent moment the workings of divine love.

Are we as open and ready for this breaking-in of Christ? If we can open windows in our walls of theological belief and stretch our expectations of God's working among us, we too may experience epiphany in ways that God wants and we need. I recall J. Edgar Goodspeed's suggesting years ago that all of us have a few rooms in our lives that need remodeling. That "restructuring" is what God has in mind for those who accompany these global wise ones in their pilgrimage to find the way, the truth, and the life.

As we allow the Savior of all humankind to remodel our beliefs, values, attitudes, and behavior, we join those early seekers from the East in bearing effective witness, honored by God.

Prayer: **"O God, you made of one blood all nations, and by a star in the East, revealed to all people him whose name is Emmanuel. Enable us so to proclaim his unsearchable riches that all may come to his light....Amen." (Laurence Hull Stookey,** *United Methodist Hymnal,* **255).**

Wednesday, January 7   Read Psalm 29.

Is there room in your life for reverence? Is the glory of God a faith-forming presence in your life? The psalmist sees God in all, which allows him to both perceive and express the proper relationship between himself and God. Awe and reverence are an important ingredient in religious experience.

However, we live in times that struggle with reverence or respect for anyone or anything. We question authority, express cynicism about government and law, debunk tradition and custom. We seem to have a need to bring all we know down to a nonthreatening, nonchallenging, and familiar level. The mathematical term *least common denominator* rules the day.

The church suffers from this lack of high regard—as do religious belief, values, and practices. Our concept of God has been eroded as well as our reverential attitude toward the crucified, risen, and redeeming Christ. A young Hollywood actress epitomized our culture as she referred recently to God as "a livin' doll" and Jesus as "my buddy."

This familiarity with the Divine obscures our understanding of our capacity for sin, which our destructive relationships and unhealthy lifestyles reflect. It dilutes the necessity for a Savior who graciously but firmly calls us to the "more excellent way." When we ignore or lose the "glory," we have only ourselves and our self-imposed alienation from the recreating God, the redeeming Christ, and the reassuring Holy Spirit. Our limited capacity to pull ourselves up by our least common denominators offers little of the hope promised to those who love God. A sense of glory impels us to "press on toward the goal for the prize of the heavenly call of God in Christ Jesus" (Phil. 3:14).

Prayer: **Pull us up, O God, to where you are. May some of your divine glory lift us beyond what we see and make life what you desire for us. Amen.**

Thursday, January 8   Read Luke 3:15-17, 21-22.

The Christian year progresses rapidly from Jesus' birth to his baptism. As we approach this sacramental time in Jesus' life, it is good to reflect on God's incarnational intent of salvation through Jesus Christ. Jesus' coming was not accidental or coincidental; it was the deliberate intervention in human affairs of a compassionate God.

Thorsten Renqvist, a Norwegian sculptor, portrays God's intent in a remarkable wood sculpture of the risen Christ. A heavy shadow-box style frame encloses the upper torso and head of Jesus. Jesus' left hand extends toward the observer, palm up in a welcoming gesture. It is the right hand, however, that is startling in its depiction. The arm extends straight out through the frame and beyond with the palm down in a gesture of blessing. The symbolism is vividly compelling. With one hand Christ invites all who are "within the frame" to come to him—the believers, the church.

With the other arm Jesus smashes through the frame that seeks to contain him so as to touch and bless those who are beyond the wall that has been imposed around him. The artist seeks to depict the decisions we make about the proper extension of God's grace. Christ will have nothing to do with exclusionary walls! The sculpture is both a blessing and a challenge to move beyond our limited understandings of grace.

As we approach the occasion of Jesus' baptism, may we remember God's interventionist act on behalf of all humankind and acknowledge with gratitude Jesus' acceptance of his part in this drama of salvation.

Prayer: **"Blessed are you, O God of our Lord Jesus Christ, for you have blessed us in Christ with every spiritual blessing. . . . You have destined us for adoption as your children through Jesus Christ according to the good pleasure of your will and to the praise of your glorious grace that you freely bestowed on us in the Beloved One" (Eph. 1:3-6, adapted). Thank you. Amen.**

Friday, January 9   Read Luke 3:15-18.

One of the well-known paintings of the artist Georgia O'Keefe is "Road Past the View." Set in the mountains of New Mexico, the painting depicts a road that curves from the valley, up into the foothills, and disappears around a bend. The viewer has the distinct impression that it continues on its journey even though it is past our view.

In today's account of the events leading to Jesus' baptism, we might regard the message of John the Baptist as a spiritual downer. His message questions some of the religious practices of his day. The Jewish people awaited the coming of the messiah who would bring good news to the oppressed, bind up the brokenhearted, and proclaim liberty to the captives (Isa. 61:1). John proclaims the near advent of this one so fervently desired. However, some drastic changes would need to be made in religious beliefs and practices before the messianic age could come. Shopping at the same old religious malls would not result in the salvation they sought. John called them to repentance for their sins and invited them to journey on a new "Road Past the View."

Part of our hope as modern-day seekers of God's "yes" in our lives rests in our willingness to respond to that same invitation— an invitation to move beyond our present ways of viewing and doing life and faith, which limit our view of God's desires and promises. John's baptism by water prepared his people for the potential of Christ's saving grace. Today we remember our baptism so that "the Holy Spirit work within [us], that having been born through water and the Spirit, [we] may live as faithful disciples of Jesus Christ" (The Baptismal Covenant IV, *The United Methodist Book of Worship*).

Prayer: **Satisfying as our religious belief and experience may be, O God, encourage us to take those enriching and vision-stretching roads past our present view of faith to the fullness of life in Christ, whose baptism we recall this day. Amen.**

Saturday, January 10   Read Luke 3:21-22.

In the Protestant tradition, a sacrament is a means of grace in which Jesus participated and asked us to do likewise. There are two of them: baptism and the Lord's Supper. Today's scripture reflects on Jesus' baptism, the act that completes John the Baptist's ministry of proclamation and preparation. God confirms it with the words "You are my Son, The Beloved; with you I am well pleased."

For Jesus, baptism was the declaration of the beginning of his salvific ministry on behalf of all humankind for all time. It was his choosing of God's choosing of him for this unique role in God's grace. Possessing both freedom of will and choice, Jesus could have decided not to accept the role God chose for him. Or he could have followed it in part. He might have elected to remain in his hometown of Nazareth, serving as a worthwhile citizen, an honest carpenter, a teacher of the Torah in the synagogue, and a moral and devout Jewish man. He apparently was all of this. Sensing the uniqueness of the touch of God in his life, however, he knew that God expected and needed more from him than this. Through baptism he committed himself to God's need, knowing that "in him every one of God's promises is a 'yes'" (2 Cor. 1:20).

Jesus' baptism encourages us to reflect on our response to God's touch in our lives. The sacrament has two parts: Christ's act of grace for us and our acts of faithfulness because of it. The remembering of our baptism calls us to fulfill our part of the sacrament in committed and effective discipleship. For it is "through him that we say the 'Amen,' to the glory of God" (2 Cor. 1:20). May God find us prepared and willing!

Prayer: **We remember our link with you in the sacrament of baptism, O compassionate, forgiving, and renewing God. May this recollection enable us to fulfill your promises through our grace-prompted discipleship of witness, caring, and serving. Amen.**

22

Sunday, January 11   Read Acts 8:14-17.

John baptized Jesus in the waters of the Jordan River, and the Holy Spirit descended upon him in confirmation and blessing. Jesus' disciples continued these two aspects of water and Spirit in their practice of baptism as the early church developed. Since that time, Christians have come to understand baptism in the Spirit in various ways. Yet whatever our position, clearly the act of baptism is a one-time occurrence, while baptism by the Spirit is a continuing relationship of formation in Christ.

Sometimes the Spirit mentors us through faithful people who guide us in the faith: Peter and John offer support through prayer and the laying on of hands. My Grandmother Taylor was such a mentor for me. Home for the holidays from college, I looked forward to visiting with her. I found her in her favorite rocking chair, reading her Bible. In all my sophomoric worldly wisdom I asked her how many times she had read the complete Bible. "The number is unimportant," she replied. "The important thing is to study it every day." At my insistence she checked a list on the last page and reported she was in her forty-second reading. "What a dull and useless waste of time," I exploded in disbelief. "Oh no," she replied. "Every time I open its pages, stories, persons, and passages greet me as old friends, and new understandings take me on wondrous journeys!" I left hurriedly in embarrassment. A few days later I found her precious Bible under the Christmas tree as her gift to me. Inscribed in it were the words, "To my Grandson: The Word of Life that will make your life what God wants and you need."

Baptism is a once-and-forever thing. It is also a journey of formation and discipleship with and through the Spirit.

Suggestion for meditation: **"As you therefore have received Christ Jesus the Lord, continue to live your lives in him; rooted and built up in him and established in the faith, just as you were taught, abounding in thanksgiving" (Col. 2:6).**

HEALING OUR HEARTS

January 12–18, 1998   **Marilyn Brown Oden**✤
Monday, January 12   Read Isaiah 62:1-2.

Healing our hearts regenerates our whole self. In the Hebrew Scriptures "heart" represents the total person; it is the center of emotions, discernment, devotion, and wisdom.

We pray this week that our hearts might begin to be healed of guilt and grudges, of grief and greed, of guardedness and generational scripts. Centering prayer helps us begin to replace these rhinestones with the precious gems of forgiveness and grace, trust and generosity, courage and maturity.

My friend who is a heart surgeon never begins his task without praying with the patient and the family. Prayer is the first step in healing our hearts. The Mount Sinai monk, John Climacus (seventh century), called prayer the spring of virtues. He described it as an illumination of the mind, a curtain to shut out despair, a victory over depression. He said that through prayer we find peace for our souls and healing for our wounds.

Prayer quiets us in our midnight brokenness, as though we hear ourselves "called by a new name" (Isa. 62:2*b*), a name whispered in the mist of mystery, a name symbolizing our belonging to God. In moments when we are centered in this relationship, as individuals or as congregations, we experience a holy healing that transforms our heartburn into burning hearts, aflame with gratitude.

Suggestion for prayer: **Pray without words, silently centering yourself upon the Holy Healer.**

✤Author of six books; laywoman, First United Methodist Church; Dallas, Texas.

Tuesday, January 13   Read John 2:1-5.

Besides the stark flatness and sparse population, a notable feature of driving through the panhandle of Oklahoma and Texas is that the trees bend toward the ground instead of reaching upward. The strong winds bow the branches. Those trees remind me of how our burdens of guilt bow us. Instead of reaching toward God and trusting God's grace, we trudge along with downcast eyes, as if looking for land mines.

Our guilt, of course, is justified. Mary told the servants at the wedding, "Do whatever he tells you" (v. 5). We, today's servants, don't do that. Our lives flash before us with all those things done that we wish we could erase, and all those things left undone that we wish we could sketch into our yesterdays. But we can't. And sometimes, laden with guilt, our hearts despair.

Even devout Saint Anthony (third century) was attacked by dark thoughts and asked God what he should do in his misery. He received the insight that the solution was a rhythm of work and prayer, work and prayer. He began to practice that rhythm, experiencing reassurance and joy.

The rhythm of prayer and work helps heal our hearts of guilt. We pray for forgiveness, and God wraps us in grace. When we trust the power of that grace, guilt is released. We find ourselves energized by gratitude for God's grace. Our bowed frames straighten, and our eyes lift to the needs around us that match our gifts.

Again and again we fall short; guilt attacks us. But again and again we can renew the disciplined rhythm of work and prayer, not choosing guilt for a partner but dancing with the Spirit, open to God's grace and purpose in our lives.

Suggestion for prayer: **Ask forgiveness of a deed for which it is difficult to forgive yourself and to trust in God's grace.**

Wednesday, January 14   Read Psalm 36:8-10.

Every time we pray the Lord's Prayer, we link our own forgivenness to our forgivingness. Being healed of guilt and being healed of grudges are related.

The Balkans are a prime example of the destructive power of grudges and how divisive leaders can inflame them. My husband Bill and I visited United Methodist refugee centers in Bosnia during the NATO bombing in 1995. We traveled in a jeep on dusty winding mountain roads. Chasms bordered the narrow way. Shelled vehicles lay where they had toppled down the banks.

As we rounded a curve in an area known for hijacking, we saw what we had feared. Before us were camouflaged tanks and armed soldiers. Danger turned to humor when we discovered that they were a lost French troop looking for the war!

In some situations we too dress for combat, unsure where we'll find a war. Hyped by grudges from the past, we venture forth expecting conflict and consciously deciding to perpetuate it. We keep our grudges locked safely in the deposit box of our soul, savoring them and avoiding reconciliation.

The psalmist says of God: "For with you is the fountain of life; in your light we see light." Grudges, justified or not, damage spiritual life. They lead us away from God and toward death and darkness. Ignatius of Antioch (first century) warned that God does not dwell where divisions and bad feelings exist.

When we pray sincerely for one who has harmed us, something changes within us. In time, with continued prayer for that person, our grudge fades. His or her power over our spirit is disarmed. The other may or may not change; but, through prayer, God brings light to our own hearts.

Suggestion for prayer: **Pray genuinely for a person that you have difficulty forgiving.**

Thursday, January 15   Read Psalm 36:5-7.

A six-hour drive separated the emergency-room call from my arrival at the community hospital. My strong mother lay vulnerable between white sheets in the intensive care unit. Tubes ran along the bed like a small brigade sent out to battle death. The monitor screen sketched the mountain range of her unstable condition. Her heartbeat raced like an Olympic runner, and oxygen pumped into her fragile lungs. I sat beside her, covered her hand with mine, and waited.

Grief wounds our hearts: grief from physical and mental change of self or a loved one; grief from separation by death, divorce, the empty nest; grief from loss of job, dream, place; grief from alienation of colleague, friend, kin. Grief slaps us with our lack of ultimate control.

Some heart wounds are like a sudden gash, severing life as it was from life as it will be. Some are more like cancer, slowly eroding our soul. Yet we can put our trust in God's protective care. The psalmist proclaims, "How precious is your steadfast love, O God! All people may take refuge in the shadow of your wings." We are not promised no grief; we are promised refuge. Wounded and weary, we can crawl into the cradle and be rocked in the shadow of God's wings while God's love hovers over us.

However long we must wait and whatever the outcome—whether we ride the turbulent waves of a storm or sink into the depths of our soul—through prayer we can trust God to be with us. We can trust God to give us refuge in the moment, each moment, every moment. We can trust God to light our pathway when we are strong enough to go forth once more, scarred but resurrected. When grief wounds us, faith in the Great Comforter brings healing to our hearts.

Suggestion for prayer: **Pray for the Comforter to wrap you in peace.**

Friday, January 16   Read 1 Corinthians 12:1-11.

Greed is a common sickness of the human heart. Greed is when God gives us manna, and we wail for a banquet. Greed is when we peer carefully around us and measure our share. Greed is when our plate of opportunities is heaped high, and we vie for seconds.

Greed is insatiable. People afflicted with it always feel a need for something else. The more they have, the more they want. Over the centuries, that hasn't changed.

Greed takes many forms. Some of us are greedy for money, some for power, some for honors, some for compliments, some for center stage, some for time alone, some for food, some for clothes, some for knowledge.

Greed uses others, routinely claiming their gifts like a dairy farmer with a human herd. Greed misuses others, guilefully usurping their gifts. Greed uses up others, draining their gifts and then tossing the givers, shriveled, away. Paul says, "To each is given the manifestation of the Spirit for the common good." Our greed eclipses "the common good."

There is a difference between greed and hungering. The word *hunger* brings to mind food and calls forth the image of sitting around a table together. Greed grabs, frowning and hoarding, from others. Hungering reaches out to receive and again to give, smiling, finding joy in sharing with others.

One early church father taught that healing comes through the practice of virtues. Healing our hearts of greed begins with praying for forgiveness for our ingratitude for the manna we have and then rising to practice the discipline of generosity.

Suggestion for meditation: **Contemplate an area of greed that you need to replace with generosity.**

Saturday, January 17   Read John 2:6-11.

The teacher of my six-year-old granddaughter Chelsea presented a lesson on good posture. Expecting to get the answer "skeleton," she asked, "What do we have deep inside of us?"

"Courage," answered Chelsea.

Oftentimes the debris of fear buries courage. We fear that friends, family, or God will forsake us; we fear that we won't get our share of possessions, power, or credit; we fear that we'll lose face, status, or security. We are even afraid we won't dress right or use the right fork. We face life with wariness rather than courage. And our dry bones rattle.

The same is true of congregations. I think of a church once known for being anti-everything. Its leaders guarded resources rather than shared them, guarded the church's narrow vision against change. When pushed to discover the source of their negativity, they realized they feared for their church's future. Their over-againstness was due to fear of dying. But rather than risk opening themselves to the fresh winds of the Spirit, they had built a wall and assigned guards—waiting for Jesus to turn water into wine, without even daring to venture forth to fill the jars with water. And their dry bones rattled.

On guard, our response to a person or group ranges from cool suspicion to heated aggression, which evokes a similar response. Neighbors quit speaking; congregations end up polarized; nations wage war.

The Spirit (*spiritus, pneuma, ruach*—related to breath and the wind) brings life. Breath by breath, life enfleshes our dry bones, healing our hearts.

Prayer: **Loving Holy One, we pray for forgiveness for huddling together, guarding the door. Please grant us courage to venture forth to the wellsprings of life. Amen.**

29

Sunday, January 18   Read Isaiah 62:3-5.

Healing our hearts of harmful generation-to-generation scripts is a difficult and painful process. Following our script, perhaps we try to be perfect instead of learning to play. Maybe we seek glib stardom instead of spiritual growth or abuse instead of nurture. Perhaps we meet superimposed career goals instead of remembering Brother Lawrence who was honored and happy if, for God's sake, he could pick up a straw where no straw should be. The scriptures do not call us to live out someone else's script but to share our own God-given gifts.

Healing comes when we can toss the script without severing our roots. As our hearts heal, we begin to speak a second language that includes compassion for the generations that scripted us and those we have scripted. That includes gratitude for life that enhances, not diminishes, the lives of those around us. Perhaps our hearts receive healing as we learn how to speak a second language.

Many more sicknesses of heart exist than we have prayed about this week. Our faith is that all will receive healing.

A bishop's wife named Virginia confirmed this for me from her bed in a Dallas nursing home. She had reached a stage in which her memory was seriously failing. However, on that day she recalled our common ties and stammered the word *Louisiana*. When Bill prayed for her, she closed her eyes—her face radiant and a holy smile on her lips.

I shall always remember Virginia lying there—in a body that had already betrayed her and a mind that was beginning to. Yet her shining eyes shone forth from a healed heart, aflame with God's love. She was "a crown of beauty in the hand of the Lord."

Prayer: **Loving Holy One, thank you for our many blessings, especially that of healing our hearts. Amen.**

THE WORD THAT GIVES LIFE

January 19–25, 1998   **Jin Hee Han**✤
Monday, January 19   Read Nehemiah 8:1-3, 5-6.

After returning to their ruined homeland, the people of Israel settled into their towns. One of their first requests of Ezra, the scribe, was that he read to them from the book of the law of Moses. Ezra brought the law of the Lord before the people, and his reading of the word brought the people together. People would remember Ezra for this act for ages to come.

The gathering took place in the square before the Water Gate, a location that would put the law within the hearing of even those ritually unclean people who would not be admitted into the Temple precinct. In this public place, the public reading of the word was forging a group of the Israelites who came back from the exile in search of home into a community of faith.

Ezra enjoyed a prominent spot, but the reading was the people's project. It was the people of Israel who "told the scribe Ezra to bring the book of the law of Moses." Ezra's fingers unrolled the scroll to read, but the people made history as they stood up in the presence of the word. They lifted up their hands and responded to the word of God with a double Amen. They were being born afresh as the worshiping community on the first day of the seventh month, which was New Year's Day in the Jewish calendar.

Prayer: **Bring us together through your word, O God. We lift up our hands with the chorus of amen, amen.**

✤Professor of Biblical Studies, New York Theological Seminary.

Tuesday, January 20   Read Nehemiah 8:8-10.

In the square before the Water Gate, about a dozen of Ezra's helpers moved through the people to help them understand and interpret what was being read. These were the Levites. For those who did not speak Hebrew, they translated the passage into Aramaic, the language of the people. These Levites also served as interpreters, connecting the proclaimed words with the people's life.

The expounded word overwhelmed the people. To understand the word of God is bound to hurt. Not knowing what the word means, we can enjoy the bliss of ignorance. Understanding tosses us from the comfort of naïveté. Awakened from ignorance, the people mourned.

Those who wept shed tears for many reasons; it would take millennia to fathom their source. We, like they, also weep. Some of us mourn lost opportunities. Sometimes we weep when an unbearably beautiful truth in God's word strikes a chord in our hearts. Whether in anguish or in ecstasy, tears tend to wear us out. The joy of the Lord returns that strength to us.

Faithful exegesis does not leave the people in sadness. The leaders of the assembly advise the people not to mourn, for it is a holy day. It is a festal occasion. It is time to "eat the fat and drink sweet wine." In celebration of the holy day, they are to send portions of food to "those for whom nothing is prepared." Those who have nothing are welcome at this feast. All provisions—understanding and interpretation, food and drink—are ready.

Prayer: **We are eternally grateful to you, O God, for the people who guided our quest for understanding. Open our minds and hearts, so that we may share the food of heaven and of earth with our hungry brothers and sisters. Amen.**

Wednesday, January 21   Read Psalm 19:1-6.

The first six verses of Psalm 19 portray God's created world as filled with ineffable exuberance. A profound language travels through time and space, passing on the knowledge of the mystery of God's creation. The whole world is erupting with glorious praise, though humans cannot hear it.

The psalmist is happy to wonder, and the poet's diction verges on Lao-tzu's *tao* (the truth that cannot be put into words). A line of discourse with no words saturates the heavens and the earth, the habitat of creation.

The psalmist ponders and finds that God's mysterious work of creation comes into dazzling focus with the sun. God has built a dwelling place for the sun, a sanctuary of a new life. From there the great luminary starts its course with excitement and sustains its joy every step of the way.

People in antiquity believed that the sun was a god, and they discovered a sense of justice in the regularity of its movement. The rays it spills from heaven serve as a delightful image of justice with no shady schemes and with no discrimination.

The earth may not talk much, but an Asian saying states that heaven does a lot of listening. It listens to the sound of creation from day to night, from the corner of our land to the end of the earth. It listens to the blooming sound of creation as it thaws from the freezing night of oppression. Look! The sun rises again, and God's created world is once more the way God intended it to be.

Prayer: **O God, may we listen for your voice in the speeches that we do not understand. May we learn from the sun that does not withhold its heat from anyone who looks up to it. Amen.**

Thursday, January 22   Read Psalm 19:7-14.

Psalm 19 is a peculiar psalm, bringing together two arenas of God's revelation that theologians have labored to hold together for centuries: nature (vv. 1-6) and the word of the Lord (vv. 7-14). This psalm is a hybrid, and its great contribution is that now we cannot think of the world without the word. Creation and Torah: They are now one poem.

The word of God has all the supreme qualities that would require a heavenly language to describe it. We get glimpses, or echoes, of God's glory being praised throughout the universe.

Just as the sun marks the boundary of the living, so the law of God marks the boundary of our life. As the sun gives life, the teaching of the law revives the soul. It is sure and pure. Its rewards are life, wisdom, and happiness.

The word of the Lord is richer than the best food that waters the mouth and opens the eyes of the hungry. It is to be desired. It comes with an everlasting warranty, "enduring forever."

The law of the Lord establishes a clear order, but God's servants live in a less than perfect world. We need the guidance the Torah offers about the manner of our conduct, so that we may not lose the reward for following the teaching of the Lord. From time to time we fail to discern God's way, and then we will need God's forgiveness. The proud ones in the world tempt and coax God's servants to follow their way. As friends of the world, we happily err under peer pressure from our contemporaries. The psalmist prays that his words and thoughts may be worthy enough to make an offering acceptable to God. We pray with him so that we may find our right place in God's creation, thanks to the guidance of the word of God.

Prayer: **O God, may the words that I say in my heart be a worthy prayer. Let my meditations bring joy to your church. Amen.**

Friday, January 23   Read 1 Corinthians 12:12-13, 27-31*a*.

Baptism is a moment charged with the power of trans-formation. "With this baptism you are a new person." "You are God's child, and we welcome you in Christian love to the family of Christ." With these words we congratulate new members on their baptism.

Though you may not realize it, the waters of baptism soak those sitting in the pew too. As the water renews our baptismal vow, the body we joined at our baptism now has a different shape of incarnation: The body has just taken on new members.

We had better watch out. This baptism has the power of turning anyone into a sister or a brother in Christ. It overcomes the barriers of ethnicity, culture, economic status, class, or whatever else pits one human being against another. In baptism, all these different people are joining the body. Some of them may be the people with whom we had never dreamed of spending eternity.

Now we are one body, which has many members. Sometimes we view this diversity as a problem, and we try to keep our varied gifts and those who possess them away from each other. Diversity is not so problematic when we keep our gifts to ourselves. But the body of Christ brings its members too close to pass by without rubbing souls with one another. In fact, the diversity itself is one of God's great gifts.

How can we coordinate these rich gifts? Paul's policy was not to contain their use but to entertain greater gifts. When the church is crowded with apostles, prophets, and teachers, what should we do? Let's ask for more. There is always one more wonderful thing God has given us to share.

Prayer: **O God, we praise you for the variety of gifts that you created among us so that we can serve one another. Amen.**

Saturday, January 24   Read 1 Corinthians 12:14-26.

Perhaps the greatest gift in Paul's list of promises has already been given: us. Us to each other. And while this gift came without assembly instructions, it offers a wonderful variety of masterpieces to work on.

We have growing pains as we try to learn to live with one another. We have produced stories of love, though we have had our full share of war among brothers and sisters. The challenge comes in keeping the body in one piece in peace.

From time to time we forget who we are as we look upon the blessings bestowed upon others. We mark our own as alien and are blind to the treasure of others in this body. We become oblivious to our bond with other members. We have regrettably said in a private act of excommunication, "I have no need of you." In truth the worth of the members of this body was never based on what they could produce for us. We were not baptized on the basis of our usefulness.

In the body of Christ Paul says we affirm the value of some more than others. We stand up to acclaim them. We defend their cause at all costs. Who are they? They are the ones some may think less honorable or weaker or less respectable. Our heart goes to the poor, the sad, the lonely, the segregated, and the underprivileged. Their stories are our discourses. Paul says God's intention in arranging the body in this way was to ensure peace. We set dissension aside to provide care for one another.

Suggestion for meditation: **In the church family you are part of, how do the members see one another? How do you see yourself? Is there more often dissension, or is there more often peace within the body?**

Prayer: **O Christ, help us hold dear what you hold dear. We thank you for the gift of one another. Amen.**

Sunday, January 25   Read Luke 4:14-21.

Jesus, who had been led into the wilderness by the Spirit to be tempted by the devil, has now come back filled with the power of the Spirit. Today's passage contains a report of the first thing Jesus did upon his return to his hometown of Nazareth.

Jesus went to the synagogue to participate in the Sabbath worship with the people of God. There he opened the scroll of Isaiah and read the portion that spoke about God's benevolence to the poor, the captives, the blind, and the oppressed. When he completed his reading, Jesus added this comment: "Today this scripture has been fulfilled in your hearing." With this single sentence from the lips of Jesus, the words of the prophet came to have a new existence through the life and death of Jesus Christ.

Luke the evangelist has an orderly temperament. He wants to say at the beginning of his Gospel what he will enjoy unpacking later. He would have loved our Sunday morning bulletins. So Luke publishes the shape of Jesus' ministry in this passage.

The first stroke of a paintbrush beckons the picture that will fill the canvas. The first note on the page of a score calls forth the music that is to unfold. The first step of a marathon runner breathes the air of hope for a gold medal. However, brushstrokes do not always finish pictures; not all wonderful notes reach the page; and many dreams never rise from the bed.

But Jesus lived exactly as he said he would, and our hope will forever be in his power to free us from anything that would hold us captive.

Prayer: **Lord Jesus, your word gives hope to the souls in captivity. May we hear again what you read in the synagogue in Nazareth. Proclaim the year of jubilee in our midst today. Amen.**

GROWING UP IN FAITH

January 26—February 1, 1998   **Cathy Barker**✚
Monday, January 26   Read Psalm 71:1-6.

This psalm is the prayer of an aging servant of God. (See v. 18.) Reflecting on a lifetime of faith, the psalmist recalls God's unchanging presence from a time before memory. Never mind doctors, nurses, or midwives; "it was you who took me from my mother's womb." This servant has grown up and grown old, trusting in God's constancy. The psalmist now bears witness to a long life of faithfulness and trust.

Ponder how the psalmist's experience compares with your own. What is your earliest memory of God's presence? Could you say, "Upon you I have leaned from my birth"? As you were growing up, how did your image of God change? How have you lived out your trust in God through your youth and adulthood? In times of difficulties, how did you know that God continued to care for you and guide you?

This psalm includes petitions for help interwoven with the confident proclamations of God's sturdy love: "Be to me a rock..., a strong fortress..., for you are my rock and my fortress." Throughout one's life the needs may change, yet God remains constant. The aging saint sang of hope and continual praise in response to God's faithfulness.

Prayer: **O God, my rock and my fortress, you have been unshakable through the years. May I continue to grow and mature in faith and trust. Hear my praise and joy as we live out this day together. Amen.**

✚Pastor of United Church of Christ; Granite Falls, Minnesota.

Tuesday, January 27   Read Jeremiah 1:4-7.

Jeremiah's call to be a prophet stands out because he had no real choice in the matter: God called him before he was born. The apostle Paul also speaks of being set aside before his birth (Gal. 1:15).

Jeremiah may not have had much choice, but like other prophets he still objects to the honor. Simply being in such close proximity to the Divine overwhelms him! He humbly reminds God that he does not know how to speak, that he is only a boy. Imagine his knees shaking, his voice trembly and cracking!

God usually does not take no for an answer in these situations. Just like a parent who brings home shoes a size too big, then confidently states, "You'll grow into them," God reassures the young Jeremiah that all will be well. The boy will grow up and grow into his calling. God, after all, is the one who will send him, and God will command him what to speak. He has an important calling: to be a prophet to the nations—not just his own people but all people. (Notice the Epiphany theme of inclusiveness.) He cannot accomplish this without God's constant presence, so God quickly assures him of it.

How often, as we grow up in our faith, do we encounter looming challenges for which we feel woefully ill-equipped? It seems impossible that we could ever fill the shoes before us. The objections spring easily to our lips! Yet once we stop our protesting, God's word of assurance is there.

Prayer: **Ever-present God, even as you hear our uncertainty when you call, reassure us again of your trustworthy guidance as you lead us into maturity of faith. Amen.**

39

Wednesday, January 28   Read Jeremiah 1:8-10.

To the trembling, terrified boy Jeremiah, God speaks the familiar, straightforward phrase: "Do not be afraid." In good company with Joshua, Ezekiel, Mary, and Paul, Jeremiah hears these words of comfort and assurance. Invariably they come in the context of great demands. God asks much but promises presence and guidance every step of the way. It is a package deal—if you say yes to one, you are assured of the other.

This is a big job for a boy: to be a prophet "over nations and over kingdoms"! God is not just talking about the hometown crowd here; Jeremiah is to be a voice to those who are not part of the Jewish faith. (Again an Epiphany theme of the universality of God.)

Jeremiah's job description sounds ominous at first. He will scold and accuse; he will foretell doom and destruction. He will be an unwelcome guest with unbidden news. Only after that can he be about the process of rebuilding, comforting, or offering hope. His future promises to be a rollercoaster of challenges! The power to take on these opposing roles had to come from God. Jeremiah would grow into the job, you might say.

What extremes make up your "job description" as you grow in faith? When have you needed the reassurance, "Do not be afraid …, for I am with you"? As you mature, what new challenges has God set before you?

Prayer: **Awesome God, I come to you with holy fear. When you ask much of me, I pray for your words in my mouth, your presence in my heart. May I grow into each new challenge of service. In the strength Christ gives, I pray. Amen.**

Thursday, January 29   Read Luke 4:21-27.

Both Jeremiah and Jesus understood their mission as being worldwide. In today's text Jesus bumps up against provincial bias in his own hometown of Nazareth; the folks there do not understand the global nature of his message.

At first the people in the synagogue were pleased and proud to see their own native son doing so well. They were delighted to hear his message of justice and healing; each person there could probably have named several needs in Nazareth that Jesus should address.

Jesus anticipated their reaction. The proverb "Physician, heal yourself" is in the same category as "Take care of your own" or "Charity begins at home." He expected that reaction and responded with two examples from the scriptures the people knew and loved.

During a drought and famine, God sent the prophet Elijah to a certain widow, a "foreigner," for food. She reluctantly shared her last bit of meal and oil. Miraculously, neither supply was exhausted, even until the end of the drought (1 Kings 17:1-16). Naaman, a "foreigner," went to Israel to seek healing of his skin disease and received help from the prophet Elisha (2 Kings 5:1-19). These two non-Jews received the benefits of God's blessings.

Unfortunately, the congregation at Nazareth was caught in an immature way of thinking. They were happy thinking that God's blessings would be showered on *them*, giving them the home-town advantage and putting them in line for particular benefits. But Jesus shook their assumptions.

Prayer: **Forgive us, God, when our self-centeredness and superficiality prevents our sharing your generosity with others. In Jesus' name. Amen.**

Friday, January 30   Read Luke 4:28-30.

Young children operate under the assumption that "the world revolves around me." As they grow up, they reach a point where fairness is important as they learn to take turns and share. If (when?) individuals reach maturity, they understand that the world does not revolve around any one person and that life is not always fair.

As we mature in faith, we open ourselves to the realization that we do not earn God's blessings, and we cannot contain God's generosity. So even though a pious person needs healing, it may be an obvious sinner who receives Christ's healing touch. Grace is not always fair.

The congregation at Nazareth had not reached a maturity of faith that permitted God's blessings to reach beyond its circle. While welcoming Jesus at first, they were troubled by Jesus' message of inclusion, which insulted their thoughts of exclusivity. In their jealousy and anger, they lost their heads! Filled with rage, they hustled him out to a cliff where they intended to kill him by throwing him down upon the stones. This time, Jesus slipped away. *This time.*

The message of justice and peace rings like a beautiful chime in our ears. Yet in reality we may be overlooked or even called upon to sacrifice, so that others may receive blessings. Does the chime become a clashing cymbal that fuels our rage, or is it the clarion call that moves us to activism?

Prayer: **God of justice, remind us once again that your ways are not our ways. Show us the generosity of your grace, and teach us to live graciously. In Jesus' name. Amen.**

Saturday, January 31   Read 1 Corinthians 13:1-7.

The Christians in the church at Corinth were behaving like quarrelsome kids on a playground—parading their piety, boasting about their spiritual gifts, and comparing one with another. One can just see Paul, pen in hand, sighing and shaking his head at this flock he was trying to nurture from a distance.

In the last sentence of chapter 12, Paul writes, "And I will show you a still more excellent way" (v. 31). This way is the way of love, outlined in chapter 13 and leading to his pointed instruction in chapter 14. Paul was not thinking about passion or marriage when he wrote these poignant sentences. They serve us well for wedding meditations, but their original purpose is even more potent. Paul speaks of *agape* love, mature love.

Paul defines *agape* love here in part by what it is *not:* envious, boastful, arrogant, rude, irritable, or resentful. It does not insist on its own way or rejoice in wrongdoing. Those childish behaviors do not befit the life of faith. *Agape* means being patient and kind, rejoicing in the truth. "It bears all things, believes all things, hopes all things, endures all things." These traits are *childlike* rather than childish. They capture the fresh, unpolluted love of a trusting child. Manifested in a grownup, this love, being wiser and deeper, embodies the love of Christ.

Prayer: **God of love, guide us in the way of your divine love that we may set aside harmful behaviors and embrace those that bring wholeness and healing. In Christ we pray. Amen.**

Sunday, February 1   Read 1 Corinthians 13:8-13.

Agape love lasts. Unlike the spiritual gifts of tongues, prophecy, and even knowledge, *agape* endures. Paul does not write off the spiritual gifts altogether, but in this chapter and the next he makes a strong statement about the place of such gifts in the community of faith.

Agape love never ends because it comes from God, made known to us in Jesus Christ. God's very being is love (1 John 4:7-8). Paul tries to embody that love and exhorts the Corinthian Christians (and us) to do the same. In this way the whole church lives out the high calling of loving.

How do we do it? We begin by putting an end to childish ways. Every text this week has offered clues:
- the psalmist, living a life of growing faithfulness and trust;
- young Jeremiah, growing into his calling as prophet and letting God take the lead in his life;
- the congregation at Nazareth, conspicuous in its self-centeredness and lack of mature faith;
- Paul, describing the generous *agape* love that is not arrogant or rude.

Paul sums it up poetically: "When I was a child, I spoke like a child, I thought like a child, I reasoned like a child; when I became an adult, I put an end to childish ways." In other words, "Grow up, people!" Grow into the understanding that you are loved and blessed by God—and so are others, including some who in your eyes may seem less deserving. Do not be afraid—God has enough love to go around!

Prayer: Generous God, we seek to grow in our faith, to reach maturity in our understanding of you and your self-giving love. In our Savior's name. Amen.

WHEN GOD COMES TO US!

February 2–8, 1998   **N. Sue Van Sant Palmer**✤
Monday, February 2   Read Isaiah 6:1-8.

We read today of Isaiah's seeing God: "In the year that King Uzziah died, I saw the Lord." Standing in the divine presence, Isaiah felt God's holiness: "The Lord [was] sitting on a throne, high and lofty." Isaiah heard the voices of the seraphs calling, "Holy, holy, holy is the Lord of hosts." He felt the shaking of the temple's foundations, and he cried out, "Woe is me! I am lost, [or "There is no hope for me! I am doomed," TEV], for I am a man of unclean lips,…yet my eyes have seen the King, the Lord of hosts!" Isaiah was doomed in God's holy presence unless God acted to protect him. God did act: The seraph brought a live coal from the altar, the place of the sacrifice, and touched Isaiah's lips.

Close your eyes and imagine the searing coal touched to Isaiah's lips; the burning pain of God's cleansing, saving action, purifying and refining. We yearn to see God, but do we really want God to come to us? We too are persons of unclean lips, marked by guilt and sin. When God comes to us, God's forgiving act may place us in a refining fire, burning away whatever in us separates us from God.

Isaiah did not flee God's presence, despite his lament. Perhaps, overwhelmed by God's power and holiness, he could not. But in remaining, he became available to God. His remaining is evidence of God's saving power and grace.

Prayer: **Redeemer God, appear to us. Do not let us flee when, in your presence, we feel the grief of our guilt and sin. Remain with us; protect us as we pass through your refining fire. Amen.**

✤Lawyer and layspeaker; church school teacher and teacher of youth *Disciple*, residing in Clarksville, Tennessee.

Tuesday, February 3   Read Isaiah 6:1-8.

In today's reading we focus on God's call to Isaiah: "Then I heard the voice of the Lord saying, 'Whom shall I send, and who will go for us?'" The words do not appear to be spoken to Isaiah, but Isaiah can hear them. Because the burning coal had seared his unclean lips, blotting out his sin and dispelling his guilt, Isaiah can hear the voice of God! Moreover, he responds, "Here am I; send me!" We know the rest of the story from the verses that follow: God calls Isaiah and commissions him to tell the people of Judah of coming destruction. Isaiah is to speak a message they will not heed until the land is "utterly desolate" (6:11).

When God comes to us, God calls us to go into the world. We fear the searing coal and the hard task. We feel burdened; we draw back. We can hardly keep our own lives together. How can we say to God, "Here am I; send me"?

We can respond affirmatively to God's request because in God's cleansing, God clears away our fear, our resistance, our disability; we have only the task and its own difficulties—and we have God's energy for the task. When we experience God, God propels us into the hard tasks: feeding the hungry, comforting the sick, visiting the prisoners, fighting oppression, preaching the word.

"Here am I; send me." Surely it is worth releasing ourselves to God and passing through the refining fire that blots out our sin, so that we can hear God's voice and respond clearly to God. God enables us to answer, "Here am I; send me." Being able to answer and to act is itself a gift from God and brings us peace.

Prayer: **Redeemer God, we want to see you, to hear your voice. We know that your children, our neighbors next door and around the world, have great needs. By your grace we will respond, "Here am I; send me." Amen.**

Wednesday, February 4   Read 1 Corinthians 15:1-11.

In our reading for today and tomorrow we hear from Paul, called and commissioned by God to preach the gospel: "Now I would remind you, brothers and sisters, of the good news…in which also you stand, through which also you are being saved." Paul recites this good news: Jesus died for our sins, was buried and then raised from the dead, and appeared to his friends and disciples. Through this good news, Paul says we are being saved, and in this good news we stand.

Consider what it means to say, "The good news gives us a place to stand." We may have come to rely on our everyday world, the security of family and friends, home and job. But this worldly security does not provide a place to stand. Everything is transient for us. We are persons whose lives are torn asunder by war or natural upheavals or destruction of relationships. We may lose our jobs, in which we anchor much of our identity; we may lose the persons we love. We may fail, betraying ourselves and others, and have no structure for our interior or exterior lives. When we lose the structure of our lives, we know from experience that we cannot provide this "place to stand" for ourselves.

Only the love of God, the power of God in the universe, stands outside this transience. This love and power of God, conveyed in God's fundamental power over physical death in the resurrection of Jesus Christ, can transform us, lifting us out of our selves and our sinful nature and offering us a place to stand.

Prayer: **Redeemer God, we best understand that we need your structure, this place to stand, when our world shifts. Touch our lives with your grace so that we become more aware each day that what passes for structure in the world is ephemeral; enable us to affirm each day our need for a place to stand in the good news. Amen.**

Thursday, February 5 Read I Corinthians 15:1-11.

God's coming to Paul on the road to Damascus turned Paul from one who "persecuted the church of God" to one who proclaimed the good news: "He appeared also to me....By the grace of God I am what I am, and his grace toward me has not been in vain."

We may not actively persecute God's church, but our lives require turning around. I fear that often we are too busy or too self-absorbed or too content with the structure created by our ordinary lives to know our need of God's grace, to recognize God's coming, to attend to God's call, and to allow God to turn our lives completely around.

We are all called: called to center our lives in the love of God and to be the messengers of God's love. Every day, an experience of God's grace is before us, available to transform us. We have the opportunity to become who we are by God's grace. And every day, God has work for us to do.

Are we able to say with Paul: "By the grace of God I am what I am"; and "[God's] grace toward me has not been in vain"? Those affirmations require a renewed commitment each day, a greater commitment than may be our custom. The alternative, however, brings us unspeakable grief: "God, the creator and sustainer of the universe, has touched my life with grace for naught, in vain."

Prayer: **Creator God, I want to be able to say, "I am shaped by God. I stand before God and the world as witness to God's power of transformation, and I am about the business of doing the work of God that is before me." Even at the cost of the refining fire of Isaiah's coal touched to my lips, of being struck blind like Paul, come to me, Redeemer God—and enable me to say that I am what I am by your grace and that your grace toward me has not been in vain. Amen.**

Friday, February 6   Read Luke 5:1-11.

We read today of God's word coming to the crowds among the fishing boats along the seashore.

Jesus, pressed by the crowds as he taught beside the sea, got into Simon Peter's boat and asked to be put out a little so that he could teach from the boat. When he had finished speaking, he directed Peter: "Put out into the deep water and let down your nets for a catch." Peter had fished that place all night with no result but said, "Master,...if you say so, I will let down the nets." He and those with him caught so many fish their nets began to break. Peter fell down at Jesus' knees, saying, "Go away from me, Lord, for I am a sinful man!"

Jesus came to Peter's ordinary working world. Peter heard Jesus as he taught the crowds. When Jesus directed Peter to "put out into the deep water," Peter began to obey—against his common sense and experience. Before the near-miracle catch, Peter called Jesus "Master," suggesting that he recognized Jesus' authority already. Having obeyed Jesus, Peter then was amazed by the nets full of fish, a result not in accord with his practical experience. He responded not only with his intellect but with his whole self: He fell down before Jesus, overwhelmed and frightened by his own sinfulness in God's presence.

God comes for us too. Perhaps God comes to our day-to-day world, working in us before we realize God's work. Our ability to experience God may follow from a weaving together of God's coming to us—our yielding perhaps only a little at first but letting go our ordinary control—and God's action in us. It is a mystery— not a matter available to our understanding.

Whenever God comes, God's holy power makes our sinful nature clear; like Peter, we may want God to go away.

Prayer: **Redeemer God, be at work in us, making us ready to experience your coming and your call. Amen.**

Saturday, February 7   Read Luke 5:1-11.

Yesterday we read of Peter's response to Jesus when he realized Jesus' nature: Peter's falling on his knees and crying, "Go away from me Lord" is like Isaiah's cry, "Woe is me!" Jesus countered Peter's fear: "Do not be afraid; from now on you will be catching people." When they came to the shore, Peter, James and John "left everything and followed him."

We cannot explain this away: "They left everything and followed him." Do we hear that? "They left everything and followed him." Matthew's Gospel carries the same message: Jesus called Simon Peter and Andrew while they were in the midst of casting their nets. "Immediately they left their nets and followed him" (4:20). James and John were in the boat with their father, mending their nets. Jesus called them and "immediately they left the boat and their father, and followed him" (Matt. 4:22). Mark's Gospel records the same response.

What shall we do? In order to be disciples, must we leave everything and follow Jesus? Is there some "secondary" kind of discipleship where we can stay partially connected but not really leave everything and follow Jesus? I fear that we behave as though a secondary kind of discipleship is an option. While we may remain carpenters or teachers or plumbers or homeless persons or prisoners or hospital patients or doctors or bus drivers, God requires that we "immediately leave everything" and follow. We cannot "call in" intermittently and still be disciples. We cannot offer excuses. Following Jesus begins immediately. For us following may not involve a change in occupation or location, but following does require us to leave everything in our interior geography. As we begin, we can hear the voice of Jesus, "Do not be afraid."

Prayer: **Redeemer God, what do you require of us? Enable us not to be afraid; enable us to leave everything and follow you. Amen.**

Sunday, February 8   Read Psalm 138.

Experience the psalm of thanksgiving and praise as a meditation: Read it once aloud. Then read each stanza; allow each
image to form in your mind. Look up even the ordinary words in
a dictionary. Then read the psalm again as though you are the
psalmist. I share with you a portion of my meditation.

Verses 1-3. The psalmist bows down—his body enacting his
reverence—toward God's "holy temple," the place of holy
mystery; he gives thanks to the "name" of God, the name of holy
mystery. The psalmist speaks to God directly, personally: "I give
you thanks, O Lord." He gives thanks with his "whole heart," a
phrase that evokes complete yielding of self to God's "steadfast
love"—a constant, unwavering love—and God's "faithfulness." I
think what a wonder it is that God is faithful to us. God answered
the psalmist's call immediately: "On the day I called, you
answered me." God increased the psalmist's "strength of soul," a
phrase that suggests God provides power and energy to the
psalmist's very self.

Verses 7-8. The metaphor of rescue continues: "I walk in the
midst of trouble." "You preserve me." "You stretch out your
hand, and your right hand delivers me." I remember Psalm 23,
"Though I walk through the valley of the shadow of death… thou
art with me" (v. 4, RSV). I am flooded with the memory of Psalm
23. I imagine the outstretched hand of God, preserving, pro-
tecting me in time of trouble. From my experience of the
steadfast love and faithfulness of God, I begin to say with the
psalmist, "The Lord will fulfill his purpose for me." I yield to
God's purpose, eager for God to be at work in me.

Suggestion for meditation: **Go early to church today and bow
down. Imagine the psalmist and then yourself, bowing down
toward the holy temple of God, giving thanks and praise with
your whole heart until your being is taken up with thankfulness
for the faithful, steadfast love of God.**

RESURRECTION HOPE

February 9–15, 1998   **Joyce Hollyday**✤
Monday, February 9   Read Luke 6:17-23.

It was a bitterly cold Christmas eve in Washington, D.C. I was working at a shelter for homeless women in a church basement. After singing a few Christmas carols, the women settled in for the night on mats spread over the floor. All was quiet for a while. But shortly after midnight, two women began arguing.

Sheila accused Mary of stealing her coat while Sheila slept. Mary charged Sheila with being a liar. Sheila responded by telling Mary she was a "no-good good-for-nothing." Without hesitation, Mary shouted, "I'm better than you'll ever be. I'm an aristocrat of the highest order—with the Rothschilds on my mother's side and the Three Wise Men on my father's!" That ended the discussion.

How reality differs today from the words of our scripture passage. Jesus—who chose to live among and minister to the outcasts and the sick—proclaimed that the poor and the hungry, the sorrowful and the persecuted are blessed. It is to these, he announced, that the kingdom of God belongs. Yet today the poor are being scapegoated for a variety of national ills. "Welfare mothers," "illegal aliens," and "criminals" are among the most despised people in our midst. How would Jesus treat them?

My friend Mary at the shelter—who had the demeanor of one who had been told most of her life that she was worthless—claimed worth and dignity for herself. The specifics of her claim may not hold up, but at its core is a gospel truth: In the kingdom of God, the poor are royalty.

Prayer: Jesus, help me participate in your kingdom by loving the poor and making their concerns my own. Amen.

✤Peace activist, journalist, author, pastor, chaplain; Woodruff Scholar at Candler School of Theology, Emory University; Atlanta, Georgia.

Tuesday, February 10   Read Luke 6:24-26.

I traveled throughout South Africa in 1988, when that country was still very much in the grip of the system of racial hatred known as apartheid. I visited the black township of Duncan Village, where Jam-Jam, a young man active in the freedom struggle, served as my host. As we walked, Jam-Jam told me that he had just been released from ten months in detention. His jailers had kept him in a cold cell, fed him cornmeal infested with worms, and tortured him.

Before long an armored personnel carrier appeared in front of us, and eight members of the South African Defense Forces, waving rifles, surrounded us. They escorted us at gunpoint to an interrogation room, where an officer of the security police briefly questioned me. Then he turned to Jam-Jam. He threatened to jail Jam-Jam again if he didn't give up his "subversive activities."

Jam-Jam's only response was to reach into his back pocket and take out his small New Testament. Putting it in front of the officer's face, he said confidently, "Sir, I am a Christian." Silence ensued as the arrogance of evil met the quiet power of the gospel.

Jam-Jam knew the power of the book in his hands. He knew its promises of justice: Mary's declaration that the poor would be exalted and the rich put off their thrones (Luke 1:52-53); Jesus' announcement that he had been anointed to "bring good news to the poor" and "proclaim release to the captives" (Luke 4:18); and the clear and direct words we read today from the Sermon on the Plain: "Woe to you who are rich,...who are full now,...who are laughing now."

The good news for the poor should disturb those of us who are comfortable. Unless we are in solidarity with the despised and the suffering, this list of "woes" is directed toward us. Jesus cast his lot among the poor and invites us to do the same.

Prayer: **Help me, Jesus, to live simply and courageously, as you did. Amen.**

Wednesday, February 11   Read 1 Corinthians 15:12-20.

Moments before he was killed, Archbishop Oscar Romero of El Salvador preached from John 12:24—"Unless a grain of wheat falls into the earth and dies, it remains just a single grain; but if it dies, it bears much fruit." Romero was one martyr among 75,000 in El Salvador's struggle to bring justice to that tiny country, where a small elite prospered while the vast majority of people went hungry. Most of those killed were Christians, including several priests and four U.S. missionary women.

El Salvador means "The Savior." It is a country that has known crucifixion. But its people also know the power of the Resurrection.

Yvonne Dilling, a friend of mine from Indiana, worked with Salvadorans who fled to a refugee camp in Honduras. All the suffering that she witnessed made her spirit very heavy.

One of the refugee women asked her why she always looked so burdened. Yvonne spoke of her commitment to the refugees and their plight and of the grief she felt. The woman gently chided her, "Only people who expect to go back to North America in a year work the way you do. You cannot be serious about our struggle unless you play and celebrate and do those things that make it possible to give a lifetime to it." She reminded Yvonne that each time the refugees were displaced and had to build a new camp, they immediately formed three committees: a construction committee, an education committee, and the *comité de alegría*— the "committee of joy." Celebration was as basic to life as digging latrines and teaching their children.

In Third World countries, I have often observed that the people who suffer most also seem to celebrate with the most passion. Those who have known crucifixion also understand the power of resurrection. Their joy is evidence that there is a power greater than the power of death.

Prayer: **Jesus, in the midst of suffering may I know joy. Amen.**

54

Thursday, February 12   Read 1 Corinthians 15:12-20.

While I was in South Africa, I frequently asked people I met, "Do you think that apartheid will end in your lifetime?" Most said no. One woman responded, "Probably not in my lifetime or in my children's; but maybe in their children's." Most people viewed the struggle for freedom as an effort that would last for generations.

The children were more confident. I asked a ten year old in the black township of Mamelodi if he thought that his children would grow up without apartheid. "I will see to it!" he declared proudly. The children often lit candles in their windows, and the police would storm into their homes and blow them out. The children laughed, saying, "They are afraid of candles." But what frightened the police was the power behind the symbol: "The light shines in the darkness, and the darkness did not overcome it" (John 1:5).

Jesus is the Light that cannot be extinguished. His resurrection was the final victory over death in all its forms: racism, poverty, war, abuse. Though the power of death often seems strong in our world, the power of resurrection is stronger. Death held no claim on Jesus.

South Africa has recently undergone its own "resurrection." After decades of strangulation by apartheid, a new nation is emerging—a nation founded on forgiveness, trust, and hope. Whenever a nation or community or individual throws off the shackles of death, Jesus' resurrection is proclaimed once again and hope is unleashed on the world.

Prayer: **Jesus, show me the way to live in the light and hope of your resurrection. Amen.**

Friday, February 13   Read Psalm 1.

As a child, I used to spend joyful days on a piece of land my family owns near Gettysburg, Pennsylvania. Fall brought an array of vivid colors to the trees. In winter, the tracks of rabbits and deer appeared in deep snow. Spring prodded forth myriad delicate wildflowers.

But I liked summer best of all. Perched above a rushing waterfall was a rock resembling the profile of a man. Every summer the "Old Man of the Falls" sprouted a mustache—a line of green moss just below his jutting nose. Each summer the moss seemed like a promise—a sign of the passing of another year and of God's steadfast faithfulness in bringing about rebirth in creation.

But to me the land's most memorable feature was a sycamore tree. My sisters and I used to sit on the vast roots of the tree, dangling our feet among the minnows in the pools of water at its base. I remember that tree as being wide and sturdy, reaching high into the sky. Its exposed roots at the water's edge formed a broad and tangled network. It seemed that nothing on earth could ever move that tree.

That sycamore is the image that always comes to mind when I read Psalm 1. Those who follow the way of the Lord are like tall trees. They take root in the soil of compassion and justice and receive nourishment from rivers of mercy and love. The image reminds us that our upward reach toward God is mirrored in our deepening roots in the needs and joys of those who surround us.

Trees planted by water never wither from drought but always produce fruit in their season. So it is with Christians who allow God's love and mercy to flow through their lives, producing fruit through faithfulness and service.

Prayer: **God, nourish me with your love so I may pass it on to a needy world. Amen.**

Saturday, February 14   Read Jeremiah 17:5-10.

On Ash Wednesday 1991, on the other side of the world, allied forces in the Persian Gulf War bombed the Amariya shelter in Baghdad, killing hundreds of Iraqi women and children. Closer to home, in the neighborhood where I lived in inner-city Washington, D.C., the sound of gunshots and the wail of police and ambulance sirens punctuated the night. I felt a great despair over the state of the world. Before falling asleep I sensed God's inviting me to keep a Lenten discipline of fasting.

Three weeks later, I joined hundreds of other Christians at the Nevada Test Site to pray for peace. My water-and-juice fast had deepened my sense of God's presence; when physical strength gave out, the assurance of God's sustenance took powerful hold. Yet still I remained closed to part of God's power.

I could not escape it in the desert. I went off by myself to a place of gravelly sand and a lone Joshua tree with spiny branches outstretched like arms toward God. There, as other pilgrims to the desert have done for centuries, I fell to my knees and discovered a great emptiness. I was finally able to weep, to allow my tears to spill and water the barren earth.

In pouring out my despair, I found that there was room for something I had been closed to since Ash Wednesday. There, on the twenty-fourth day of my fast, I felt embraced by the gentle arms of God and nourished by hope.

In stark contrast to the image of the tree planted by water in both yesterday's and today's scripture passages is the "shrub in the desert." The shrub without roots becomes the tumbleweed that is vulnerable to every wind, blown across the desert without destination or home. But those who are rooted in God's love are sustained in hope.

Prayer: **God, help me to live in the power of your hope. Amen.**

57

Sunday, February 15   Read Jeremiah 17:5-10.

Several years ago, just before Christmas, I preached in a chapel service at Gettysburg College. Afterward, the chaplain invited me to her home for lunch, where I met her five-year-old son, Kyle. Kyle's proudest accomplishment that season was that he had memorized the biblical story of Jesus' birth. He (as well as his mother) was anxious to display his talent.

Kyle started out strong, but he began to falter just when he hit his favorite part: when the angels appear to the shepherds and shout, "Glory to God in the highest, and on earth peace." He remembered the "Glory to God" part, but then his mind went blank. His mother offered a few encouraging words, and Kyle thought hard. Suddenly, his face brightened and he began again: "And the angels appeared to the shepherds and said, 'Glory to God in the highest…and I'll huff and I'll puff and I'll blow your house down.'"

God's intent is for peace on earth. But gale-force winds of war and greed blow away the homes of the poor in our nation and around the globe. The winds of destruction catch up many people, whose actions increase the suffering of the poor and the homeless. But those who are rooted in God's love and justice can stand up to such winds and offer a vision of the kingdom of God—a realm in which all have shelter and food.

Prayer: **God, help me to live as a witness to your kingdom. Amen.**

TRANSFORMED BY FAITH

February 16–22, 1998   **H. A. Harrington**✤
Monday, February 16   Read Exodus 34:29-32.

As we begin this week of meditations leading to the Transfiguration, we need to remember that in God's scheme of things, all of creation is in a journey of continuous transformation. Continents shift; rivers change their boundaries; marriages grow, struggle, and rebound; lives and perspectives pass through countless alterations. This has always been the way of all things.

However, no transformation has as profound a ripple effect as the transformation effected by God. When a person or a people have come face to face with the Creator and realize for the first time that God knows them and calls them by name, they know that neither their world nor their own souls will ever be the same again.

As Moses concludes his forty days with God and approaches the Hebrews, his changed life so profoundly manifests itself in his face that they scarcely recognize him until they hear his familiar voice. How can any of us remain the same after God has looked unflinchingly into our eyes? How could any of us not throw open our arms and receive with joy the transforming holy presence that knows us and claims us and calls us God's own!

God's encounter with Moses is precisely the kind of experience God wants for us all and is ready to offer. Are we prepared for a genuine encounter with God? We will never be the same.

Prayer: **Eternal God, help me to be receptive to your Spirit, so all that I am and all that I do and say might be molded by your will. Amen.**

✤Author; pastor of St. Matthew's United Methodist Church; Metairie, Louisiana.

Tuesday, February 17   Read Exodus 34:32-35.

As we pursue this Exodus passage that relates Moses' transformed appearance after the Sinai encounter with God, we could examine Moses' practice of veiling himself. But the more we focus upon this curious act, the more we miss the transcendent truth of his actions after receiving the second set of Commandments.

The more powerful lesson for us is that Moses viewed himself not just as a recipient of God's word and grace but as a teacher and sharer of the same! Unlike the Dead Sea, which receives fresh light and water but hoards it until no life remains in its depths, Moses immediately knew that he had received life-giving truths of wisdom and deepening, and those could not possibly stop with him. So...he taught, shared, explained, and gave witness. The fresh waters of God's unending desire for humanity spilled over Moses like an overflowing cup and poured into the lives and hearts of the people.

None of us is an end product of God's reaching out. There is no room for an attitude of "It's just you and me God, nice and cozy." God intends that we share the word, becoming channels of hope and affirmation to everyone we meet. Heaven only knows the sheer volume of people whose lives have been renewed, blessed, inspired, and affirmed because those blessings flowed through someone else.

Moses didn't remain on Sinai, basking in a mountaintop experience. Such "peak" experiences and special moments rarely last. God reaches out to enable us in the everyday grind, the nitty-gritty, to say, "Have no fear; I go before you...." Is this not our task: to offer this saving wisdom, just as Moses, to all we meet?

Prayer: **Gracious and loving Lord, help me be a daily witness to your grace, that persons might see the power of your Spirit in every moment of my life. Amen.**

Wednesday, February 18   Read Psalm 99.

The Israelites began each new year with a festival that underscored the kingship of God in all things, which reinforced their sense of an in-control God. They needed that assurance, just as our needs require that same assurance.

Is anyone in control anywhere? Does anyone know my name? Does anyone really care? We find people withdrawing into themselves in increasing numbers as they perceive the answers to these soulful questions as "No." From Bosnia to Rwanda to Peru to the Balkans to the struggles within our own cities, more and more people cynically assert that they are "on their own."

Yet the natural longing of the heart is a desire to be part of a transcendent plan or purpose and to know that each of us is not incidental but a vital participant. The psalm thunders an affirmation to this longing! From the very beginning, the psalmist declares, "The Lord is in control!" The first five verses leave no question that the architect of all creation is firmly at the wheel. Have no doubt; have no fear.

And we today, as with Israel then, also long to be known, to be heard, to be wanted. We cannot abide being nameless chess pieces on the board of life. To this deepest of all spiritual needs the psalm responds: "Moses and Aaron...[and] Samuel...called on his name. They cried to the Lord, and he answered them."

With a deepening sense of fulfillment and edifying, transforming conviction, each of us affirms, "I am a cherished child of God, who calls me by name. I am an invaluable part of God's orderly process that is continually unfolding."

***Prayer:* O Lord, our Lord, for the gift of being known and named, called forth and sent out to do your work, we are deeply thankful. Amen.**

Thursday, February 19   Read Psalm 99.

We continue to absorb the power of Psalm 99. Through its magnificent proclamations of God's reign and our role as God's called, claimed, and chosen ones, we can scarcely hold back an exuberant little tap dance and a few "Hallelujahs!"

But in the midst of our celebration we come to verse 8, and a sobering reality stares us in the face. Yes, God loves us. Yes, God calls us by name. Yes, God has chosen to use us in building the world; and yes, God is a forgiving God. Then right in the middle of all this affirmation, verse 8 tells us that God will also hold us accountable for our wrongdoings. *There is no cheap grace with God.* Life with Yahweh is a joyous, transforming experience. It enables us to become all that is within us to become. But…life with God demands a lifestyle of justice, fairness, faithfulness, and discipline.

We have become a people who want to feast at the banquet of God's love and glory, but we would prefer that someone else wash the dishes. We sing songs of praise behind stained glass windows but recoil from touching the hungry and outcast whose faces press against our hearts in need and hopelessness. All the exuberance in the world over God's grace isn't worth a thing if our lives do not follow holy guidelines. We must keep God's decrees and live according to God's statutes. God repeatedly clarifies the guidelines for obedience and the definition of transgression.

Do we seek the mountaintop without living faithfully in the valley? Do we want the moment in the sun but not the discipline of discipleship?

***Prayer:* O Lord, for your gift of unconditional love and your expectation of our own accountable lifestyles of faith and service, we give you thanks. Amen.**

Friday, February 20   Read 2 Corinthians 3:12-16.

As we read this second letter to the church at Corinth, we cannot help but sense the surge of hopeful confidence in the faith, almost as though it was the opening announcement in a revival meeting. The writer's use of the word *boldness* is not the same as *arrogance* or the obnoxious *self-righteousness*. It *does* carry the flavor of certainty and assurance that faith in Christ is a transcendent truth, an ever-present lifeline to the Almighty. When faith undergirds you, how can you *not* be bold and confident! Paul's words written several years later to the church at Philippi seem to echo these words: "I can do all things through [Christ] who strengthens me" (4:13).

The world is full of those whose only apparent spiritual drive is to proselytize another: "Hey buddy, if you're not of my religion, then you're lost. Wanna talk?" Paul reminds us of the inner power that comes when your heart is full, your life is directed, and God is meeting your needs. It is a life of profound security; a life that needs no sense of shame for the faith—and no need to look elsewhere.

A financial advisor invited a friend to a tax seminar. The friend noted that his advisor kept nodding affirmatively throughout the presentation. Afterward, he said to the advisor, "You've been to this seminar before, haven't you? Why come back to something you've obviously been to many times?" The advisor smiled and said, "Because I never tire of hearing that which I know to be the truth."

And so it is with faith. God fills us with such hope that our only response is a continually renewed certainty. And *that* is a transforming lifestyle!

Prayer: **Great and gracious Lord, in a world of uncertainty and instability, we cling to your strong and faithful Truth with us; you hold us in your heart....we are not alone. Amen.**

Saturday, February 21   Read 2 Corinthians 3:17–4:2.

As I stood at the ATM machine filling out my deposit slip, I realized the floor was littered with carbons, crumpled copies, and withdrawal slips. One of them had writing on it. The words said, *Why can't I be you?* I wondered who wrote it. What was happening in his or her life? Who did this person want to be like? Why? What was his or her deep unhappiness? I felt an urge to find the person and talk, but the bank lobby was empty. All I had were the poignant words on a slip of paper.

This person is not alone. Millions of us are desperately unhappy with ourselves. The media reminds us each day that we are too tall, too short, too fat, too skinny—too much of this and not enough of that. So we spend billions of dollars trying frantically to adjust, color, change, alter, or in some way become something we are not. It is a tragic and often life-destroying obsession.

But Paul tells us that when we stand in the presence of the Lord we are free; we have no need to hide, only to be wonderfully transformed by the spirit of God. God's freedom means being free to love yourself, to see yourself as a Rembrandt of God. It means you no longer have to dream of being someone else because now you know God has claimed you just as you are.

Jesus spent every moment affirming and undergirding the very people society had declared unlovely and unworthy. He lifted spirits; they flew as eagles. As we read this passage we feel a surge of victorious faith. "I am God's. I am free. I am worthy in God's sight. I am made in God's image."

Prayer: **O God, because you love me I can love myself! Because you seek me and claim me, I am free! Amen.**

Sunday, February 22   Read Luke 9:28-36.

Of all the lessons from this hallowed account, found also in Matthew and Mark, few surpass the simple sequence of events that begin the entire narrative. Jesus, knowing what lay ahead, was surely filled with anxiety and perhaps even self-doubt. Who wouldn't have such inward fears when betrayal, confrontation, humiliation, and death lurk just around the corner? And what does Jesus do? He goes straight to God and prays for guidance, support, and direction.

While praying, Jesus is dazzlingly transformed—a great testimony to God's presence at the crossroads of life. A popular phrase may apply here: "When you reach the end of yourself, you reach the beginning of God!"

Throughout biblical history, God has said unfailingly, "Come to me." Throughout human history as well, those who place their lives in God's care and depend upon God's presence in struggles and in victories, in good times and in bad, have been transformed. It is not a helpless dependency but rather a holy empowerment. Jesus ascends to the mountaintop, not to escape the harsh reality of life, but to be strengthened for the journey.

As a student pilot, I flew with a professional friend in an old biplane. As we roared across the cotton field, I wasn't giving enough engine power or control angle to clear the onrushing treetops. My friend yelled, "Call on it man; call on it!" He grabbed the controls, jammed the throttle full, and pulled the stick as far back as it would go. We shot straight up and cleared the forest edge.

Our scripture says the same: If we will only call on God to receive power for the day, God will always provide it.

Prayer: **Dear God, who empowers me in all things, always help me seek your guidance first in every moment of my life. Amen.**

THE HABITS OF SPIRITUAL LIVING

February 23—March 1, 1998
Monday, February 23

Wayne E. Oates✤
Read Psalm 51:1-17.

The habit of confession

The Bible attributes this psalm to David, after the prophet Nathan confronted him with his sins. (For the story of these events, read 2 Samuel 11:2–12:23.) David responded to Nathan's charges by lamenting, "I have sinned against the Lord" (2 Sam. 12:13). Thus David began practicing the habit of confession.

This psalm offers a prayer formula to keep our minds from wandering when we confess our sins. It does not speak of sin in generalities; David's sins were specific. We can name specific sins in our own life story.

With intense self-examination we can *know* our transgressions. Our sin is right before our own eyes. God "requires truth in the inward being" and "wisdom in [our] secret hearts." These words are not just a public litany we say in church. They are face-to-face, personal conversation with God—a heartfelt prayer for God's cleansing forgiveness that heals us like a medicinal herb and washes our besmirched spirits "whiter than snow." The habit of confession is a prayer for joy and gladness in exchange for a broken, depressed being. It is a yearning for a clean heart, a right spirit, and a restored joy of God's saving grace.

This habit is a covenant, a promise to keep—a promise to teach transgressors God's way and to be a minister of encouragement. This is no vain practice of ritual sacrifice but the offering of a "broken and contrite heart." Confession, forgiveness and compassion for others are inseparable.

Prayer: **Lord, have mercy upon me, a sinner. Amen.**

✤Professor of Psychiatry Emeritus at the University of Louisville.

Tuesday, February 24   Read 2 Corinthians 5:20–6:10.

The habit of reconciliation

Paul speaks as an ambassador for Christ to you and me. He entreats us; that is, he asks us urgently to be reconciled to God. God has taken the initiative toward us in Jesus Christ. For a Christian, reconciliation is a way of life, a habit of the spiritual life.

Reconciliation with God implies that we are estranged or alienated from God by sin. This reconciliation has both a vertical and horizontal dimension to it. We are reconciled to God by the sacrifice the Lord Jesus made for us in his life, death, and resurrection. To be reconciled with God means just this—to take the way of Christ in his life, crucifixion, and resurrection as a daily walk of life with God through the power of the Holy Spirit. The Holy Spirit is our counselor and comforter, the one who activates the gifts in our lives. This is the vertical dimension of reconciliation.

The second, or horizontal, dimension of reconciliation is to live the life of forgiveness. Not to forgive our neighbor and kinspersons is to shut ourselves off from God. To bear grudges, to hate, or to live in unreconciled relationship to others and to God clutters up our relationships. As Paul puts it in Galatians 6:1: "My friends, if anyone is detected in a transgression, you who have received the Spirit should restore such a one in a spirit of gentleness. Take care that you yourselves are not tempted." (Read further instructions of Jesus in Matthew 5:23; 18:15-20.) Such reconciliation is strong medicine for ailing spirits, but the God of reconciliation will give you courage and spiritual robustness.

Prayer: **God of peace, grant me the discipline and spiritual integrity that reconciliation with you and fellow human beings provides as I take up my cross this day and follow the Lord Jesus Christ. Amen.**

Ash Wednesday

Wednesday, February 25   Read Isaiah 58:1-12.

The habit of practicing righteousness

Ash Wednesday begins the Lenten season. Its name comes from the practice of persons' putting ashes on their foreheads as a sign of repentance for sin.

Isaiah 58:1-12 addresses the meaning of a day such as Ash Wednesday. The call to worship by the priest is to be like a trumpet, declaring to the people their transgression. The people seek God daily and delight to know his ways. They "delight" to draw near to God and to fast. Yet this piety in worship differs vastly from their behavior in daily life. The Lord specifies the inconsistency of the people's worship and their mistreatment of their neighbors. The people fast only to serve their own best interests. This is not the kind of fast the Lord chooses.

Genuine repentance is the fast God chooses. Repentance loosens the bonds of wickedness. It frees the oppressed. We are prompted to share our bread with the hungry and bring the homeless into shelters and to clothe the naked. What a redemptive habit!

With this inseparability of worship and appropriate fasting, light breaks forth and healing springs up. The Lord answers our cry and says, "Here am I." God's presence is the joyous reward for consistency of worship and justice toward the oppressed and needy.

Prayer: Lord God, by the grace of your Son Jesus Christ and the leadership of your Holy Spirit, enable us to live lives of sincere worship that lead us to care for the oppressed, to share bread with the hungry, to shelter the homeless, and to loose the bonds of injustice. Amen.

Thursday, February 26   Read Deuteronomy 26:1-11.

The habit of remembering

A great habit of spirituality to form at any time, but especially during the Lenten season, is that of *remembering* the great acts of God's deliverance in our lives. This prompts us toward gratitude and thanksgiving to God. Psalm 103:1 says it well: "Bless the Lord, O my soul, and all that is within me, bless his holy name. Bless the Lord, O my soul, and do not forget all his benefits."

This discipline of gratitude is the beating heart of the message of Deuteronomy 26:1-11. The reading reminds the Hebrews of their deliverance from slavery in Egypt. It reminds them that they have come into the land that God has given them to possess and settle in—a "land flowing with milk and honey."

These verses call them to remember the deliverance and the gift. With gratitude they were to practice these habits of gratitude, as are we.

As a sign of their faithfulness in remembering, the Hebrews were to give the first fruits of the land to God. We are to share with God *first* the results of our work in this land. Remind yourself and your faith community of your gratitude to God for God's deliverance of you. As Psalm 103 again says of God: "who forgives all your iniquity, who heals all your diseases, who redeems your life from the Pit, who crowns you with steadfast love and mercy, who satisfies you with good as long as you live."

Prayer: Almighty God, in whom we live and move and have our being, establish us in great habits of gratitude and remembrance of your mighty acts on our behalf. We thank you for all of your benefits. Amen.

Friday, February 27   Read Psalm 91:1-2, 9-16.

The habit of holding fast to God's promise

We live in times that try our souls and threaten us with destruction. At such times despair overcomes us, and we do not know where to turn. Psalm 91 speaks to this dilemma. It extols the providence and protection of God in the worst of times. It is a psalm of blessing to steady those who need endurance, the habit of holding fast to God's promises.

Verses 1-2 address us personally; they subtly command us to live in the shelter of the Most High and the shadow of the Almighty. Nebuchadnezzar threatened to throw Shadrach, Meshach, and Abednego into a fiery furnace if they did not serve his pagan gods. (Read Daniel 3:13-17.) They put themselves in the shelter of the Most High and in the shadow of the Almighty. They were thrown into the fiery furnace; a fourth person appeared with them and delivered them. Psalm 91:14-15 says, "Those who love me, I will deliver. I will protect those who know my name."

It is true that those who love God are not always saved from hardship, pain and death. Six million Jews were not saved from the evil of the Nazis. But God does not promise immunity from hardship, pain, or death; God offers a deeper protection. "Protect" in this psalm has to do with God's honoring us, setting us on high, satisfying our very souls and giving us life in the midst of and beyond the darkness of this world. Shadrach, Meshach, and Abednego believed that; even if they were not delivered, they would remain true to God.

In the Christian faith, through the resurrection of Jesus Christ, we live in the faith that "neither death, nor life…will be able to separate us from the love of God in Christ Jesus our Lord" (Rom. 8:38, 39). Whatever we face, let us hold fast to this promise.

Prayer: Strong Deliverer, steady our faith as we face tribulation, suffering, and even death. Amen.

Saturday, February 28   Read Romans 10:8*b*-13.

The habit of being near the word of God

Today's scripture combines the strength of the Old Testament Law and the gospel of our Lord Jesus Christ. The apostle Paul says that "the word is near you, on your lips and in your heart." Deuteronomy 30:14 is more graphic: "The word of the law is very near to you; it is in your mouth and in your heart for you to observe." God was near to Israel in the law by which God anticipated and laid the foundation for the gift of God's very being in Jesus Christ. What does the nearness of the word have to do with daily living?

First, it means that in our minds and hearts we, by reading and study, store up words of scripture. The words cannot be "in our mouth" until we have learned them. We learn the stories of the Bible; the dramatic story of the life, death, burial, and resurrection of Jesus. We tell that story to our loved ones and friends. Being encouraged by this word of Christ, we and they have hope and not despair.

Second, we have specific guiding words by which to function in daily living. We do not harbor grudges because scripture urges us to confess our brokenness to God. We seek reconciliation. We walk the walk; we talk the talk. We do those things that are acceptable in the sight of Jesus Christ. We do not run away from testing times but face them with courage and personal discipline. We treat others as persons made in the image of God and for whom Christ died. All of this because the word of God is near us, on our lips and in our hearts.

Third, we cultivate an awareness of God's presence in the Holy Spirit, the one who walks alongside us, enabling us to bear adversity.

Prayer: **"Let the words of my mouth and the meditation of my heart be acceptable to you, O Lord, my rock and my redeemer" (Ps. 19:14). Amen.**

71

First Sunday in Lent

Sunday, March 1   Read Luke 4:1-13.

The habit of refusing to be an exception

The devil tempted Jesus to deny his humanity, to admit he was an exception to the demands of being genuinely human. Often we routinely deny Jesus' humanity and our own by making him and ourselves an exception to the laws of life.

Therefore, on this first Sunday in Lent, let us confess this great temptation. Let us ask for strength to begin the habit of refusing to consider ourselves an exception to the demands of being human.

Jesus was hungry. The devil tempted him to take a shortcut in satisfying his desire by turning stones into bread. Jesus refused to be an exception. We are tempted to take a shortcut to affluence, to success in the work world, to sexual satisfaction, and so on. We choose to rush rather than taking the long, disciplined route. And in our rush we fail to develop patience—the power to wait.

The devil showed Jesus *in an instant* all the kingdoms of the world and promised him all authority and glory if he would worship the devil. Here again gratification seems immediate—in an instant. The devil tempted Jesus to lay aside his humanity. Only *after* his life ministry, death, and resurrection would Jesus say, "All authority in heaven and on earth has been given to me" (Matt. 28:18). God the Father gave the authority; Jesus did not take any shortcuts.

Finally the devil tempted Jesus to jump off the temple, to test not only the natural laws but to test God's promise that God would send angels to bear Jesus up—the laws of gravity notwithstanding. The secret to living is to refuse to allow tempters to deceive us into thinking we are exceptions. Begin and continue the habit of refusing to be an exception.

Prayer: Lord, help me to partake of Jesus' humanity and refuse to be an exception, as he did. Amen.

TRUST AND OBEY

March 2–8, 1998   **Mariellen Sawada**✤
Monday, March 2   Read Luke 13:31-35.

This week's lectionary scripture lessons have to do with trusting.
- In Genesis (Genesis 15:1-12, 17-18), Abram must trust in a God who is making some unbelievable promises.
- In his letter to the Philippians (3:17–4:1), Paul writes of trusting in the fullness of heavenly citizenship.
- In Psalm 27, the psalmist writes of trusting God amidst the fears that abound.
- And in the Gospel story, Jesus trusts in the work and ministry that God would have him to do.

Trust is an unwavering legacy of these Bible characters. Can you imagine how a lack of trust might have changed or distorted all of these Bible stories? What might have happened if Jesus had wavered one single bit when faced with the doubts and fears of the Pharisees? What would have happened had Jesus decided to hide behind barriers of fear? What would have happened had he run from the evil he was trying to conquer?

Trust is not all. That trust enabled the "Bible-times" characters to do the work and ministry of God. God challenged the people to trust and to *obey*. From long ago to now, to further in the future than we can ever know, God asks, encourages, and challenges all of us to trust—and to obey.

Prayer: Thank you, Lord, for asking, encouraging, and challenging me to trust—and to obey. May trusting and obeying become an intentional part of my everyday living, every day of my life. Amen.

✤Pastor, Wesley United Methodist Church; San Jose, California.

Tuesday, March 3   Read Luke 13:31-35.

As Jesus is teaching and "casting out demons and performing cures," some anxious Pharisees visit him. In a heroic act, these Pharisees attempt to save Jesus' life by warning him about Herod's actions: "The best thing you can do, Jesus, is to stop doing what you're doing and flee."

Jesus responds something like this, "You're talking to the wrong party here. I'm doing what I'm supposed to be doing. It's Herod who's out to lunch."

This warning could have stopped Jesus in his tracks, over-whelming him with its evil, frightening him with its reality. Instead, Jesus' concern rests with the Pharisees who deliver the message. If the Pharisees see the evil in Herod, why don't they confront Herod? Why do the Pharisees seek to change the one doing what is right instead of seeking to change the one who is doing what is wrong? Perhaps because

- it is easier?
- it takes less courage?
- it seems the most logical answer?

In the midst of it all, Jesus teaches through this situation. Jesus tells the Pharisees and all who would understand, "Go and tell that fox for me...."

When have you gone to tell "that fox"—for Jesus?

When is it that you need to speak up—for Jesus?

When will you trust in the need to support good instead of evil?

Prayer: **Lord, thank you for challenging the Pharisees and challenging me to speak up for you. During this Lenten season, hold this challenge of love and trust before me. Amen.**

Wednesday, March 4   Read Philippians 3:17-4:1.

My friend Pong is building a legacy that now includes a new country. Pong has just become a citizen of the United States. After lots of protocol, paperwork, interviews, and waiting, citizenship was granted.

While holding dear his country of birth, Pong is now beginning to realize the opportunities and the responsibilities of being a U.S. citizen. He is realizing
- I'll be old enough to vote for the next U.S. president.
- I can get a job now.
- I have a new identity.

These realizations are exciting and sobering. With citizenship comes the expectation of privilege and struggle, of strength and vulnerability, of assurance and doubt. But through it all Pong vows to stand as a good citizen.

The apostle Paul writes about these realizations of citizenship in his letter to the people of Philippi. Paul writes of a heavenly citizenship offered to all who will accept and embrace it.

Having embraced this identity, Paul tells the Philippians and all who read his words to stand firmly with it, no matter what happens. He seems to say, "Don't waver in your heavenly citizenship. Remember your opportunities and responsibilities Hold fast to the new identity given to you."

Paul speaks these words to us today as we experience this Lenten season. He reminds us that we have a heavenly citizenship to embrace today and all days.

Hold fast to the identity of being a Christian, a member of Christ's family, a citizen in the realm of God.

Prayer: **Dear God, may I always honor my heavenly citizenship. May I stand firm in the knowledge of my heavenly legacy, no matter what. Amen.**

Thursday, March 5   Read Genesis 15:1-12, 17-18.

Abram speaks with the Lord. He bemoans the fact that he has no hope of leaving the earth a living legacy. He says that he is childless; he has no heir.

"Well," says the Lord, "that's not quite how it's going to be. In fact, nothing could be farther from the truth." The Lord then attempts to tell Abram about what is yet to be; what life will be brought forth; what righteousness will come about.

Abram responds skeptically. In this conversation, Abram just cannot see the possibility of God's promises. The predicament of his life limits his vision; the promises don't make sense...

...until God suggests, "Let's work on your range of vision, Abram. Let's go outside." There, outside, in the night, God expands Abram's vision with the sight of the heavens and the stars. Outside, under the stars, God enables Abram to trust and to look beyond himself. God helps Abram realize again that there is more to life and living than meets the eye—promises and possibilities exist beyond predicaments and limitations.

Maybe you wonder, like Abram, about God's plan for your life. Maybe you wonder, like Abram, about your ability to follow that plan. Maybe, like Abram, you wonder, *God, do you have promises and possibilities...for me?*

If you wonder, like Abram, then go outside under the evening sky and spend time counting the stars with God. Be likened to Abram and realize God's vastness beyond your own understanding. Realize the power and wisdom God can instill in your life.

Prayer: O immense God, thank you for enabling Abram and the rest of humanity to count the stars with you. Help us look beyond what we humanly can know to envision the vastness of your presence and the value of your promises. Be with us, Lord, as we count the stars with you. Amen.

Friday, March 6   Read Psalm 27.

Psalm 27 reflects the psalmist's legacy of trust in God, beginning with confidence and writing with courage.

But get real.

If evildoers were to assail you to devour your flesh, wouldn't you be even a little bit afraid?

If an army were out to get you, wouldn't there be some fear in your heart?

If you were falsely accused so that your job, your home, or your reputation were in danger, wouldn't there be some cause for concern?

Is the psalmist saying that if I trust the Lord to be the "stronghold of my life," then I must not fear anything?—not disease and disaster, "downsizing," the loss of quality time, global warming, or nuclear disaster?

Is the psalm writer saying that the presence of trust is the absence of any fear?

No, I don't think the psalmist is saying it's wrong or faithless to fear. Instead, this writer inspires us to be courageous enough to believe and to "wait for the Lord" amidst our fears. This writer encourages us to be strong so that fears do not overtake us or keep us from seeing "the land of the living."

This week—amidst fears that may threaten or assail you—take courage, be strong, and keep sight of "the land of the living." Surround your fears with courage and strength that only the Lord can offer.

Prayer: **Today, now, in this moment, O Lord, surround me with your strength and courage—amidst my trust, amidst my fears. Give me the vision to see more—amidst my trust, amidst my fears. Amen.**

Saturday, March 7   Read Psalm 27.

Talk about the power of prayer!

My friend Renee and I are in awe as we remember the prayers of our grandmothers. We remember their praying with energy and anguish. We remember their trust in God not only to understand their prayers but to act on their prayers.

Renee tells of her grandmother who prayed "mighty prayers" that always found immediate and miraculous response. I remember my grandmother's praying long-standing, long-suffering, heartfelt prayers that would begin at 4 A.M. every day of her Christian life.

These grandmothers leave a legacy of faith to us, their grand-daughters. They are contemporary examples of the power of prayer. In the same way, the writer of Psalm 27 leaves a legacy of faith, having revealed a life of prayer.

Psalm 27 is about the psalmist's life of prayer; the writer's experience of talking with God, inquiring of God, crying to God, singing to God,...and waiting for God. What energy and anguish in the life of this pray-er!

Do you wonder about the power of prayer in your life? Do you imagine its experience in your life? Do you wonder what would happen if you were to offer God a "mighty prayer"? Do you think about what would happen if you intensely prayed some long-standing, long-suffering, heartfelt words and feelings, hopes and dreams?

If you offered such prayers, perhaps you and the world would be transformed, changed, enhanced, encouraged. Perhaps God would enter your life and speak. Don't just wonder or think about these prayers. Don't just imagine them. Talk about them. Talk about the power of prayer...with God.

Prayer: **Lord, help me pray to you with heartfelt words and feelings, hopes and dreams. Enable me during this Lenten time to talk about the power of prayer with you. Amen.**

Second Sunday in Lent

Sunday, March 8 Read Luke 13:35.

There's nothing I like better, no matter what season of the year, than to go to my favorite Japanese restaurant to eat some good tempura. At its essence, tempura is a delicious Japanese dish consisting of fresh vegetables quickly fried in a light batter. The secret for good tempura seems to rest in the recipe of the batter. It's the batter that must be tasty—and light.

Amazingly enough, tempura is a Lenten food! Recently, I learned that fifteenth-century Japanese Christians conceived of tempura. They wanted a delicious meatless food to serve during Lent—their attempt to keep the dietary discipline during the days of remembering Christ's passion. It was their way of preparing for "the one who comes in the name of the Lord." All this time, I just thought I was eating good food!

Tempura remains a traditional food in my life and experience. But this year during Lent, it becomes more. It becomes a legacy of faithful Christians whose witness to Christ has affected me unconsciously and now, consciously.

This week we remember many legacies resulting from the trust of the faithful.

- Abram gives us the legacy of his family.
- The psalmist offers a long-standing, poetic legacy of praise and prayer.
- Jesus teaches a legacy for righteous living.
- Paul offers us a legacy of heavenly citizenship.

All of these legacies, including tempura, whet our spiritual palates. During Lent, partake of these legacies and find your way to proclaim to the world, "Blessed is the one who comes in the name of the Lord."

Prayer: **O gracious, grace-giving God, nourish me with the legacies of faith. May they bless me and challenge me to offer my legacy of faithful living to others. Lead me, Lord. Amen.**

PRAISE GOD! ALL THE TIME

March 9–15, 1998   **James R. King, Jr.✤**
Monday, March 9   Read Psalm 63:1-4.

Praise God!

This week the scriptures remind us of the most important lesson we will ever need to learn: Keep God in the center of all we do. Listen for this lesson.

When you want something to live, give it attention. When you want something to die, turn your back on it. We must learn to give God attention if we want God to live in us. One of the primary reasons for the church's existence is to maintain worship. When a congregation worships, it praises God. When we praise anything, we give it attention; we help to maintain its existence in our minds and hearts. When we praise God, we are building up the presence of God in our lives.

The psalmist is clear. Our primary concern is to connect with God. Why seek and praise God? "Because your steadfast love is better than life, my lips will praise you." We are children of God, connected to the greatest source in the universe.

When we acknowledge who God is and consider how satisfying it is to be in God's presence, our natural response is to praise God. One thing is for sure according to the psalmist: When God is in the center of our lives, we shall not want; peace that passes human understanding fills our existential moments, and our faith in God secures our future.

Prayer: **O God of life and love, we praise your holy name and thank you for your steadfast love. Help us keep you in the center of all we do. In Jesus Christ's name we pray. Amen.**

✤Executive Director of the Tennessee Conference Council on Ministries of The United Methodist Church; Nashville, Tennessee.

Tuesday, March 10   Read Psalm 63:5-8.

God is good all the time.

God is at work in the world and in our lives. One cannot underestimate the revival that comes when we pause to reflect, meditate, pray, and praise. These pauses refresh and fulfill us whenever we drink from the spiritual well of God. To receive satisfaction, we may not deceive ourselves into thinking that we can break from the presence of God in our lives. It is important to distinguish between physical maturity and spiritual maturity. When we emphasize physical maturity, we recall situations where independence is appropriately applauded as when children learn to tie their own shoes or they are able to go to school without the assistance of their loved one. Spiritual maturity recognizes that one is always dependent on God. To think of living independently of God is ludicrous.

The psalmist in verse 5 reminds us that it is natural and appropriate to use the physical anatomy (the mouth) to express gratitude and praise for spiritual fullness and satisfaction. God's goodness emerges during times of reflection and comes forth through all we say and do.

Because God is good all the time and provides for all our needs, staying close to God day and night allows us to joyfully declare, "It is well with my soul."

Prayer: O God of life and love, thank you for being there for me anytime and all the time. Help me make you the foundation of all that I am and all that I do, for only you can satisfy my soul. In Jesus Christ's name I pray. Amen.

Wednesday, March 11   Read Isaiah 55:1-9.

God is spirit.

God is the spiritual parent of us all. When we acknowledge God as spirit, it carries us a long way in our understanding the connection among people of all nations and races. The prophet has a clear sense of God's will for the world family when he writes in verse 1, "Everyone who thirsts, come to the waters." God invites all—even those accustomed to being excluded by virtue of their poverty or society's oppression. The prophet makes it plain in the same verse, "And you that have no money, come, buy and eat!"

How unfortunate it is that we use the name of God to justify our dislike for one another. How sad that so many people of faith find division under the name of God. Surely this separation in our attempt to serve God is rooted in something other than the generous will of our spiritual parent.

What do we get when we accept the invitation to come to the waters? We get all that we need, all that truly satisfies—water, bread, wine, and milk. In God we find the essentials for life. We need God! No one can be full without God; and for those who are empty, fullness is available.

All one has to do is to turn to God. This is the message of repentance and grace. With all our mistakes related to our selfish ways, God—who loves more than most can imagine—is willing to accept us and meet our every need.

For those who seek to understand from a logical point of view, this understanding is unclear. In order to understand God's way we must activate our faith capacity, for God is spirit. The prophet guides the open mind when he writes, "For my thoughts are not your thoughts, nor are your ways my ways, says the Lord."

Prayer: **O God of life and love, fill us with your spirit that we may do your will. In Jesus Christ's name we pray. Amen.**

Thursday, March 12   Read Luke 13:1-5.

Repent.

In these words from Luke's Gospel, Jesus chastises the Jews for being too concerned about physical suffering and death and failing to understand the significance of spiritual death. Jesus' words again contradict the Jews' belief that one suffered in direct proportion to one's sins, while reminding them that their spiritual lives are in danger without repentance.

The will of God is that spiritual living will influence the world. Light should overcome darkness; love should overcome hate.

A loving God has blessed us, and yet too many will not take time to worship God. It is easier to complain about the problems facing our young people than it is to use our gifts to teach a Sunday school class or to support a program that offers a healthy alternative. We have misplaced our values; our concerns are exclusive.

To fulfill God's purpose and know satisfaction, repentance is necessary. Our concern is not physical death but spiritual death. A spiritually dead person cannot participate in his or her purpose for being, which is to glorify God. A spiritually dead person cannot help usher in the good news of God's intent for all God's people. After all, can we not see the world is perishing more from a lack of spiritual perspective than a physical one? We have enough food to feed the world; but if we are spiritually dead, selfishness prevents us from sharing. We have enough resources to give all children an education and to provide for our elderly. Unless we repent and turn to God's will, we will not see the kingdom of God. We cannot save ourselves. We must turn to God, for true life is with God.

Prayer: **O God of life and love, our selfishness entraps us. Forgive us and help us to be more obedient to your will for the world. In Jesus Christ's name we pray. Amen.**

Friday, March 13   Read Luke 13:6-9.

Use what you have.

An older brother was teasing his younger six-year-old brother. The older brother invited the younger to come to the bathroom. When the younger boy arrived at the door, the older brother said, "Look, there is a small bear in the bathtub." Rather than look in the bathtub, the younger child ran back to his room. As the older brother pleaded with him to come see the little bear, the younger brother yelled back with a tearful sound in his voice, "I'm not, because I'm supposed to be happy."

As children of God we will have our share of problems, but it is the will of God that all of God's children be blessed (happy). Our blessedness is linked to our willingness to live into God's plan for us where, by grace, we grow into our potential and help shape the world into a reflection of God's will. We must be willing to use our gifts to the best of our ability for the glory of God.

The story of the barren fig tree reminds us of God's expectations that we be fruitful and thus participate in our vital role of kingdom building. Thousands of Christians across the world have missed this important lesson as they repeatedly refuse to share their gifts with a congregation or with some community effort that glorifies God.

Jesus also uses the parable to make it clear that all of us live under the grace of God. However, we need not misunderstand God's graciousness and take it as a season in our lives to make more excuses and do nothing. In fact, as long we have breath and health we have time. Yet we know not the time or the hour, but our time will run out and the opportunity to serve God's purpose will be gone.

Prayer: O God of life and love, deepen our appreciation of the privilege you have given us to travel on this earthly journey. May all that we can be rise to serve your purpose. Amen.

Saturday, March 14   Read 1 Corinthians 10:1-5.

History and wisdom

Have you noticed how difficult it is to get one athlete in competition to talk negatively about the opponent? In fact, even when some athletes know that their talent and record are superior to their opponents', they speak with respect about the other. What warrants such caution when commenting on the outcome of a game? Two reasons come to mind immediately. One: History teaches us that while confidence is good, overconfidence is bad. When a person or community becomes overconfident, it is possible to relax too much and lose the necessary intensity that keeps one alert and at the top of his or her game. Two: Overconfidence can motivate an opponent; who wants to be taunted? In reality, on any given day, one is subject to being defeated by a more energized and highly motivated opponent.

Paul uses the history of the Hebrews to remind the early church in Corinth that you can be right in the midst of God's blessings or active in the life of a congregation and still miss the mark because you take things for granted and become content and comfortable with the status quo. Samson's experience with Delilah, Sarah's laughter at the announcement of giving birth at her age, or the disciples' going to sleep rather than watching while Jesus prayed are just a few examples of how none of us is immune to the tendency to believe and act out of our limited human understanding, rather than to look beyond our self-centeredness to God's ever-creating power.

Prayer: O God of life and love, may the wisdom of history and remembering keep us alert to your will from day to day and hour to hour. In Jesus Christ's name we pray. Amen.

Third Sunday in Lent

Sunday, March 15   Read 1 Corinthians 10:6-13.

There is no place to park.

My loving father reminded me over and over again during my childhood years that there was no place to park. There was no place to pull over and say you have it made. My father did not go into much detail, but I think he was trying to communicate to me the same lesson that Paul wanted to get through to the Corinthians. Temptation will never die. Distractions will come at the least expected time; and, to that extent, we must always be ready. Not only must we be ready for the temptations of the world, but we must remain so centered on God's will through praise that we interpret the temptation as a test to help build our Christian character by reminding us to cling to God in all circumstances. So Paul writes in verse 12, "So if you think you are standing, watch out that you do not fall."

Paul leaves the Corinthians with the essential warning about the physical trap of temptation but quickly embraces them with encouragement. Paul writes, "No testing has overtaken you that is not common to everyone. God is faithful, and he will not let you be tested beyond your strength, but with the testing he will also provide the way out."

So often we hear among some who have been tested by trials and tribulations, "God will make a way out of no way." In the end it is good to know that grace wins. God will not let us down because God cannot fail us. Let us then, in every season, keep God in the center of all we do, for God is worthy of praise.

Prayer: O God of life and love, it is reassuring to know that when we have done our best and sometimes find ourselves still marked by failure, you do not give up on us but love us into victory. Thank you God! In Jesus Christ's name we pray. Amen.

GOD RESTORES US TO WHOLENESS AND JOY

March 16–22, 1998   **Elaine Eberhart**✤
Monday, March 16   Read Joshua 5:9-12.

Transitions mark our lives, transitions that are often as memorable to us as the periods that come before and after them. Marked by baby showers, graduations, and retirement parties, these hinge points in our lives contain pieces of what was and possibilities of what is to come, mixed with a good measure of grief, anxiety, and exhilaration.

As communities of faith, we also mark the transitions in our church year—some with celebrations and some with times of self-examination. Many of us begin the Lenten season with the words *repent and believe the gospel*; ashes are placed in the sign of a cross on our foreheads. With those ashes, we commit ourselves to the Lenten journey and remember that God is with us.

This passage from Joshua relates a transition point in the covenantal relationship between God and the people of Israel. God has given the land to God's people, and their observance of Passover signals the transition from the wilderness to the land that was promised to their ancestors. Although their life as a community radically changes in this transition, one thing remains constant: The God who saved them from the disgrace of Egypt, who provided manna and now gives the produce of the land, is yet present with God's people.

Suggestion for meditation: **Remember with thanksgiving a transition in which you have felt God's presence.**

✤Director of Development at Candler School of Theology at Emory University; clergy member of the Holston Conference of The United Methodist Church.

Tuesday, March 17   Read Psalm 32:1-5.

I once kept a shamrock in a sunny window. Every afternoon I arrived home to see its slender stems and broad leaves all reaching toward the sun. I would turn the pot so that the plant would have a more uniform appearance, but each day the result was the same: The shamrock oriented itself toward the light.

Confessing our sin reorients us toward the God who loves us and wills our good. Through confession, we name before God the times we have strayed from God's way of love. The very act of naming our sins turns us back toward that way of love in which God is ever working in and for us.

The psalmist speaks of the consequences of keeping our sin hidden. Like many secrets, our secret sin causes us pain and depletes us of our strength. Most of us have spent sleepless nights plagued by the worry of a broken relationship for which we were at fault.

That worry brought both emotional and physical pain. The psalmist says relief from that pain comes in exposing our sins to the light of God's love for us. When we confess, God is quick to forgive; and the heavy weight of guilt is lifted. We turn again toward God and our neighbor in love, because we no longer devote our energy to the futile hiding of secret sin.

God is present when we hide from God, shining the light into a darkened corner of our lives. God prompts our confession as God moves in us speaking of the possibility of forgiveness and restoration to a life of joy. Happy are we who name our sin in response to a light-offering God.

***Suggestion for meditation:* Name before God one thing that is keeping you from fully loving God and neighbor.**

Wednesday, March 18   Read Psalm 32:6-11.

In the second part of Psalm 32, the psalmist testifies about the experience of confession and restoration and counsels his hearers to follow his example and trust in God. From his own experience he advises the hearers to listen for God's gentle leading and not be obstinate, like a mule who must be curbed with bit and bridle. Those who trust in God and dare to name their sins will know God's forgiveness, will receive assurance of God's steadfast love and restoration to a life of joy.

Traditionally Lent has been a time in which the church has focused on repentance and forgiveness. Early Christians used the season to make final preparations for the baptism of converts. Those persons who were cut off from fellowship with the church because of particularly egregious sins were given the opportunity for restoration to the community. With the careful training of converts and the process of reconciliation for those who were cut off from fellowship, the entire church was called to self-examination, confession, and a new commitment to the baptismal vows to love God and neighbor.

Lent is a time of reflection, and that reflection brings both regret and joy. The ways that we have not honored God's command to love God and neighbor confront us, yet we receive assurance of God's forgiveness as we commit ourselves anew to the way of love. The freedom to turn again to God and neighbor brings joy even as we remember the one who suffered for us.

Prayer: **For the assurance that you forgive me, for your steadfast love, for the many ways that you fill my life with joy, I give you thanks, O God. Amen.**

Thursday, March 19   Read 2 Corinthians 5:16-21.

A recent issue of a news magazine envisioned life in the twenty-first century and suggested the advances we might anticipate. It is hard to imagine the world that scientists and engineers predict, but we know that the advent of computers and new medical technologies has changed our lives greatly over the past ten years. Technological advances may enhance the quality of life, but we wonder whether they will address the problems that will likely outlive our generation: problems of physical and spiritual hunger, of violence, of poverty.

Although our technological advances lead us to affirm Paul's words "everything old has passed away; see, everything has become new," we know that he is writing of a different and more radical transformation of the world. Paul asks the Corinthians and us to see life in a new way. The coming of Christ has recreated the entire universe; God's choosing to share the lot of creation by becoming one of us inaugurates a new era.

The reordering of the universe is work that also occurs in each person who is related to Christ. God's renewing work affects every part of our life. If we are in Christ, the renewal of creation that began with Christ continues in us.

Signs of reconciliation, God's mission in the world, mark the renewal of creation. Just as we who are in Christ become part of the renewal of creation, we also share that mission, becoming ambassadors of reconciliation in Christ's name. It is that work of reconciliation, prompted and enabled by a loving God, that holds hope for the future.

Prayer: **Use me, O God, to take the good news of your reconciling love to a hurting person today. Amen.**

Friday, March 20   Read Luke 15:1-3, 11*b*-32.

This parable's setting is important, because the identity of Jesus' hearers provides insights into the meaning of the story of the prodigal son. Jesus has attracted tax collectors and sinners. Seeing them, the Pharisees and scribes grumble about the disgrace of one who "welcomes sinners and eats with them."

Before we fault the Pharisees too much, we have to remember who they are and how much they resemble most of us. The Pharisees see their charge as maintaining the integrity of the law and rituals. Jesus' new friends are ritually unclean, which threatens that integrity. And the Pharisees have ample reason to hate the tax collectors. They are not simply working for a government in which the Pharisees have no voice; the tax collectors make their living by doing the bidding of the foreign government that occupies Israel. They are exploiting their own people.

Those ideas are not so alien to us as we would like to think. It is not a great distance from the Pharisees' grumbling to that of our own: Will the hospitality we offer persons we see as sinful be understood by them as condoning their sin? How can we advocate high standards of moral behavior and yet offer a welcoming hand and God's good news to all?

Jesus' vision in the parable instructively answers those questions. The radical nature of the vision says that God reaches out with extravagant love for all. Jesus does not reject the Pharisees; he broadens the circle to include even those the Pharisees have declared unworthy.

Prayer: **Enlarge my vision of your love, O God, so that I may reach out to others with your mercy. Amen.**

Saturday, March 21   Read Luke 15:20-24.

We might rename the parable of the prodigal son the parable of the prodigal father. This story tells of a son's ill-chosen path and subsequent return home, but its chief focus is the love that the father lavishes on his son. In contrast to the son's extravagance in squandering his inheritance, we see the father's prodigality in the extravagant actions of love he pours out at the return of his beloved.

The father's extravagance is what makes this story so striking. It is unremarkable that a father would meet a repentant son with forgiveness. A father who observed the law might have granted his son pardon, even when the son had asked for his inheritance early thereby treating his father as if he were dead.

This father goes beyond what was required, however; his love knows no bounds. He is watching for his son, for he sees him when he is still far off. He runs to meet him, risking indignity, because men in Palestine did not run except in cases of danger. He embraces his son, and then calls to his servants to bring gifts and begin a time of celebration. The gifts are lavish: the best robe, a ring, sandals, a fatted calf reserved for festival days. The lavish gifts publicly mark the restoration of the son to his family.

Such is the extravagance of the God who welcomes all of us home when we have strayed to explore the attractions of a far-off land. God scans the horizon, awaiting our return. God runs to meet us. Before we can force the words of our confession, God embraces us, and there is joy in heaven and on earth at our return.

Suggestion for meditation: **In what ways has God lavished love on me?**

Fourth Sunday in Lent

Sunday, March 22   Read Luke 15:25-31.

We who are oldest children can identify with the elder son in this parable. We have often seen our parents relax standards of behavior where our younger brothers and sisters are concerned. When we were children, it was easy to point out the seeming hardships of being the oldest even as our siblings argued that the way of the middle or youngest child was far more difficult.

The elder son voices some of our feelings, but his case is perhaps stronger than ours. He hears the music and learns that it is for his brother, but he will not join a party given for one who has dishonored the family with dissolute living. When his father urges him to come inside, the older son hurls his words angrily. He has labored long for his father, and where has it gotten him? What he has earned by merit, his wayward brother is getting for free.

In his explanation, the father tries to restore the elder son to his place in the family just as he has done with his younger son. While he tells the elder son of his love for him, he also affirms that the celebration for the younger son is necessary. The story ends without resolution; we do not know whether the elder son will go inside.

All of us who like to believe that we merit God's favor because of our good behavior must also ask ourselves whether we will join the party. The problem with relying on our merit is that it limits our access to God's grace. The party begins for us when we celebrate with others who, like ourselves, enjoy the grace that God lavishes on all of God's children.

Suggestion for meditation: **What do I need to give up to join the party?**

RIVERS IN THE DESERT

March 23–29, 1998   **Anne Horton**♣
Monday, March 23   Read Isaiah 43:16-19.

Today's scripture calls the Hebrew people to remember—but not dwell on—the past. In the first two verses the prophet reminds the Hebrew people of the crossing at the Red Sea (Exodus 14–15). If you turn to that passage you find these words: "Do not be afraid...the Lord will accomplish....The Lord will fight for you, and you have only to keep still" (Ex. 14:13-14).

Remembering is important. Remembering that the Lord made a pathway through the sea and through the wilderness engenders the courage and strength of this people in exile to face the present and the future. God made pathways in the past, and God is making a pathway from exile to Jerusalem.

A recent children's retreat focused on the journeys of the Hebrew people. It skimmed the surface in an experiential nature. The different groups traveled (hiked) to the towns of Haran, Hebron, Egypt, the wilderness, and so on. Each group received the "essentials": raisins, crackers, and water. Over a period of three hours they walked, listened, read scripture, and learned about the experiences and the lives of the Hebrew people. One child commented on the many times God called the people to remember. To be so young, this child had learned a significant biblical truth.

During this season of Lent, where do you need to see or remember evidence of God's presence within your life? What pathways do you need to recall to face the present with strength and courage?

Prayer: **Almighty God, help me to reflect and see your presence within my life. Amen.**

♣Program Coordinator for Sumatanga, North Alabama Conference.

Tuesday, March 24   Read Isaiah 43:18-21.

"I am about to do a new thing;...I will make a way in the wilderness." As amazing as God's support of the Hebrews has been in the past, it is as nothing compared to the wonderful things God is bringing about now. The path through the sea will become a path through the wilderness; God's redemption is ongoing.

Many signs and wonders accompanied the Hebrews in their journey through the desert. Possibly the most memorable was the gift of water in the desert—a gift that refreshed God's chosen people to the end that they would declare God's praise. God had brought forth water in the desert. What a great thing God has done!

This provision of water causes much of creation to honor God. Even the animals of the desert rejoice in God's provision for a wondrous future. With the flowing of water in the desert, that which once was a place of dryness and death becomes a place of respite and care.

When our well is dry or when we are in a desert time within the journey, we may lose sight of the great things God *has done* for us. We may lose sight of the great things God *is doing* for us. Only through eyes of faith may we "perceive it." We need to attempt great things for God, but we also need to expect great things from God.

Prayer: **Lord, in this time, open my mind and heart to see the great things you are doing in my life. Amen.**

Wednesday, March 25   Read Psalm 126.

I can only imagine the excitement and joy the exiles must have felt when Cyrus of Persia allowed the Israelites to return to Palestine. The people had been praying in the hope they would be able to return to their homeland. The psalmist identifies himself with the people of the return. The return was probably like a dream—too good to be true. What an opportunity for joy and laughter. Even other nations recognized the power of God's mighty acts.

The people pray for a new restoration of fortunes; they liken their desire to "the watercourses in the Negeb." The Negeb is a dry territory to the south of Palestine (Judah) that autumn rains can quickly change into a place of life-giving streams. The Hebrew people pray that their tears of disappointment may issue in a harvest of joy. The psalmist assures them that God will answer their prayer.

A close friend was diagnosed with cancer. She shared with me her ups and downs with treatment as well as her physical and emotional lows. What helped her through was her practice of meditating on God's word each day. When doctors told her she was cancer free, what joy and jubilation she expressed. A restoration had occurred. Joy remembered—joy anticipated!

Where does each of us need restoration? Is it in health? in work? in our relationship with God or others? in faith? Wherever it is, let us give thanks and seek God's word in our own restoration.

As the Hebrew people remembered what the Lord had done, we too remember. In this time of Lent, let us approach the Lord with tears of repentance that we may enter into the joy of "the great things" the Lord has done for each of us.

Prayer: **Where do I need restoration, Lord? Show me and restore me. Amen.**

96

Thursday, March 26 Read Philippians 3:4*b*-11.

Paul promotes himself as a model Jew by enumerating his privileges and achievements. And what these privileges and achievements gave him was a self-righteous confidence in his own abilities—a "confidence in the flesh," rather than a confidence in God. Paul's language of loss and gain calls to our minds a ledger sheet, a system of checks and balances. Yet he goes on to say, "I regard everything as loss because of the surpassing value of knowing Christ Jesus my Lord." Pitch the ledger sheet out the door; Christ has given Paul a new way of looking at and assessing the world.

For Paul, knowing Christ involves an intimate, personal, and obedient relationship. He moves beyond the intellectual knowing of the mind to a knowing that incorporates the will and the heart. Paul juxtaposes the righteousness of the law with "the righteousness from God based on faith."

Our society demands that we live in certain ways: eat this, do that, wear this. Only then will we be successful and accepted. We stockpile privileges and achievements as we operate from the ledger sheet, rather than opening ourselves to the transforming power of Christ who gives us a new way of seeing.

I often find myself caught up in religious traditions, and I lose sight of the God I love and know. I have to stop, humble myself before God, and once again put my trust in God.

During this Lenten season, allow yourself to be known and transformed by Christ in heart, mind, and will.

Suggestion for meditation: **What part of your life needs the transforming touch of Christ?**

Prayer: **God, we resist transformation of the heart, mind, and will. Help us shed that reluctance and be open to your transforming love. Amen.**

Friday, March 27   Read Philippians 3:10-14.

The language of Philippians 3:12 in the Revised Standard Version often gave us difficulty: "Not that I have already obtained this or am already perfect; but I press on to make it my own" (v. 12, RSV). The New Revised Standard Version has "remedied" the verse: "Not that I have already obtained this or have already reached the goal; but I press on to make it my own." But many Christians today still come back to the question: Can a Christian obtain perfection? We are looking for a way to justify our actions.

In this passage Paul tells the Philippian Christians that he has not reached perfection, but this is how he's trying to get there: "It is not to be thought that I have already achieved all this. I have not yet reached perfection, but I press on, hoping to take hold of that for which Christ once took hold of me. My friends, I do not reckon myself to have got hold of it yet. All I can say is this: forgetting what is behind me, and reaching out for that which lies ahead, I press towards the goal to win the prize which is God's call to the life above, in Christ Jesus" (vv. 13-14, NEB).

We are not to rest on our laurels—remembering what we have done; we are to remember what we still have to do in Christ. We do not become perfect by obeying the law. In 1 Corinthians 2:6 and following, Paul defines perfection as a moving toward a mature faith, a continual process of growth. I believe Paul is saying that every person is grasped by Christ for some purpose.

Many of us spend our whole life trying hard to figure out what that purpose is. When we keep Christ as our focus (goal), he will reveal that purpose. We are not to relax with that purpose but be fervent in it.

Suggestion for meditation: **What are you needing to put aside so you can continue to strive toward God?**

Saturday, March 28   Read John 12:1-8.

Bethany is only two miles from Jerusalem. In the full knowledge of a plot against his life, Jesus returns to the vicinity of Jerusalem. The now-raised Lazarus and his sisters, Mary and Martha, host a dinner. Once again we find Martha serving.

Not weighing the cost of the perfume or the extravagance of it, Mary anoints Jesus' feet and wipes them with her hair. This anointing is an act of appreciation for where Jesus has trod and where he will go—his journey to the cross. What a compassionate and costly love she shows!

This picture brings to mind the story of *The Gift of the Magi* by O. Henry. The story centers around two people in love, both of whom are poor. Each had a unique possession. Each gave the other all there was to give by sacrificing that unique possession.

Mary humbles herself and shows no self-consciousness as to what others think as she wipes Jesus' feet with her hair. Mary's act is a priestly and prophetic sign, confirming Jesus' imminent work of reconciling God and humanity. Mary's focus and love center on Jesus. She wants to take in as much of Jesus as she can before he goes to Jerusalem.

No doubt people with whom we have wanted to spend as much time as we could have crossed our paths. Their knowledge, insights, and ideas have intrigued us, challenged us, and helped us grow spiritually. When we come face to face with Jesus Christ—however Christ may be revealed to us—we must learn to disregard what others may think of what we do or say. We must focus only on our love for Christ and our willingness to obey the Lord of our lives.

Suggestion for meditation: **What blinds you or hinders you from loving Christ?**

Fifth Sunday of Lent

Sunday, March 29   Read John 12:1-8.

Judas! What is your problem? Why is it so hard for you to look at the generosity of others without embarrassment or wanting to control? I imagine this might have been Jesus' reaction to Judas. Judas had seen an act of kindness, of loveliness; but he construed it as being wasteful. Judas is reacting to the generosity of someone's bestowing something precious on someone else. If Mary had poured the perfumed ointment on Judas, would he have reacted differently? Or was he so money conscious that he could not see the beauty of the gift?

Recently a young woman came to me and shared the love she had for her husband who had been killed in a tragic accident. Several times she made the comment, "I wish I had told him how much I enjoyed his interruption in my day." It seems he had a passion for wanting to be in the out-of-doors. He would pack a picnic lunch, call his wife to meet him, and eat lunch with her beside a nearby lake. They would spend those times sharing dreams, concerns, and life. She realized the beauty of the gift too late to say thank-you or to tell him how much she really had enjoyed those times.

Whether it is interruptions or planned experiences, why do we hold back? Risking is a part of growth. Mary was wanting to show her deep love for Jesus.

Often it seems that we are unable to receive the goodness of others or even to affirm it. We would all benefit from remembering to do and say things now—as Mary did—because the chance may not come again. It is well worth the risk in sharing life with others.

Suggestion for meditation: **What is getting in your way of seeing the beauty of other people's generosity?**

100

GOD DOES NOT WANT SUFFERING

March 30—April 5, 1998   **Carolyn Stahl Bohler✤**
Monday, March 30   Read Luke 19:28-40.

This week we reflect upon the "Passion" narratives. Liturgically, *passion* refers to the suffering of Jesus. In a broader sense, *passion* means strong feelings. Jesus was passionate about justice, God's love, health, and living responsibly in relationship.

Jesus tried—passionately—to enable people to claim God's power in their lives. There were those who could not imagine that such an effective prophet would not want political power—power over others. He sought to expand their imagination, to help them see their power with God.

A God of compassion never *wants* anyone to suffer nor requires suffering to bring about good. Yet suffering exists. When suffering occurs, it is not the last word; good can reemerge. God's constant pull is in the direction of good.

Jesus chose to ride into Jerusalem amidst the noisy, jubilant crowd. If necessary, he was willing to suffer for what he believed. (This scenario differs greatly from the understanding that God willed Jesus' suffering.) Indeed it was *through* Jesus' suffering, which resulted in part because of people's inability to grasp Jesus' message of empowerment, that Jesus' message and power survived.

Suggestion for meditation: **Reflect upon some expectation of good you have had in your life. Consider how it was fulfilled, thwarted, or altered. Imagine an empowering God helping you understand relevant guidance regarding that expectation today. Jot down any thoughts, images, or ideas that you receive.**

✤Professor, United Theological Seminary; Dayton, Ohio; author of several books.

Tuesday, March 31   Read Isaiah 50:4-9*a*.

This one we meet in Isaiah is such a confident teacher! Verse 4 marvelously describes the empathy good teaching requires: "[The Lord God] wakens my ear to listen *as those who are taught*" (emphasis added). It is not surprising that one who listens *as* a student to one's own teaching—putting oneself in the student's place—would be an assured educator. The speaker's security of self is connected to attentiveness to and interest in the students. This reaching out is possible because of trust in a God who helps.

Years ago, I gathered courage to make a decision regarding my profession while singing "Take my life, and let it be consecrated, Lord, to thee." That hymn's verses about using my intellect, voice, hands, feet, and consecrating all to God persuaded me that I must do what I could with my gifts. God the Good Teacher uses all the aspects named in the hymn to help us find our calling *and* to gain a measure of confidence to pursue it.

The assured one who speaks in Isaiah suffers even while doing what seems to be God's call. The called one does not seek out suffering or think that God sends it. Instead, he or she relies on guidance and strength from God while facing the challenges.

Believing in a God who calls and teaches goes hand in hand with taking concrete action in our communities. If we use our intellect, voice, feet, and consecrate all to God, we can hardly avoid issues. We act and speak, anxious at times but God-assured.

Suggestion for meditation: **Repeat a dozen times, then recollect occasionally during the day a phrase such as these: "The Good Teacher guides; I am God-confident"; "God, help me to be self-assured, attentive to others, and confident in you."**

Wednesday, April 1   Read Psalm 31:9-16; 118:1-2, 19-29.

What a passionate way to begin the day! Myriad Jews and Christians repeat the words exclaimed by the psalmist, "This is the day that the Lord has made; let us rejoice and be glad in it." Yet many of us also cry out the sentiment of the psalmist who said, "My eye wastes away from grief, my soul and body also. For my life is spent with sorrow, and my years with sighing."

We will grieve, age, and face death; these are aspects of created life. We may at times be sorrowful about these features of life, but we realize we cannot avoid any of them. These experiences are necessary elements and can provide meaning when we express our feelings honestly with people we love.

Is it possible to be authentic and to claim *both* rejoicing and sorrow on the same day? Can one laugh and mourn within twenty-four hours?

Jesus and his disciples shared this same array of emotions. Just as our bodies have fevers that convey to us the need for attention, so do the depths and heights of our emotions convey to us the need to pay attention; we may have something important to learn.

Several years ago Alanis Morissette wrote the lyrics to a provocative song. She employed the phrase "you learn" after each of a list of human experiences, such as "you cry," "you lose," or "you bleed." The psalmist rejoiced and learned, grieved and learned; so can we.

Suggestion for meditation: **Using verbs, review recent experiences. Explore what you learned from each of these events. Reflect upon God's presence in your passions and God's passion in your presence.**

Thursday, April 2   Read Philippians 2:5-11.

Paul claimed in Philippians 3:4-6 that when he was Jewish, he was confident of his stature in the community—he was zealous, righteous, and blameless. Now, as a follower of Christ, he willingly gives up his status. It is rare that a person gives up status. Paul speaks to others who have political or religious power, asking them to transcend their own desires too. This task is not easy for anyone, but it is especially difficult if one has control or wealth. Those without political power or wealth can fantasize what it would be like to have it—but why would those with status try to empathize with others who do not? Paul urges them to do just that. In fact, he suggests that the ones to whom he speaks should become servants to the others.

The hymn Paul cites in this passage starts with the declaration of Christ as equal to God. From that position, Christ Jesus empties himself, seeks to do God's will, and then dies in a manner that is inconceivable in God's desiring. Yet out of the emptying comes fullness. Jesus truly becomes the Christ, the anointed one.

Notice that neither Paul nor the hymn he cites suggests that people who are already servants or enslaved submit themselves further to emptying or injury. It is those with power and status who must yield their attachment in order to be open to God and to other humans. Neither imprisonment nor suffering is glorified—God is.

Suggestion for meditation: **Reflect whether status, role, or wealth is getting in the way of your having confidence in God or your being compassionate towards others. Honestly notice whether you are tempted to ask those who serve you in any way to be subservient. Reflect whether you do claim your worth as a child of God, not subservient but equal.**

Friday, April 3   Read Luke 22:14-27.

The disciples just don't get it, but neither do we very easily. Again and again they ask, and so do we, "What makes us great?" We have an obsession with greatness. Again and again Jesus told his disciples that to be great is to serve—not to be subservient but to serve others in the community, as a service to equals.

An equation that I use to understand authority, whether over our own lives or in regard to other members of a community, is this: Authority + Vulnerability = Integrity. This equation is a strength + a strength = a strength. Vulnerability is openness to influence. In our culture, we often take the myopic view that to be effective, those in authority should never let other people influence them toward change. Yet, with a little thought, we realize that leaders have far more wisdom and integrity when they are sensitive to the influence of the community members. Changing one's mind can be a sign of great strength—integrity. The one in authority may even be open to God's influence!

Some of us need to claim authority. We are so sensitive to influence that we hardly know where we stand. Others of us need to accept our vulnerability. We would discover more relational power if we were not so stubborn or closed to others' opinions and ideas. In this passage Jesus reframes authority to include service. The greatest becomes like the youngest. The leader serves but not to show his or her humility. The leader serves because service is a vital, connecting link to all people; service invites everyone's participation.

Prayer: **God, who has authority and yet is responsive to all creation, may I not take myself so seriously that I presume to be certain what is best. Rather, may I genuinely hear others and be responsive to them. Amen.**

Saturday, April 4   Read Luke 23:1-49.

We might consider God to be like a puppeteer, tugging at our strings, making us do what God wants. We might consider that God is like a jazz band leader who seeks to create aesthetic beauty along with creation. The jazz band leader has themes, emotions, moods, and rhythms in mind and assumes authority to initiate those ideas with the musicians. Yet the musicians are truly free. They can attend to the nods of the leader and play cooperatively, energetically, and beautifully for the good of all. Or they can mess up (intentionally or unintentionally).

With God as a puppeteer, God's will supposedly is accomplished. *What is* is God's will. With the second view of God as jazz band leader, God's power is relational; God's will is the most significant factor in the outcome, but God's will can be thwarted.

It is easy to assume when reading this passage that God is a puppeteer. Yet what we have here is a description of events, not a printout of God's will. *What is* is not always what God intended.

Many did not want Jesus' death. Pilate forthrightly says he does not find Jesus guilty of any of the charges against him. He points out that Herod has not found Jesus guilty either. The shouting of the crowd thwarts Pilate's wisdom, though many in the crowd do not want Jesus killed either. Women wail.

The community itself thwarts God's will for the community. And in the next instant, God pours out God's will again. Nothing that happens can be reversed, but amazing new possibilities may be in sight!

Prayer: **Dear God, like a jazz band leader you provide amazing new possibilities. May I look toward you and be attentive to others, so that I may play a part in the music of your kingdom. Amen.**

Palm/Passion Sunday
Sunday, April 5   Read Luke 23:50-56.

Joseph, from the Jewish town of Arimathea, was a member of the council who had *not* agreed to the council's plan and action to get rid of Jesus. *It had not been a unanimous decision!* Joseph and the women took down Jesus' body, wrapped it, and laid it in the tomb. They returned home to prepare spices and ointments. Because the Sabbath was starting, they rested.

We do not know what God had envisioned as the best alternative for Jesus and those gathered in Jerusalem. God, like Joseph of Arimathea, may not have agreed with their plans. However, God's power to evoke new possibilities is strong enough to jolt people's religious expectations.

Christians understand the meaning of Christ in a variety of ways today, just as the people around Jesus had differing opinions about who he was and what was happening. Was Jesus the prophet sent to announce that God is the God of the poor, the heavy laden, and those who suffer injustice? (theology of Elisabeth Schussler Fiorenza) Is Christ the Christa/Community that seeks connectedness among the members who live on the basis of love? (theology of Rita Nakashima Brock) Does Christ usher in New Being? (theology of Paul Tillich) Is the affirmation that Jesus is God a reminder that White people are not God? (theology of Jacquelyn Grant) What was special about Jesus' relation to God? Was he "God's supreme act of self-expression"? (theology of David Griffin)

We do not need a unanimous opinion. The important thing is to make visible Christ's presence through our being and actions "day by day."

Suggestion for meditation: **Do I agree to the plans and actions of others, even if I honestly experience God's guidance to dissent?**

FOR CHRIST'S SAKE

April 6–12, 1998   Jan L. Richardson✤
Monday, April 6   Read John 12:1-11.

In John's Gospel we find Mary at Jesus' feet again, only this time she is not content simply to listen while her sister Martha tends to the tasks of hospitality. As Jesus sits at table with the other guests, Mary brings out not a little perfume but a whole pound, made of pure nard, and begins to pour it on Jesus' feet. She uses so much, John tells us, that the whole house is filled with the fragrance. All those present are enveloped in the scent.

It is an extravagance, an excess, a waste. It is nearly a whole year's wages, for Christ's sake.

For Christ's sake. Yes. Where Judas criticizes Mary for her wastefulness, Jesus blesses her for her extravagant gift. She has seen what lies ahead for Jesus in a way that Judas has not, and Jesus gratefully recognizes her desire to help prepare him for what lies ahead. It is not that she cares so little for the poor, as Judas implies. Rather, she is willing to make herself one of them, to give away her costly gift in order to share her love for Jesus.

The question haunts me this week: What am I willing to waste on Jesus?

Prayer: **God, you love us with an extravagant love and an abiding passion. May your love flow through my actions and envelop those around me. Amen.**

✤ Artist-in-residence at the San Pedro Spiritual Development Center in Winter Park, Florida.

Tuesday, April 7   Read Isaiah 49:1-7;
John 12:20-36.

The night before I left Atlanta to take a pastoral appointment in Florida, I gathered with friends at Lori's apartment. Candles around the room cast light on the shadows as we talked for a long time. As I left, Lori gave me two purple candles to take with me. Especially during that first year, I lit them when I longed for a sense of connection with people who knew me well. Though I tried to use them sparingly, after a time they had burned down to nubs.

I wrote Lori and told her what the candles had meant to me, about the light they had provided in a time of shadows. I told her that certainly I could go buy more candles but that I was also trying to learn how to ask for help when I needed it. Could she send me another candle?

One grey day during a difficult season, a package from Lori appeared in my mailbox. I opened it and caught my breath as I pulled out a beautiful pottery oil lamp. I kept it lit most of the day and still use it frequently. Unlike a candle, it does not spend itself as long as I keep oil in it.

The gift of light was a gift of grace. It did not take the shadows away, but it reminded me of those who were present with me in my questions and in my sorrow. Today's passages from Isaiah and John speak of the God who gives light and who comes to us in the midst of our brokenness and our uncertainty. Journeying with Christ does not mean that we will never again be enveloped in darkness but that we do not journey alone through the shadows.

Prayer: **God of daylight and of darkness, I give you thanks for every grace-filled gift, for each light in the shadows. Amen.**

Wednesday, April 8   Read Isaiah 50:4-9*a*.

In the eight years of military rule that followed the ousting of President Isabel Peron in Argentina in 1976, an estimated 30,000 people became *desaparecidos*, "disappeared ones." Anyone who attempted to protest, organize, or speak out risked being branded a subversive and arrested. The authorities often hid from their families both their location and the charges against them. Many were tortured and killed.

Many of the mothers of the "disappeared ones" began individually to search for them, going to the prisons, police stations, military offices, and government buildings. As they searched, the mothers became aware of one another and decided to combine their efforts. They began to gather in the Plaza de Mayo across from the Government House in Buenos Aires each Thursday afternoon at half past three, recognizing one another by the pictures they carried of their loved ones who had disappeared and by the white kerchiefs they later adopted, decorated with the words *aparacion con vida*—"reappearance with life."

The authorities began to recognize them too. Many of the mothers received threats; others disappeared; and some were killed. But the Mothers of the Plaza de Mayo, as they named themselves, had begun the work of justice, their actions giving flesh to the words of the servant in Isaiah: "Who will contend with me? Let us stand up together. Who are my adversaries? Let them confront me. It is the Lord God who helps me; who will declare me guilty?"

Prayer: **God of the outcast, you provide home to the exiles and proclaim liberation to the captives. Bless all who work for the freedom of your people; strengthen all who labor for the healing of your world. Amen.**

Maundy Thursday

Thursday, April 9   Read John 13:1-17, 31*b*-35.

Just a few days ago, he had sat at another table and received Mary's gift as she poured the precious perfume on his feet. Now it is Jesus' turn to give as he gathers at the table with his companions for their final meal. And so, basin in hand, he begins to wash the disciples' feet and to dry them with the towel he has wrapped around himself. Water splashes over the sides of the bowl as he moves from friend to friend, kneeling before each one.

Water has connected Jesus and the disciples since the beginning of their journey together. By the shores of the lake of Gennesaret, Jesus had first met and called Simon Peter, James, and John. On a stormy lake the disciples had become terrified until Jesus calmed the waves. Another time they had watched as Jesus walked toward them on the water. They had listened with some perplexity as Jesus spoke of his life-giving water. And they had watched tears roll down Jesus' face as he wept over Jerusalem and again as he stood at the tomb of his beloved friend Lazarus.

This last meal is a meal of memory. Jesus gives them not only the gift of bread and wine by which to remember him but also the gift of water. In the washing bowl they see the reflections of all they have shared together. Yet Jesus impresses upon them that their shared journey does not end with this gift of washing. Rather, they are to continue to wash one another's feet, even as he has washed theirs. Water will continue to connect them and all who walk in the path of Christ, offering grace and comfort.

Prayer: **Even as I receive your gifts, O God, may I pass them on to others. Even as I know your touch, Divine Companion, may I extend your embrace. Amen.**

Good Friday

Friday, April 10   Read John 18–19.

They did not leave. Three Marys stood at the cross with Jesus: his mother Mary, her sister Mary the wife of Clopas, and Mary Magdalene. And beside his mother Mary stood the one identified as the disciple whom Jesus loved. While the others stood at a distance or had fled into hiding, these four kept the death-watch, breathing with Jesus as he breathed his last.

I have seen their faces. I saw them as I stood with a congregation member at the bedside of her dying mother. The woman who had been mother for more than sixty years was small and still and soft against the crisp, white nursing-home sheets. Periodically she drew a slow, ragged breath. Her daughter became her midwife, breathing with her through the labor. Finally her mother breathed out, and the breath was not returned.

The faces of those who stayed at the cross were there as a friend watched a beloved companion lie in his bed at home and breathe raggedly during his final hours. They were there as we gathered in the church to celebrate his life and lifted the strains of the hymn he had chosen for his memorial service, "I'll Praise My Maker While I've Breath."

The beloved family and friends who stood at the cross offer breathing lessons on this day. They knew that in the passage from life to death they could offer nothing but their presence; and so they freely offered that, staying with Jesus, breathing with Jesus, holding on to one another as he released his hold on the life they had known together.

Prayer: **While we have breath, God, may we praise you; while we have life, may we stand with those who struggle. Amen.**

Holy Saturday
Saturday, April 11   Read Matthew 27:57-66.

Several years ago, I stood at the graveside of an infant as a small group of her family members gathered for her service. She had been born on the Wednesday of Holy Week, died on Maundy Thursday, and now we stood by her tiny casket on Holy Saturday. I had agonized over what to say as the presiding pastor, knowing how inadequate words would be in the face of such a loss.

Standing at the grave, I spoke of others before us who had waited by another grave. By Matthew's account, Mary Magdalene and the other Mary were sitting there as the stone was rolled in front of Jesus' tomb. They waited, not knowing what was going to happen, weighted down by their loss and clinging to each other. They waited, perhaps in time joining the other followers of Jesus who waited together—their minds filled with memories of what he said would happen after his death, but their hearts filled with questions about what would actually unfold.

Today we wait, hovering between the tomb and the resurrection. We may feel the weight of whatever losses we have encountered in the year past. And although we may read the story with the eyes of those who know resurrection is coming, we still have yet to discover how God's resurrection power will unfold in our own lives.

There are few words to comfort us on this day, only the memory of those who knew what it meant to wait, to watch, and to wonder; only the presence of those who abide the silence with us.

Prayer: **When silence inhabits my life and the questions gather around me; when sorrow fills my hours and the waiting goes on forever; in your mercy, God, come and wait with me. Amen.**

Easter Sunday

Sunday, April 12   Read John 20:1-18.

In her book *Pilgrim at Tinker Creek*, Annie Dillard writes of when surgeons first discovered how to perform cataract operations and began to operate on people who had been blind since birth. The surgeons were able to give them the gift of sight but not the gift of understanding what they saw. Because they had not learned to see as children, the colors and shapes they now saw held little meaning.

Some found it an overwhelming experience. One teenage boy threatened to tear his eyes out. Another young woman kept her eyes closed for two weeks after her operation to shut out the brightness. When she finally opened her eyes again, she still did not understand what she saw; but as she looked around, the girl cried out again and again, "Oh God! How beautiful!"*

This must have been something like Mary Magdalene's encounter with the resurrected Jesus. She saw him but could not at first make sense of what she saw. Her eyesight had not been trained for resurrection. But her heart recognized the sound of her name. Understanding settled in, and she exclaimed with the knowledge of what she had seen.

Perhaps this, then, is the invitation of Easter: to see what we have never before seen, to look at the familiar in a new way. In the presence of the risen Christ, we are invited to gaze at what has been dead in our lives and to cry out, as we see with new eyes, "Oh God! How beautiful!"

Prayer: **Open our eyes, God, to perceive what we have never seen; open our hearts to know your resurrection. Amen.**

---

*Annie Dillard, *Pilgrim at Tinker Creek* (New York: Harper & Row, 1974), 29.

THE LAW OF LOVE, THE RULE OF FEAR

April 13–19, 1998   **Jeff Blum**✤
Monday, April 13   Read Acts 5:27-32.

Tattoos are an ancient and profound form of folk art very prevalent among those incarcerated in jails and prisons. The most poignant tattoo I experience is the common practice of etching the letters of the word *LOVE* across the knuckles of one hand and the letters of the word *FEAR* across the knuckles of the other. It is a wonderfully graphic illustration of the opposing forces at work in our human lives.

Peter and the apostles were no strangers to jails: They appeared before the Sanhedrin as escaped prisoners. They listened to the familiar message of the Sanhedrin: Out of fear of our power to incarcerate and kill you, we order you to desist preaching. Just like modern judges who work out of the hand of fear as their ultimate weapon, the Sanhedrin fully expected the apostles to stop preaching.

Peter and the apostles, however, were working out of the other hand. Their obedience was not born out of fear but out of love. As witnesses to the defeat of death by Jesus' resurrection, they were not motivated by fear. More powerful than the lack of fear was the overwhelming presence of love. Whereas fear limits, love compels. They had no choice but to preach the good news that God had placed in their mouths.

Faithfulness both enables and is nourished by our ability to overcome the *FEAR* written across our one hand and live exclusively out of the *LOVE* written large upon the other.

Suggestion for meditation: **Out of which hand do I most often speak and act—love or fear?**

✤Minister in the Christian Church (Disciples of Christ), having worked in jails and prisons for the past twenty years.

Tuesday, April 14   Read Acts 5:27-32.

At a conference for people involved in prison ministry, an unknown grey-haired priest told the story of a chaplain at San Quentin prison.

Among the inmates in this chaplain's charge was a longtimer known for his cunning. Using his street smarts, the convict constantly conned the chaplain out of special visits, extra phone time, and numerous other activities considered luxuries in the stark prison environment. Since the difficulty of the con is part of the game, the convict eventually grew exasperated at the stupidity of the chaplain and upbraided him for being such a patsy. The chaplain replied that in life one must choose whether to be a sucker or a cynic; for him, being a sucker was preferable.

Having told the story, the priest quietly sat down. It was only when he was goaded to admit that he was the chaplain in the story that the priest revealed that in reality he had been the convict. After a lifetime in prison, he finally was released and was now—in his elder years—studying for the priesthood.

Cynics, whether robbing a convenience store for their next cocaine fix or sponsoring legislation that provides more bombs and less bread, live out of fear. Fear breeds cynicism, and cynicism feeds fear. There is no room for vulnerability and trust for those given over to the rule of fear.

Love, on the other hand, allows one the luxury of being a sucker, a fool, a disciple. How silly and foolish, what profound suckers Peter and the other disciples must have seemed to the powerful and cynical Sanhedrin. Yet their foolish acts laid the groundwork for the kingdom that offers us forgiveness and love even on this day.

Prayer: **O God, you call us to demonstrate love in all the arenas of our life. When we have to choose between loving sucker or fearful cynic, give us faith to choose love, to gladly be a fool for Jesus Christ. Amen.**

Wednesday, April 15   Read Psalm 150.

These words of the psalmist are a mystery to me and most modern Christians. Ours is a joyless faith more comfortable with the drudgery of good works or obedience to law than the ecstasy of praise.

We know of ecstasy and emotion in our secular lives: the sensual aspects of eating, sexuality, the arts, and sports. We are not embarrassed to release impassioned signs of celebration, satisfaction, sorrow, or enjoyment when indulging in these activities.

Our religious life is different. A person who would think nothing of sobbing through a movie sits stoically through a retelling of the crucifixion. A fan who leaps to his feet cheering as a touchdown is scored shows no emotion as a young person comes forward to join the church.

It is fear that robs us of the joyful expression of our faith. Modern religion reins in these spontaneous feelings lest we plunge down some slippery slope of emotionalism and lose control of our carefully controlled lives. We fear that our faith is not sufficient to keep our expressions of love for God and our fellow human beings from deteriorating into expressions of our base humanity.

The majority of my married life depends upon a life of good works: staying true to the boundaries of the marital covenant. Our marriage would be empty, however, if not for those moments when my wife and I give ourselves over to the emotion of our love. Our intimate relations inform our life in a way beyond the rational communication of daily calendars and shared agendas.

Faithfulness in marriage is giving myself over to my wife holistically—mentally, emotionally, physically. Can faithfulness to God be any different?

Prayer: **Loving God, free us to give ourselves—our praise, our sorrow, our joy, our fear, and our love—fully for one another and for you. Amen.**

Thursday, April 16   Read John 20:19-23.

As Jesus breathed the Holy Spirit into the disciples, he vested them with a wonderful power: the ability to forgive and not to forgive sins. As a minister's spouse who works as a social worker in a metropolitan jail, I live in a strange dualistic world. I spend my weekends with the "righteous" people of our church community while I spend my weekdays among the "sinners" who populate our jails. I often find it difficult to embody this gift of the Holy Spirit in either venue.

Invariably, there are rational explanations for the criminal behavior of the "sinners" of the jail—mental illness, poverty, inadequate social development, brutal addictions. The law of love requires that I look beyond the act, embrace the child of God, and offer healing and forgiveness. The fear that often rules my life encourages me to do the opposite: stand complacently by while society labels God's children as criminals, unworthy of forgiveness and compassion.

We "righteous" people of the churches live lives of complacency and self-satisfaction. Convinced of our righteousness, especially in comparison to the "unclean" of the jail, we abide by the bare minimum—or less—of what faith requires. In this setting, the law of love requires that I shock the seemingly righteous out of their complacency, acknowledging that what we fail to do is an equally serious sin. But the fear that rules my life too often leaves me silent while we smugly live on, believing in our inherent righteousness.

The call to forgive and not forgive sins is not some mystical power given to Christians for their own edification. It is the power to grant life to those to whom love and forgiveness are strangers and meaning to those whose lives have deteriorated to rote religiosity. It is the core of the good news.

Prayer: **Open our hearts, hands, and lives with your love, O God. May our lips declare your praise and forgiveness to all. Amen.**

Friday, April 17   Read John 20:24-31.

Afficionados of pop psychology personality typing would have a clear category for Thomas. The man is all judgment and no intuition. The extreme nature of his requirement to believe, actually having to place his fingers in the wounds, sets this man apart and earns him the title of "Doubting" Thomas.

Titles, labels, nicknames, diagnoses can be freeing: They give us insight into the gifts and graces God has provided for our journey. They can also be boundaries that deny us the ability to become the people God has called us to be.

My life in the criminal justice system is rife with labels: hooker, judge, junkie, attorney, schizophrenic, prosecutor, thief, guard, and countless variations on four-letter words unprintable in this book. The way that labels empower and impair in the secular world is vividly demonstrated to me on a daily basis.

Confronted by the risen Christ, "Doubting" Thomas becomes "Believing" Thomas far short of plunging his fingers or hands into open wounds. The Gospels contain story after story of the ancient equivalent of hookers, junkies, and schizophrenics, as well as lawyers, attorneys, prosecutors, and guards, who were born anew when confronted by the living Christ. The interesting thing about many Gospel stories is that those with shameful titles were often the first to embrace Jesus, while those with honorable labels walked away in disgust.

As followers of Jesus Christ, the only labels of concern to us are those we willingly embrace for ourselves. The first is "sinner," for it is only in the understanding of our own fallen nature that we can fully appreciate the loving power and forgiveness of God. The other is "Christian," for it identifies us as people who, having recognized their fallen nature, follow him who has brought us into forgiveness.

Suggestion for meditation: **What is my label, nickname, or title? Does it empower or impair me in my walk with God?**

119

Saturday, April 18   Read Revelation 1:5.

We love the word *criminal*. We love it because most of us are not criminals: Our society has not defined us as persons outside the boundaries of acceptable behavior. We are good people.

The problem is that *criminal* is a subjective and fluid word. Behavior defined as criminal changes with each meeting of the legislature. Adjoining countries, counties, or even towns may have radically different laws. Behavior defined as criminal by one generation may be defined as heroic by the next. The exact same act, such as the taking of human life, can be either a crime or an action worthy of praise depending on the circumstances.

Many of the people we revere as the saints of the Bible were considered criminals by their contemporaries: Moses and David were murderers, Jacob a thief, Jesus a revolutionary.

I have sat across from a "criminal" born the same day, month, and year as I. As she related the terrifying circumstances of her life, I understood why her sins took the form of behaviors that society considers criminal. Simultaneously, I questioned why, given my privileged life, I have not freed myself from those behaviors that are so clearly sinful.

As Christians, we are compelled to eschew the secular word *criminal* for the more inclusive *sinner*. Suddenly the boundaries of acceptable behavior have dramatically shrunk, and we find ourselves living under a negative label. Whereas crime is usually defined as something we commit, sin is all too often something we omit. We may be able to avoid the dip net of secular justice, but the purse seine of God's judgment surrounds and gathers us all in.

Prayer: **Lord Jesus Christ, have mercy on me a sinner. Free me for joyful obedience in your love. Amen.**

Sunday, April 19   Read Revelation 1:4-8.

Bruce Springsteen has penned a song about a man named Billy who had the word *LOVE* tattooed on his right hand and the word *FEAR* tattooed on his left. And Billy, like many of us, was never really clear as to which hand held his fate.

God did not stop speaking to us through writers and psalmists when the last word of the Bible was penned nearly two millennia ago. As earthen a vessel as rocker Bruce Springsteen can pen lines that reveal the choices God has set before us.

Turn on your TV or radio and listen. That hand with *FEAR* etched on the knuckles will start to twitch and come to life. Crime, economic instability, international crisis, ecological disaster, all cause that fearful hand to sweat and reach out to take control of your life. Advertising coaxes you into an increasingly private and isolated life.

Turn off the TV and open your Bible or some modern revelation of God's word. Be reminded that the birds neither reap nor sow, that the meek inherit the earth, that death has lost its sting, and that a man named Schindler saved hundreds of innocent lives. Feel that hand of fear come to rest at your side as the sure and steady hand emblazoned with *LOVE* reaches out to take the cross placed before it and begin the journey.

As people who must remain in the world, we know that the difficulties of secular living can bring the cynical hand of fear to life. As people who strive not to be of the world, we must never cut ourselves off from the history and community that empowers our hand of love.

The fact that you are reading this book of meditations indicates that you have chosen not to be victimized by the hand of *FEAR*. You want clarity regarding which hand holds your fate and the fate of the world, and you have chosen *LOVE*. Continue to make that choice every day, every minute of your life.

Prayer: **God of grace, displace our fear today with your love. Amen.**

SING OF GOD'S GREATNESS!

April 20–26, 1998   **Nancy Otto Boffo**✤
Monday, April 20   Read Revelation 5:11-14.

Imagine a choir of angels. What do you see? A hundred celestial beings singing heavenly songs with angelic voices?

Now, imagine thousands upon thousands, and ten thousand times ten thousand encircling God's throne (see Rev. 5:11). In a loud voice you hear them sing, "Worthy is the Lamb, who was slain, to receive power and wealth and wisdom and strength and honor and glory and praise!" (Rev. 5:12, NIV).

Other voices now join in. Do your ears deceive you? It is "every creature in heaven and on earth and under the earth and on the sea, and all that is in them, singing" (Rev. 5:13) praises of honor and glory to the One who has created and redeemed them.

Does this scene seem surreal? According to John's vision, as recorded in the Book of Revelation, he was privileged to witness this event.

Although some may debate the symbolism of this book, the truth remains that the Lamb who was slain is worthy to be praised. When we read Revelation 5:9-10, we find that the four living creatures and the elders who encircled the Lamb's throne "sang a new song." They sang of the Lamb's worthiness "to take the scroll and to open its seals." They also sang that by his blood, the Lamb redeemed his people from the bondage of sin, making them priests to serve God.

The Lord deserves our highest praise. Since God will wipe every tear from our eyes, we too can sing a new song!

Suggestion for meditation: **Psalm 96 tells us to "sing to the Lord a new song." After reading this psalm, take time to praise the Lord with your prayers of thanksgiving.**

✤Author; contributing editor for *Devo'Zine*; codirector and founder of Titusville Christian Writers Fellowship.

Tuesday, April 21   Read John 21:1-14.

At daybreak, my son and I carefully stepped along the rocky shoreline to find the best place to fish. Finally, after hours of waiting, I felt a tug on my line. While reeling in my trout, I lost my balance atop an algae-laden rock. Teetering, I prayed, *Jesus, help me!* Immediately I felt his comforting presence and miraculously regained my balance. And I was still holding onto my fish!

I love to fish, and I like to tell "fish stories." I can tell you about the one that got away or about the one that was so big I couldn't even get it into the boat.

I'm sure the disciples who fished at the Sea of Tiberias had lots of tales to tell. After fishing all night, they'd caught nothing. Then Jesus called from the shore and told them to throw their net on the right side of the boat. When they did, their net was so full that they couldn't haul it in!

If the disciples failed to recognize their master on the shore, this miracle opened their eyes. Realizing it was Jesus, Peter jumped into the water to reach his Lord first. The others followed in the boat. Jesus greeted the tired and hungry disciples with the words, "Come and have breakfast" (John 21:12, NIV). The resurrected Christ had prepared a meal to nourish his beloved disciples. And he still nourishes our souls today.

The Lord who watched over the disciples from the shore watches over us. As we struggle with our daily tasks, we receive the assurance that Jesus is nearby. With joy, we can give thanks that the resurrected Christ still cares for those who labor, for those who are tired and hungry.

Prayer: **Living Christ, help me be aware of your presence and look for your miracles. Amen.**

Wednesday, April 22   Read Acts 9:1-6.

How can anything so ugly turn out so beautiful and useful? I wondered. But as I watched, the skilled potter fashioned the grey lump of clay into a beautiful vase.

In the hands of a master craftsman, a miracle can happen. Such is the case of Saul in his life-transforming experience on the road to Damascus.

The high priest endorsed Saul's mission of hate. This commission allowed Saul to question persons as to their belief in Christ. Saul would bind followers of the Way, bringing them to Jerusalem as criminals.

But as Saul approached Damascus, a light from heaven blinded him, and he fell to the ground. A voice asked, "Saul, Saul, why do you persecute me?" It was there and then that Saul met the Lord. Saul, the very man whom Christians feared and hated, would become a respected apostle for the faith, establishing many churches in the Lord's name.

At one time or another, each of us may find ourselves traveling a Damascus road. On a mission of our own undertaking, we may be headed on a path of destruction for ourselves or others. But God's love is the light that can illumine our headstrong ideas and sins. When we fall to our knees and cry out, we discover that Jesus' grace is sufficient and redeeming. In the hands of the Master Potter, Jesus can make us beautiful and useful.

Suggestion for meditation: **How has Christ's transforming power changed you? Consider the ways in which Jesus' "grace is sufficient for you" (2 Cor. 12:9) and meditate on his grace.**

Thursday, April 23   Read Acts 9:7-20.

Things aren't always as they seem, nor do they necessarily turn out the way we plan. In yesterday's reading, the Lord spoke to Saul on the road to Damascus. Today we discover that Saul has been blinded by the light from heaven and must be led by his hand into the city of Damascus.

What a change in events! Saul had planned to lead his prisoners, the disciples of Christ from Damascus, along this very road. But instead, it is he who is being led.

Meanwhile, the disciple named Ananias also has plans. He no doubt intends to stay away from the terrible man named Saul. In a vision, however, the Lord tells Ananias to "go to the house of Judas on Straight Street, and ask for a man from Tarsus named Saul." Frightened, Ananias reminds the Lord that Saul plans to arrest God's saints. Why should Ananias restore his sight? What good could this persecutor of God's people possibly do?

But the Lord tells Ananias that he has chosen Saul to do great things and that Saul has already seen the disciple in a vision. Saul knows Ananias will restore his sight. Ananias is part of the big picture.

Many times in our lives we can't see how we fit into the whole puzzle. But that's the good news—we don't have to! God will guide our lives and the lives of those around us. God can exceed our expectations, restore our limited vision, and make us new. Like Saul and Ananias, we too are God's chosen instruments; we can trust in God's vision and sustaining presence.

Prayer: **Lord, open our eyes so we may see you; open our ears to hear your voice; and open our hearts in response to your call. Amen.**

Friday, April 24   Read Psalm 30:6-12.

A prayer meditation in praise of God's greatness

O Lord, there are times when life is good,
    and I feel like I'm on top of the world.
During those times it's easy to feel positive
    —that I can do all things because you are near.

But, O Lord, when I fall from those mountaintop moments
    into the valley of despair,
I feel so alone and so far from you—
    and I'm scared.

In my pain I cry out to you,
    "O Lord, where are you? Help me!"
I find myself praying day and night because
    I can't stand the thought of being far from your presence.

But always, Lord, you hear my prayers and deliver me.
    Only you could turn my mourning into rejoicing.
My heart sings of your greatness and
    I will forever praise you and give you thanks.

                                        Amen.

Suggestion for meditation: **When have you felt secure in God's support? When have you felt far from God's presence? How did you experience God's reassurance?**

Saturday, April 25   Read John 21:15-19.

What must Peter have been thinking while he ate breakfast with his resurrected Lord? He had to be conscious of his having denied Jesus three times. In John's Gospel, Peter has seen his Master twice since the crucifixion and neither has mentioned that betrayal. Had Christ seen Peter's tears and repentance and forgiven him?

Indeed Jesus had, and this story portrays the Lord's tenderness toward penitents. Knowing that Peter has repented after denying him, Jesus believes in his disciple's sincerity and forgives the offense. At breakfast, Jesus makes it clear to Peter that he still loves him, and he asks Peter to commit his life to ministry.

Three times Jesus asks Peter, "Do you truly love me?" and three times Peter responds, "Yes, Lord, you know that I love you." After each question and answer, Jesus commends the care of his flock to Peter: Feed my lambs; take care of my sheep; feed my sheep. The living Christ asked his disciple to care for his flock—his most precious treasure on earth. In trusting Peter with this responsibility, Jesus demonstrates his forgiveness.

That day, Peter's occupation changed from fisherman to evangelist. He had repented, been forgiven, and was now entrusted to feed the word of God to all he encountered. As the Lord's redeemed people who still today say, "Yes, Lord, you know that I love you," we too have a responsibility to shepherd the flock. We answer the living Christ's question, "Do you truly love me?" when we willingly serve and follow him.

Suggestion for meditation: **Seek Christ's guidance as to how you can best feed his sheep.**

Sunday, April 26   Read Psalm 30:1-5.

In this psalm of thanksgiving, the psalmist opens with praise for God's delivering him from his enemies and for healing him. The psalmist seems to have come to a new understanding of God's work in his life. In verse 4, he invites all God's "saints" to "sing to the Lord" and "praise his holy name." The psalmist's acknowledgment of God's lifetime commitment allows him to realize that our purpose is fulfilled in rejoicing rather than weeping.

This psalm's superscription tells us that the psalmist wrote these verses for the dedication of the temple—one of a handful of psalms written for a specific event. One can imagine these words being chanted or sung by the worshiping community on such an occasion. Instruments such as cymbals, tambourines, trumpets, ram's horns, harps, and lyres often accompanied the singing.

According to 1 Chronicles 15:16; 23:5, as many as 4,000 professional musicians accompanied worship in the temple in the time of David and Solomon. Can you imagine what it must have been like? We might guess that quite a joyful noise was made unto the Lord!

Beyond our imagination lies the knowledge that God sustains us in our weeping and brings us to a time of rejoicing. Knowing that God changes our lives, we too have experienced deliverance and healing. Our gratitude manifests itself in songs of joy for who God is, for what God has done, and for what God is going to do.

Suggestion for meditation: Read Psalm 100. In praise and thanksgiving, sing or hum a favorite hymn as part of your devotional experience today.

MOVING THROUGH CRISES

April 27—May 3, 1998   **Stephen Martyn**✚
Monday, April 27   Read Acts 9:36-43.

Tabitha, the dear woman of God whose life was "devoted to good works and acts of charity," had come to the end of her life. But those who loved her stubbornly refused to capitulate to an inevitable fate.

All of us face circumstances that bring us to the end of our own resources. Financial collapse, physical illness, severe loss, or relational breakdowns drag us beyond the edge of our limited selves. We question whether life will be meaningful or even if we can carry on.

Such situations confront us with a crucial question: Are the only sources of life within our own selves? If so, then crises become truly overwhelming, for we have nothing left to draw upon. But is the universe greater than our limited selves? Is there a God who cares and who has overabundant loving wholeness to share? If so, then our crises become great opportunities to receive and surrender to resources beyond ourselves.

The bereaved disciples of Joppa sought Peter, the great man of God. Their hope was in the resurrection power that had been witnessed through Jesus. Their firm confidence in the power of the gospel brought joy in Joppa.

Prayer: **Lord Jesus Christ, Son of God, have mercy on me, a sinner. You know that the crises of my life have vividly demonstrated my arrogant self-reliance and my overattachment to people and things before you. Come Lord Jesus, for your severe mercy has allowed me to be carried to the end of myself that I might gain true life in you. Amen.**

✚A pastor of St. Stephen's United Methodist Church in Albuquerque, New Mexico; highly involved in writing, conferencing, and teaching in the discipline of spiritual formation.

Tuesday, April 28   Read Psalm 23:1-3.

When we come to the end of our selves and cry out for help from God, we are surprised by the gift of loving guidance. We find that we are indeed "the sheep of his pasture" (Ps. 100:3). God's care for our stress-filled lives demonstrates itself through an inexplicable sense that God will provide for all our needs. The nurture and care of "green pastures" and the "waters of rest" flow over us with the favor of divine wholeness. Our life is "restored," or handed back to us. We have a knowing beyond our circumstances that the good shepherd will lead us in exactly the "right paths."

The issue for us is, Will we be sheep or goats? Sheep will be led—indeed sheep have to be led. Goats will not be led. They prefer to follow their own path. Sheep are aware of their true condition: poor and helpless. But in their stubbornness, goats only want self-rule, even if it means their demise. The crises we move through inevitably separate the sheep from the goats (Matt. 25:32).

What blessed relief awaits any person who calls out in absolute trust and personal abandonment to the God who has been revealed to us as savior. Our dimly burning wicks and bruised reeds are not doused or broken. The Lord is indeed our shepherd! And we know in our hearts that the Shepherd's immeasurable care will lead us forward.

Prayer: **Dear Lord and master, come now to my side. See, I am but a poor sheep in need of your care. Save me, I pray, from my fallen tendency to follow the goat-self; and through your mercy, allow me to abandon all that I am into your shepherding care. My heart bows to you as the great shepherd. Amen.**

Wednesday, April 29   Read Psalm 23:4.

One can picture in the mind the "valley of the shadow of death": a dramatically steep and narrow canyon that runs through the barren wilderness of the desert mountains. During most of the year little sunlight ever strikes the bottom of this watercourse. Its depths represent everything threatening to the Israelite, including death.

Yet it is precisely *through* the alarming and threatening circumstances of crises that we must walk. They frighten us because we do not know if we will make it safely over their rough terrain. Anxiety fills us; we question whether our lives will have meaning with the loss that seems to be upon us.

But the psalmist did not fear any evil. Rather, he maintained a profound trust in the presence of the Holy One of Israel. No weapons of his own gave him assurance. No, it was the presence of God, "for you are with me." He was confident that the strength and protection of God would carry him over any threatening path. Only the presence of God can give us such strength of soul.

Prayer: **Father God, Shepherd of my life, assist me now to seek your strength and your courage in this hour of trial. I am overwhelmed by the bad news about me. Turn my heart, I pray, that I might receive your light and your love that is always present, and lead me in the way of life that triumphs over all dark circumstances. I praise you and thank you for your comforting presence. Amen.**

Thursday, April 30   Read Psalm 23:5-6.

David, the ascribed writer of this psalm, shares from actual experience his affirmation that no enemy can tear us from God's plan for our lives. The "enemies" are those forces that threaten to undo us. Whether the predicament of personal sin, the pain of conflict, or the threat of losing his life, David knew the trauma of major crises. But he also knew that the Lord would hold him together through the suffering of any predicament.

David's joyous song, "Surely goodness and mercy shall follow me all the days of my life," praises God for the sheer wonder that the crises had actually brought surprising goodness and mercy rather than dreaded darkness and destruction. He has learned the great lesson of abandonment to the Holy: Only when we place our uncertain lives in God's hands are we able to receive the surprising gifts of hope, wholeness, peace, and restoration of relationships. We discover that God wills love toward us, not destruction.

And where does it all lead? Our lives were created to be led into the house of God, into the very presence of the Lord. When all is said and done, God's presence not only takes us *through* our testing but also *beyond* our limited, fallen, broken selves.

Prayer: **Dear Lord, this dark valley has brought me into your very presence! Please forgive my lack of faith that saw only destruction. You have overwhelmed me with your love. Let me never doubt from this moment on that your will is to bring forgiveness and wholeness into my fractured life. I long to be in your house "my whole life long." Amen.**

Friday, May 1   Read Revelation 7:9-17.

The presence of God gives us the assurance—even in the face of overwhelming and impossible circumstances—that all shall be well. In the presence of God, our deepest hunger is satisfied and our thirst is no more. In the consuming presence of the Holy, the scorching heat of any crisis is overshadowed by a greater reality. That presence is none other than the Lamb who was slain and who rose again!

Crises offer us the great opportunity to stop the mad rush of our lives, allowing us to fall to our knees in absolute dependence upon the Lord of all. In this newfound and surprising encounter with goodness, we are turned from one direction in life to another. In our turning, we are receptive to the Lord's leading. Beyond knowledge, we simply know that the Son will be our shepherd and will guide us to springs of life. With joy we anticipate every tear's being wiped from our eyes.

If our end is in praise, then we must allow that end to be in this new beginning—even as we praise the Lord for the miracles of love and deliverance that renew our commitment to wait for the unveiling of the Lord's new directives. Our courage is a gift from God, and the attentive patience we now experience is a result of God's confidence in us.

Prayer: **Father, I pray with the psalmist, "Be gracious to me and answer me!...Your face, Lord, do I seek....Teach me your way, O Lord, and lead me on a level path" (Ps. 27:7, 8, 11). Help me wait for you in the confidence and courage that you so graciously share with me. I pray this through your son's powerful name. Amen.**

Saturday, May 2   Read John 10:22-29.

If we allow it, every crisis will lead us into the arms of Jesus. In his loving embrace not only are we called by name, but we know that the power that holds us can preserve us from all evil. Literally nothing can snatch us from our shepherd's care.

In this profound security of eternal care, we are far more attentive to the voice of the Lord than prior to the particular crisis at hand. We have heard the call of the Great Shepherd, and we want to follow Jesus with unreserved willingness. Because Jesus has touched our lives, we receive a deep, inner knowledge that we belong to him. The works of grace in our lives assure us that our peace, our wholeness, and our future lie in the mystery of the Trinity. Our heartfelt desire is to say "yes" to the goodness that the Lord is bringing into our lives.

In the painful situations of our lives, we tend to focus so keenly on the negative that all we can see is the crisis at hand. But in the gracious arms of God's love, we can begin to see the larger, more complete picture. The shepherd's hug enables us to see love marvelously at work all about us. Even as the wounds of yesterday heal, we have firm confidence that our future will be blessed. Therefore, we experience joy in the now of this eternal embrace.

Prayer: **Lord Jesus, shepherd of my soul, your embrace of this poor, distracted life has flooded me with transforming love. I see now that only your wholeness will bring completeness in my life. Only in your love will I find my purpose and my way forward. Help me to hear rightly and follow you willingly in all things great and small. Amen.**

Sunday, May 3   Read John 10:30.

In the broad horizon of God's love, perhaps now we can come to the first day of this new week with a profound sense that it is not just crises that lead us into God's presence but all of life. Crises help us let go of everything that keeps us from fullness of life in Christ, and, in turn, enable us to hold on more faithfully to the eternal. But our everyday, mundane lives also lead to God's presence. Whether in crises or joy, suffering or pleasure, loss or gain, every person, event, and thing in this life is meant to bring us closer to God.

Jesus boldly declared himself to be one with the Father. Only the messiah could make such a statement. But what is just as shocking is the fact that Jesus desires to be one with us. He wants our absolute loyalty so that he can be our absolute Lord. He wants to take the "me" out of the selfish center of our hearts and place God's love and service to humanity as the wellspring of our lives. "Those who love me will keep my word, and my Father will love them, and we will come to them and make our home with them" (John 14:23). Through Jesus, we too will be one with God.

Prayer: **Dear Lord Jesus, I am in awe over your actions in history. I praise you that you have enabled me to see that my greatest freedom lies in love and obedience to you and service to others. Because you are one with the Father, I declare you as my Lord. Help me seek you first in all things this week for you are the way, the truth, and the life. Amen.**

TENDING TO THE HOLY

May 4–10, 1998   **Amelia Chua**✤
Monday, May 4   Read Acts 11:1-18.

Over the ages, believers have been called to defend their faith. Persons offer this defense as often for the community of faith itself as for those beyond it. Sometimes this defense flows into a treatise supported by a climate of tolerance. Any challenge to inclusivity within the church requires defense—even today.

Acts 11:1-18 includes Peter's defense. The passage opens with criticism of Peter from the apostles and believers in Judea. They demand an explanation of his actions. Rather than accusing him of baptizing people upon whom the Holy Spirit fell, they chastise Peter for going to uncircumcised men and eating with them. Six circumcised brothers who witnessed to the coming of the Holy Spirit among the Gentiles could not dispel the prejudice against the unclean.

There comes a time when a believer is called to challenge the prejudice of the faith community. Institutions do not change easily, and yet God calls us to be the agents that bring in the new wind of the Spirit with new paradigms of love in fulfilling God's plan for the reconciliation of all peoples. As disciples of Christ we know our defense may be costly, and repentance by the community may or may not be forthcoming as it was with Peter. Yet we follow in the great tradition of the saints who understood the unity of wisdom, courage, and love for neighbor.

Prayer: **We thank you for choosing us to be agents of love, O God. Help us to live out our calling. Amen.**

✤Clergy member of the California–Nevada Conference of The United Methodist Church; spiritual director; Pacific Grove, California.

Tuesday, May 5   Read Acts 11:1-18.

I ardently believe that the God we worship is one who actively tries to reach us. Often, however, our frame of mind causes us to miss the revelation. This frame of mind includes incessant busyness, lack of attention, fatigue, and sometimes a sophistication that doubts forms of grace that do not fall within the ordinary.

The worldwide resurgence in the ministry of spiritual direction arises out of a desire to tend the holy in our lives. People of faith are awakening and listening to what God has to say. Often the primary task in spiritual direction is to create a space that helps the faithful remember and listen deeply. To remember is to collect the pieces and put them into a whole that one can understand and appreciate. This remembering and collecting often entails our retelling our experience.

This passage basically retells Peter's experience as recorded in Chapter 10. Generally Peter is accepted as the apostle who held closely to the Jewish Christian tradition. In reviewing his story step-by-step with a group of believers, Peter has the opportunity to understand a vision and integrate it with his experience in Cornelius's household. His challenge in growth is to understand that God's grace extends to all people, far above and beyond what Peter has ever imagined. To Peter's credit, he moves forward to be an instrument of that grace.

God is actively working to extend our horizons of belief and understanding. In pausing to remember those moments when the Mystery touched our lives, we savor the Holy in our midst. As a result, our faith increases, our joy abounds, and we are empowered to follow God more closely.

Prayer: **May I remember your goodness, O loving God. Let me pause to savor your presence with me. In Christ's name. Amen.**

Wednesday, May 6   Read Psalm 148.

Sometimes living in the modern world gets to me. Last Thursday it was the traffic jam that started at 2:47 in the afternoon. On Saturday it was the computer that froze halfway through the writing of this meditation. Today it was being bounced along an advanced technological phone system for twenty-five minutes, waiting for a real person who could do something to answer my call. I accessed the "Express Service Line" with a monitor for quality control.

Though telling the stars, the snow, and the trees to praise the Lord may seem like an unusual perspective, I can relate to the author of Psalm 148. More and more, it is when I turn to nature that I feel grounded and keep a perspective on what is real. Looking up at the stars late at night, I experience the depths of the universe and remember what "big" means. Catching a snow-flake on my tongue, I marvel at the cold and the seasons. It is a cycle of providence, of seeding and harvesting, of using and recycling. Arching my back to look up at the tip of a sequoia tree, I wonder at what it has seen over its lifetime, what visions lie embedded in its rings of age.

Human beings create technology, utility, and complex systems. Often these systems now determine our day-to-day reality. However, there is a vast difference between what will stand the test of time and what will not. God and our relationship to our Creator is still the ground of reality on which we stand. As the world swirls at ever greater speed around us, it is often nature that reminds us of what will remain.

Prayer: **May your beautiful creation ground me, O God, for you are the Rock of my Salvation. Amen.**

Thursday, May 7   Read Revelation 21:1-6.

As we approach the turn of the millennium, the media is promoting images that seek to capture the spirit of a certain age, like the Ming dynasty in China or the Post-Modern Era in Europe. Some are still pictures; others are fast-forwarded in a time sequence to project them into the future. Some of the "Brave New World" projections I have seen have been rather bleak: They depict scarcity of world resources, authoritarian rule, violence, darkness, and weary masses.

The vision of the new heaven and new earth in Revelation 21 is very different—full of light, hope, and joy. As we juxtapose this vision of the future with a hard look at the world in the present, what surfaces is the deep, deep longing in our hearts for all creation to live in the harmony (*shalom*) planned by its Creator. Our hearts yearn for the time when everyone will have an adequate share of daily bread, and hunger will be no more. We long for healing and wholeness, a time when tears will not reveal hearts shattered by pain. We dream of the earth's people living truly as neighbors in peace because justice prevails.

As people of faith, we hold the tension of the present with our hope for the future. In the most troubled spots in the world, a spark will ignite and maintain a steady glow. Each spark of love for neighbor as self adds harmony; each spark of justice adds peace; and each spark of love for God adds glory. Many people of faith and people of many faiths share the vision of the new heaven and earth. In their time, these sparks will burst into bright light.

Prayer: **God of all ages, let me live in the new heaven and earth today. In Christ's name. Amen.**

139

Friday, May 8   Read Revelation 21:1-4.

The minister turned to her and said, "Julie, repeat after me." Julie glanced at the minister, nodded slightly, looked at Jonathan shyly, and resolutely repeated each phrase: "I, Julie Mei-Ling, take you, Jonathan Wei-Ang, to be my wedded husband, to have and to hold, from this day forward, for better, for worse, for richer, for poorer, in sickness and in health." Julie paused and her eyes brimmed. Jonathan squeezed her hands to pass her his energy. The minister picked up and Julie followed, "to love and to cherish . . ." Her tears overflowed, she lowered her head, and a tear dropped to her glove. Jonathan smiled, reached into his trouser pocket, and took out a linen handkerchief. He reached out, brushed aside a wisp of her hair, and lifted her chin. She smiled, closed her eyes, and offered her cheeks. He gently dabbed her cheeks and wiped the traces of her teardrops. The audience held their breath.

We all recognize those moments of holiness when a scene of love takes our breath away, and we too stand on holy ground. The beauty both captivates us and inspires fear in us. In that moment, we too believe that all will be well and all hopes will find fulfillment.

The new Jerusalem, the holy city, will be prepared as a bride adorned for her husband. God will lead her forth and dwell with her. God's home will be with mortals, and God will wipe every tear from our eyes. I can imagine no more tender scene of love than this. With a touch of God's hand, we can leave behind the past and walk into a new future. We will not look back, for the picture of love we see ahead will transform our history.

Prayer: **Come, my Beloved, and tenderly lead me forward in my walk with you. In Christ's name. Amen.**

Saturday, May 9   Read John 13:31-33.

When I hear of so-and-so being at the height of his or her glory, I visualize someone at the pinnacle of success, in robust health and vitality, having accomplished something so outstanding as to be recognized by the community as having made a significant contribution. This person has power, prestige, and influence.

When Jesus talks about God's having glorified him, he refers to the culmination of a long, hard road of meeting resistance; fighting the religious, economic, and political establishment; back-breaking work, misunderstanding, and betrayal by friends; and impending death. The contrast stuns me.

Each step of the way to his glory, Jesus had a choice. It was within his power to turn away, if not to downscale or slightly distort the gospel. He read people's hearts; he knew that the consequence of each decision led him closer to a final confrontation with death-dealing powers. Having a God-consciousness of good and evil embodied in a human self made the choice for God's glory a very painful one indeed.

We praise Jesus for his faithfulness. In choosing obedience to a death he freely accepted, he redefined glory for all believers. Just as we continue to face choices for good or evil and battle death-dealing forces, we have a Savior of the world who we know has won our glory for us.

Prayer: **Praise to you, Lord Jesus Christ. May I be glorified in you. Amen.**

141

Sunday, May 10   Read John 13:34-35.

As a young girl, I loved new things. I couldn't wait to tear off the wrappings and put on whatever new thing I received. I loved to put on new shoes and go out somewhere, anywhere. When I planted my first narcissus bulb, I got up at night hoping to catch its flowers coming out. When I got my first pair of goldfish, I paid them so much attention and fed them so much that they floated on the surface the next morning.

Though impatience has diminished with age, I still delight in new things. New things catch our attention because they are un-soiled by use and dirt. Newness brings a sense of not being weighted down: a fresh perspective, an excitement of something not tried before, a hope of something better.

The essence of Jesus' teaching was actually familiar to the disciples. For centuries God had tried repeatedly to convey the message. Jesus' message of forgiveness and hope, his actions of healing and providing for needs, his embrace of his disciples as friends actually recall an old, old message: God's faithfulness through the ages.

Yet by leaving what he calls a new commandment, Jesus wraps up his message and presents it to us in a memorable way. He tells us that loving one another as he has loved us will become the distinguishing mark of those who bear his name. Stated this way, it is new and it is easy to remember. This new commandment not only embodies teachings of the past, it is an invitation to look for and create new opportunities for love.

Prayer: **May your love, O God, find new forms and expressions within me. Amen.**

GOD'S BLESSINGS

May 11–17, 1998   **Janice L. Frederick-Watts✤**
Monday, May 11   Read Psalm 67.

Worship in its deepest sense is recognition of and thanks-giving for the grace of God. It is response to the warmth and authenticity of God's love, which surrounds, fills, and draws us to God. Worship is the essence and power of God's blessings.

One of the significant attributes of the psalms is their expression of the inner life. During a time of anguish in my life, reading a psalm aloud helped me articulate my deepest feelings and experience release.

But the psalmist does not confine his thoughts to the individual; rather, he speaks of the universality of God's love. The world God created is also the world God seeks to save. The world that has lost touch with the source of its life is the world God seeks to heal and make whole. The beauty of this healing is that all nations will know and praise God.

Blessings go beyond what we receive as a result of God's goodness. God's blessings are also an invitation to respond to God's purposes for healing, health, and wholeness. God's blessings are an invitation to be partners with God as instruments of grace.

Prayer: **Lord, I am thankful for your presence, your goodness, and your mercy. Your blessings constantly remind me of your love. Show me what I can do to demonstrate my love for you. In Jesus' name I pray. Amen.**

✤Pastor of the Centenary-Kingsville Charge of The United Methodist Church; Hartsville, South Carolina.

Tuesday, May 12   Read Acts 16:9-15.

Paul received a vision in which a man pleaded with him to come to Macedonia. The scriptures suggest no delay between receiving the vision and Paul's immediate response, which was grounded in his belief that God had called him to go.

The extraordinary aspect of Paul's move was that it would take him into another culture to bring the good news: Philippi was a Roman colony. Paul was taking the message to gentile Romans. In Philippi the Jewish-Christian believers had no meeting place, so they gathered by the riverside.

On the Sabbath, Paul and his companions met women by the riverside who had come to pray. Paul's speaking to the women reminds us of Jesus' speaking to the woman of Samaria. Neither let cultural traditions keep him from sharing the word of God.

Cultural traditions in our day can sometimes imprison us and give us faulty perceptions of others, hindering us from freely relating to one another. Among those cultural traditions is the matter of relating or not relating to persons of other ethnic or racial groups. We sometimes encourage ourselves to fear persons simply because of our differences. We conjure up negative images of them and scare ourselves to death. Then when we meet, our fear causes us to relate to the image rather than the person. In other words, sometimes we demonize one another, which increases the isolation and alienation.

Jesus set the pace for breaking down barriers that demonize and dehumanize. Jesus came to liberate and set free. Therefore, the church is called to be a forerunner in breaking down barriers and lifting up the value of all persons.

Prayer: **God of all, help me be open to other people, remembering that, like me, they too need love and acceptance. Let me be open to others, remembering that each person is an expression of your love and your creation. In Jesus' name we pray. Amen.**

Wednesday, May 13   Read Acts 16:9-15.

Lydia was quite a woman of her day—a merchant of wealth, but more importantly a woman of faith. She had gathered by the riverside with other women for prayer. There Paul and his companions joined them. There Paul shared the word of God with Lydia and her companions. The scriptures plainly state that though Paul was the messenger, it was the Lord who "opened her heart."

The story reminds us that the gospel message is for everyone—rich or poor, young or old, male or female. God embraces us all in love. The thirst we all have is our thirst for God. The psalmist said it well: "As a deer longs for flowing streams, so my soul longs for you, O God" (Ps. 42:1).

No matter how we may differ in our likes and dislikes, how we look or what we think, one basic yearning binds us together: the yearning to know God. Getting in touch with that deep yearning opens our hearts to God and to one another.

Lydia's conversion was not just a turning point in her own life; Lydia's conversion demonstrated the freedom God brings to all people—people of different classes, cultures, and races. God created us for freedom, but freedom is not doing anything we want to do. True freedom is acting in accordance with our highest good.

Acting against God, we misused our freedom; sin entered in. With sin came anxiety, inner compulsions, hatred, malice, revenge, imprisonments of our own making, and the loss of freedom.

In Jesus, God offered us a new burst of freedom. As a liberator, Jesus came to set our spirits free. Through Christ, God restores our lost freedom.

Prayer: **Open my heart, O Lord. Let your love flood my soul and bring me new life. In the name of Jesus who liberates and sets free. Amen.**

Thursday, May 14   Read Revelation 21:10, 22–22:5.

When I think of home, I think of a place where I am loved and cherished and valued. It is the place I belong. To think of having *no* home unleashes feelings of fear, anxiety, and uncertainty about who I am and about my place in the world.

John's vision of being at home with God comforts me. Part of that comfort comes from knowing I have a place with God—I belong. And I delight in knowing that with God I am not left out.

I visited a parishioner who had been sick for some time. She spent much time going back and forth between hospital and home. In her movement back and forth she felt isolated and abandoned by a community she deeply needed at a crucial time in her life—the church. In speaking of her feelings of abandonment, she said, "I don't mind being shut in. I just don't like being shut out." None of us likes being shut out—abandoned or forgotten.

Being at home with God in the new Jerusalem responds to our hopes for being known, for being loved, for being remembered, for healing and wholeness, and for security. All that we need and thirst for we find in God's presence.

The gates to the city are always open and welcoming, a symbol of God's openness to all. The light of the city is the loving presence of Christ. And the sounds of the city are songs of praise to God.

Home with God is where my soul has its rest because I have learned to trust in God. It is where I am my true self, and I receive all the good things God gives to those who walk in the ways of God.

Prayer: **Gracious God, help me make my home with you. I need the nurturing comfort of your presence. Amen.**

Friday, May 15   Read John 14:23-29.

John 14 has been a source of comfort for many believers. Remember, however, that Jesus first spoke these words to disillusioned, confused, and fearful disciples. To strengthen the faith of his disciples, Jesus speaks these much-loved words, "Do not let your hearts be troubled."

Jesus' preparation of his disciples for his departure was a loving act. In the months leading up to my mother's death, even though we did not realize it at the time, she prepared her family for that time. It was not any one act. She prepared us most through her love, care, and encouragement all the years of our life together. Her love comforts our hearts now in these days of grieving.

Jesus' scared disciples think they have lost all they have hoped for. Jesus looks into their frightened faces and says, "Do not let your hearts be troubled, and do not let them be afraid." He calls them to move from their preoccupation with safety and security and from their limited understanding.

Jesus invites the disciples to lean on the everlasting arms of God. He directs their focus toward God and away from their fear. Obedience would demonstrate their love for God as well as their trust in God's purposes. Our love for God is evidenced in our faithful living out of God's word. Those who follow Christ have a home with God.

Jesus offers the gifts of the Comforter (Advocate): presence, peace, and remembrance. These precious gifts are part of our inheritance as God's children. Each reminds us that God is with us. In God's presence alone we can find the peace we need.

Prayer: **Lord, be my comfort and my peace. Amen.**

147

Saturday, May 16   Read John 14:23-29.

"Peace I leave with you." How like the Lord to bring comfort when we are filled with fear. I am so thankful for the healing that comes with the Lord's presence.

"Peace I leave with you." May you be saved from trouble. "Peace I leave with you." May God give you every good thing.

When Jesus speaks of peace, it is not the absence of trouble— it is the gift of assurance that in everything there is always that which makes for our highest good. For me, an important part of the peace that Jesus offers is the peace of victory. No experience of life can take from us the peace that God gives. Indeed, God's peace passes our understanding.

When my mother died, I didn't think I could survive the loss or pain. I felt a mixture of pain, disorientation, anger, disbelief, and numbness. I spent many sleepless nights remembering and longing for my mother. I wanted to see her face again and embrace her again. I wanted to see her walk into the room again. I wanted to hear her voice and her laughter again. I wanted someone to wake me up and tell me it was just a dream. But no one could, because it was real.

Shortly after her death, as I mindlessly moved from room to room in our home, in an unanticipated moment I was lifted beyond myself; I felt peace and assurance. A lightness, wonder, and fullness in my soul unburdened me. It was the peace, the love, the presence of God. And I had the assurance of my mother's victory over death.

I believe the gift of peace is a call for us to trust God with our lives now and through eternity. It is the assurance that God is always present with us.

Prayer: **Dear Lord, in the seasons of my life, grant me your peace. In Jesus' name I pray. Amen.**

Sunday, May 17   Read Psalm 67.

We always need God's mercy. We always need God's blessings. We always need God's favor.

The nations of the world are wrought with problems. Whether it is hostility between nations, oppressive government, the poverty of the people, or the need for health care, all of the nations of the world need the "saving health" that God can provide. The problems that surface in every nation clearly indicate the need for God's kingdom. Any instances in which people are dehumanized, not treated with dignity or respect, are situations that need God's healing and grace.

Psalm 67 is a clear call, not only to the nations of the world but to the variety of peoples within a nation to confess the breaches among them and to receive restoration in their relationship. For this is God's will concerning us.

The blessings of a restored relationship benefit all with a renewed sense of community. Recognition and appreciation of each person's gifts and the use of everyone's gifts will enhance quality of life for all.

Can we not understand that the well-being of one nation is linked irrevocably to the well-being of other nations? Can we not understand that the Lord God made us all? Can we not understand that restored relationships with one another mean a restored relationship with God?

Prayer: **Gracious God, bless this nation of ours. Help me to be a repairer of breaches among peoples. Bless the nations of the world with the healing and wholeness only you can give. Grant us a renewed sense of community and well-being. Fill us with praise and thanksgiving for your love and mercy. Grant us all your saving health. In the name of Jesus I pray. Amen.**

REMEMBERING THE GREATNESS OF GOD

May 18–24, 1998   **Jaydee R. Hanson**✤

Monday, May 18   Read Psalm 97.

We live at the top of one of the highest hills in the Washington, D.C., region. Lightning and thunder are a very real part of our lives. Nearly every tree is scarred by lightning. The power and grandeur of nature is a reality, as is the possibility of destruction. I do not park too near trees for fear they might collapse when struck by lightning or when the wind is too strong. I like these reminders of nature and God's power. My children and I gather inside during storms, awed at the spectacle of a lightning storm.

The psalmist calls the earth itself to rejoice and for the coastlands to be glad. The mountains melt like wax before God. The ancient Hebrews knew God's power in nature firsthand. You could not wander in the desert for forty years and fail to appreciate God's power. The psalmist understands that God's power is not merely the power of nature; God's power is rooted in and founded on righteousness and justice.

Just as one seeks protection from the power of a lightning storm, so too does one seek protection from the power of God's righteousness and justice. That protection comes from hating evil and living righteously. There is for the righteous a better day. The psalmist sings that the dawn is sown for the righteous and joy is sown for the upright in heart.

Prayer: **God of lightning and thunder, God of righteousness and justice, help me not to fear the stormy times in my life, but rather to remember that you are always creating a new day. Let me join with all the earth in seeing and celebrating your power. Amen.**

✤United Methodist layman; Assistant General Secretary, United Methodist Church Board of Church and Society; Washington, D.C.

Tuesday, May 19   Read Acts 16:16-34.

A fortune-telling slave girl is following Paul and Silas around the Roman colony of Philippi, proclaiming them to be the slaves of the "Most High God." At first glance, the girl, who is possessed by a spirit, seems to be praising Paul and God. So why would Paul get annoyed?

The girl in the story is not praising God of her own accord. Her purpose is to earn money for her owners. Her praise of Paul and God may well echo her praise of followers of other religions. It is done for effect.

The girl's praise reminds me of the prayers I've heard at political gatherings and annual meetings of corporations. The prayers serve as an implied blessing of the status quo. Even leaders caught in major ethical and legal scandals end their speeches praising God and calling for a return to religious values. Yet their behavior does not seem to change. Day after day they ask God to bless them and their enterprises. They host prayer breakfasts and open shareholder meetings with prayer. They have all the public trappings of piety but act otherwise.

Paul's exorcising the spirit from the girl deprives her owners of income. For that Paul and Silas are beaten and put in jail. When an earthquake breaks open the jail, they do not escape. Rather, they prevent the jailer from killing himself. The jailer does not just praise Paul; he asks what he must do to be saved. He intends to change his life. Belief for him requires acting differently. His entire household rejoices.

The spirit-possessed girl, like hypocritical leaders, praises Paul's leadership but has no intention of changing.

Prayer: **Dear Christ, keep us from hypocritical prayer, from praising you and your leaders with no intention of changing our lives. Keep us from listening to those spirits who would appeal to our vanity. Help us be more like Paul and Silas's jailer—able to recognize your power and change because of it. Amen.**

Wednesday, May 20   Read John 17:20-26.

My local church uses the "Godly Play" materials developed by Jerome Berryman for Sunday school for young children. As part of the Godly Play liturgy, we extinguish the candle that represents Jesus' words and say that the light of Jesus is now everywhere. A five-year-old girl in the class always exclaims excitedly, "Now Jesus is everywhere!"

Jesus prays in these passages that the disciples might be one with God and him. He prays that through the disciples the world might believe that God sent and loved Jesus and loves the world too. Jesus understands that future believers would have to rely on the witness of the disciples who knew him. Our task two thousand years later is to witness to the love of God and Jesus that we know through scripture, through the witness of disciples across the millennia, and through our own experience.

The five-year-old girl is always one of the few children to offer a prayer. For her, Jesus is real and everywhere accessible. She is not yet a skeptic. The continued accessibility of Jesus and God's love to everyone is the promise of Jesus' prayer.

Children, like the five year old in my Sunday school class, understand God's love directly. Many of us who are older struggle with the meaning of God's love even as we try to live a life based on that love. Jesus prays that his disciples and those who come to believe through them will all be one in their knowledge of God's love. If this knowledge were automatic or something that would come to us without doubts at any time, Jesus would not have had to pray about it.

Prayer: **Dear God, you love us as a parent loves a child. You love us even when we doubt your love. Help us in the midst of our doubt to love you as simply and clearly as does a child. Guide us as we seek to live our lives as examples of your love. Amen.**

Thursday, May 21   Read Luke 24:44-53; Acts 1:1-11.

The author of Luke and Acts makes clear that these disciples are to be Christ's witnesses. Witnessing is hard. I have had to be a witness in court on two occasions. That witnessing requires that you wait until the right time; then under oath you relay what you heard, saw, experienced—what you believe happened, not what you wish had happened.

Jesus' disciples are impatient. It is bad enough that he died, but then after his resurrection he only stayed around forty days. They still want the old kingdom of Israel restored on their timetable. Instead, they are told to be patient, that God alone knows the timetable. They are to wait for a blessing. All they are to do is be Jesus' witnesses to the entire earth.

That Jesus expects his disciples to be witnesses who proclaim repentance and forgiveness of sins and not the coming of a new political kingdom still confuses his disciples. On this Ascension Day, as we recall Jesus' earthly departure and the task he entrusted to us, we need to remember that the Holy Spirit assists us in the difficult tasks of repentance and forgiveness. Luke acknowledges the necessity of waiting for the Holy Spirit before witnessing. When you cannot act as if you fully believe that to which you bear witness, you lose credibility.

Jesus knew what he was doing when he suggested that we pray daily for God's forgiveness, just as we forgive others. That is the way God's reign works: Divine forgiveness and human forgiveness are tied together.

Prayer: **Dear Jesus, your message of forgiveness and repentance sounds easy but is hard to practice. I need help to witness to your words and life. Please send me a renewed sense of the Holy Spirit's presence soon. I am growing impatient again. Amen.**

Friday, May 22   Read Psalm 47.

Awesome is a word I seldom hear shouted by anyone other than my children's friends. This psalm has all peoples proclaiming the "awesomeness" of God. In it God is the king of the whole earth and all its nations. At the end of this short psalm, the princes of the peoples gather as the people of God, and the shields of the earth belong to God. What a wonderful place the world would be if all the military defenses were in God's hands.

In the years since the end of the Cold War, dozens of new wars have broken out. We spend vast sums to arm our border guards and expand our police forces to defend us against enemies, real and imagined.

It is a terrible irony that the United States, one of the most religious, most Christian nations in the world, still spends so much on military might. The military budgets of the United States and its closest allies total eighty percent of all money spent on the military in the world. What would our world look like if we really believed that all the shields belonged to God?

To live differently, we need a different vision. Psalm 47 calls us to praise God as the ruler of all nations and all the earth. In its vision, God will be highly exalted when all the shields belong to God. What a different world it would be if we all believed that our protection comes from God.

Prayer: **Dear God, ruler of the earth and all nations, help us find the faith to join with you in breaking "the flashing arrows, the shield, the sword, and the weapons of war" (Ps. 76:3). We look forward to the day when the youth of nations are not cut down in war and when children have enough food to eat. Help us build monuments to those who prevent war, not just those who had to fight. Help us make the victory of Christ over death the only victory we celebrate. Amen.**

Saturday, May 23   Read Revelation 22:8-21.

As we approach the end of the second millennium since Jesus, we hear more and more discussions of the end of time. Various cults promote one theory or another. This passage in Revelation, the last words in the Bible, offers Christians a glimpse of what to expect when Jesus returns.

It is a difficult passage for me, in part, because of the last exchange I had with a friend. Annie died nearly twenty years ago in Jonestown, Guyana. She was bright and articulate, a nurse and a minister's daughter. She wanted a better world. I remember her passion at having found a group that was interracial, that lived Jesus' teachings, and that could use her nursing skills. Ironically, the last use of her nursing skills was injecting cyanide into the children of Jonestown, following not Christ but Jim Jones.

The last thing Annie gave me was a button that said simply, "Omega"—not "Alpha-Omega"—just "Omega." Ever since Jonestown, I have taken that button as a metaphor for those who get just half of the message of Christ. Christ is not just the end but the beginning and everything in between. Christ is not coming again to take us away but to bring a New Jerusalem, a new earth (Rev. 21).

The amazing thing about this Christ is that his coming does not require us to behave differently than we are required already. We simply are expected to live as he taught, to keep our robes "clean" by following his commandments (Rev. 22:14). It is not easy to follow Jesus, but that is all that we need do to be ready for his coming. We are not called to follow Jim Jones, David Koresh, or the Hale-Bopp comet. We are to follow Jesus' commandments to love God and our neighbors.

Prayer: **Dear Jesus, you are our beginning and our end. Help me every day to follow you in such a way that I will always be ready for your return. Help me live out your commandments where I am. Amen.**

Sunday, May 24   Read Ephesians 1:15-23.

Paul, the ascribed writer of Ephesians, offers a powerful prayer for us all. Paul prays that God might give a spirit of wisdom and revelation as the Ephesians come to know Jesus. With enlightened eyes of the heart, they might know the hope to which they were called.

In my work for the General Board of Church and Society, I meet many people who are struggling with what they are called to do as Christians. Many times they are not, in fact, struggling with what they are called to do but how to have the strength to do it. It is terrifying to realize that our calling by Christ may mean that we have to live our lives in profoundly different ways. Some of these persons fear that they do not have the strength or clarity of vision to live out their calling. They worry about their children's education if they decide to move to a new place, about challenging the political power system. They worry a lot as they try to understand their calling.

Paul understood these worries. He prays that the Ephesians might know the *hope* to which they are called. To counter economic worries, he prays that they might know the riches of God's inheritance. To address political fears, Paul reminds them and us of the immeasurable power of Christ for those who believe.

We need to pray for one another constantly. It is hard to remember the *hope* of our calling in the face of today's challenges. The demands of work life, family life, and maintenance of material things can erode the clarity of our calling by the risen Christ. Remembering God's greatness helps free us from worry to do the work of our calling.

Prayer: **Dear God, you are our Redeemer and Protector, strong enough to raise Jesus from the dead. Free us from worry, so we may know the hope of our calling. Help us to know that your greatness is greater than that of any corporation, coalition, congress, or ruler. Amen.**

INCARNATING THE SPIRIT

May 25–31, 1998   **Walter Wink**✤
Monday, May 25   Read Psalm 104:24-34, 35*b*.

This psalm's concern is the creation as a manifestation of God's providential care for the entire created order. That is an appropriate context in which to couch Pentecost, for the pouring out of God's spirit on "all flesh" will have cosmic consequences. The whole creation is craning its neck for the revealing of the children of God (Rom. 8:19). Perhaps, as the "anthropic cosmological principle" of modern cosmology suggests, the creation *has* been waiting for the emergence of a species that can bring creation to consciousness, that can articulate praise for the incredible wondrousness of the created order.

The universe had to have those properties that would allow life to develop within it at some stage in its history. Any less helium, any more oxygen, the absence of carbon, and life as we know it could not have emerged. The universe, it appears, has been awaiting our arrival, awaiting voices that can cry out, "O Lord, how manifold are your works!" Waiting for minds that can trace God's "wisdom"; that can be awed by the earth's self-renewal and creativity, its profligate abundance of creatures. Waiting for an organism able to be aware of the sheer improbability of everything. Thus the psalmist pledges to "sing to the Lord as long as I live," for this is what the universe itself needs from us.

Suggestion for meditation: **On behalf of the universe, how do I give voice to God's wondrous works?**

✤United Methodist minister; Professor of Biblical Interpretation at Auburn Theological Seminary in New York City; published author.

Tuesday, May 26   Read Acts 2:14-21.

Over millennia God is growing a body, patiently and persistently trying to incarnate in human flesh. What God had been able to do with solitary prophets, God wanted to be able to do with all: to find human beings capable of containing divine Spirit. In Israel, the Spirit spoke through judges, kings, priests, prophets, seers, dreamers—sometimes shattering them. But always one person addressed the many on behalf of the One.

But then the prophets began to envision a time to come when God would no longer speak through a single prophet, but God's spirit would be poured out on all Israel, indeed, all humanity.

It is difficult to comprehend this. Almost six hundred years before our Pentecost (over seven hundred, if we consider Isa. 32:15), God was preparing Israel for this new thing. Apparently it was not an easy feat to incarnate Holy Spirit. *Knowing* the promise was not the same as *living* the promise. It took Jesus to live the Spirit into flesh—not as a personal possession but a Spirit to be shared. Pentecost was the beginning of that fulfillment.

Joel, some four hundred years before Jesus, portrayed this longing most dramatically: "I will pour out my spirit on all flesh"—not on just the elite, the religious enthusiasts, the rich and famous, the saints and prophets but everyone: the undeserving poor, the religiously negligent, the notorious sinners, the crooks and prostitutes—in short, the kind of folks Jesus hung out with. Everyone, young and old, even "daughters" and "female slaves," would be filled with the Holy Spirit. The Spirit was being democratized. God would now govern from within the heart (Ezek. 36:26-27).

Pentecost is not the fulfillment of that hope but its inauguration. Only Jews were present. But now the gospel has reached the ends of the earth.

Suggestion for meditation: **Is the Holy Spirit incarnate in us yet?**

Wednesday, May 27   Read Acts 2:1-4.

Questions, so many questions: What new thing is the Spirit doing at Pentecost? What role in this experience was played by the fifth-day community incubation that the disciples went through together? What dangers of ego inflation are implicit in receiving the Holy Spirit? In what ways do I characteristically *contaminate* the Holy Spirit? What in me needs to die in order for me to become "God's temple" (1 Cor. 3:16-17)? Could I stand to let the Holy Spirit make me ecstatic? Can I deal with so much power? If the Holy Spirit were to come on all flesh, what new problems would arise? How can we help prepare the way for this new mutation in the Spirit's presence?

In some Old Testament texts, the spirit of God seizes or rushes upon (*tfalach*) a person (Judg. 14:6, for example). What new experience is described by the Spirit's being *within*? What is the difference between being dominated by the Spirit and being indwelt by it? between being possessed by the Spirit and integrating the Spirit into our personalities? What new thing happens when the Spirit moves into the substance of our beings? What has been the gift of the "charismatic" movement (Pentecostalism and Neo-Pentecostalism) in the recovery of the Spirit in our time? What problems has this new influx of Spirit-power created? Are we willing not just to revel in the Spirit's power but to try to incarnate it, relating it to our sexuality, our reason, our bodies, our ego-drives, our neuroses, our hatreds, and our weaknesses? Sensational displays of spiritual power are all the rage; the hard daily work of integrating the Holy Spirit is the task of the next millennium.

Suggestion for meditation: **Try writing a dialogue between yourself and the Holy Spirit.**

Thursday, May 28   Read Acts 2:5-13.

More questions. If Luke intends this story as a kind of reversal of Babel (Gen. 11), when the nations were separated by a confusion of tongues, why does he feature only Jews from the Diaspora (the scattering of Jews among the nations), rather than Gentiles? Why does he use an old astrological list of the "twelve" nations of the world, altering it to include Rome and others? Why does he leave in the list nations that no longer exist (Medes and Elamites)? Is he trying to extend his list of nations back in time to encompass all the nations symbolically? Perhaps he means to imply that all the nations, scattered at Babel, are now being brought back together through these Diaspora Jews who will bear to them the new reality of the Spirit that is to be poured out on all humanity.

Is this a miracle of tongues or of ears? Is each person *hearing* the gospel in his or her own tongue, or are the disciples of Jesus *speaking* in foreign languages? Was this originally a narrative about *glossolalia* (like the "speaking in tongues" one finds in 1 Cor. 12–14, which is unintelligible unless interpreted by someone else) that Luke changed into a miracle of translation to account for the first burst of the church's growth? Notice how determined Luke is to show that the gift of the Holy Spirit did not issue in religious self-indulgence as happened in Corinth. The Spirit does not provide religious pyrotechnics to entertain people who are spiritually souped-up but rather leads immediately to mission, to public action, to challenging the authorities, to stints in jail (Acts 4). This Spirit is the breath of a new world order breaking into the world and the power to achieve it.

Do we find that credible? Or are we the kind of scoffers who put it all down as being "filled with new wine"?

Prayer: **Fill me, Lord, with the power of your Holy Spirit. Then empower me to be ready for the changes that will come in my life. Amen.**

Friday, May 29   Read John 14:8-14.

Why does Philip think that seeing the Father will prove satisfying if he has seen Jesus and is not satisfied? What more does he want? What is it that Philip doesn't know yet? Seeing Jesus is seeing the Father: How are we to imagine this? Is Jesus like a windowpane through whom we see God? Or a mirror that reflects back to us the same divine indwelling that he calls abiding in God? Is Jesus the human face of God, now revealed as preeminently familial? "I am in the Father and the Father is in me"—is this like digging a hole beside the ocean, in which the ocean is wholly and solely in the hole but not the whole ocean? Or is Jesus equal to the whole ocean? The latter seems to be denied by the use of the preposition: Jesus does not say that he *is* God, but only that God is *in* him and he *in* God. "The Father is greater than I" (14:28). Logically, B is in A, but A is greater than B. The same, then, is potentially true of us: God is in us and we in God. If that is true, then the same power that animated Jesus and worked miracles is available to us as well—and even greater power, because the heavenly Jesus is now its everlasting dispenser.

But how can we be expected to do the works Jesus did and greater ones as well? Why does his going to the Father make such works possible for us? If we understood that God is available to do God's work within us, that might free us from the ego's anxiety at failure.

Have we done such "mighty works"? Do we know others who have? Share stories with others. We need to rehearse the expectation of miracles, to set ourselves in their path, to "ask for anything" out of that oneness of abiding in God. Then we need not be afraid of asking wrongly, for the real benefit of "abiding" is the personal relationship with God, not the answers we get.

Suggestion for meditation: **What miracle are you asking for? What expectations do you have?**

161

Saturday, May 30   Read John 14:15-17, 25-27.

The great theologian Augustine (d. 430 C.E.) said, "Love, and do what thou wilt." John's Gospel says, "If you love me, you will keep my commandments." Is there a difference? Augustine assumed that we would "will" to do only that which is pleasing to God if we love God. These are radical statements. For followers of Jesus whose religion had been defined largely as obedience to divine law, this marked an astonishing departure.

A look at history devastatingly confirms that human beings are not up to such responsibility. We need a helper, an inner spirit guide, who can "teach [us] everything," and remind us of all that Jesus said. This Advocate is that helper, our advisor, pedagogue, and peace. Is this Advocate capable of new revelations, or does it only teach us "all that I have said to you"? Clearly the former: the Advocate is a revealer, "for he will not speak on his own, but will speak whatever he hears, and he will declare to you the things that are to come" (John 16:13).

The Advocate serves several functions in John. With the death of the original eyewitnesses, it guarantees an inner connection to the event of Jesus. If the author of the Fourth Gospel received instruction from the Advocate about what Jesus said, we get an idea just how free the Advocate could be with those traditions. Likewise, the Advocate answered the delay of the Second Coming; *it* was the second coming of Jesus, and all Jesus' followers would ever need. As the "Spirit of truth," it still teaches us what Jesus said.

How can we receive "what Jesus said" with the same creative freedom as the Fourth Evangelist, plumbing the depths for meaning, making connections to our lives?

Suggestion for meditation: **What words and actions in my life lately have pleased God? What words and actions have not?**

Sunday, May 31   Read Romans 8:14-17.

Paul never refers to the outpouring of the Holy Spirit at Pentecost. But then, he seldom mentions anything described in the Gospels or Acts. But he does describe, in his characteristically intense way, what happens when the spirit of God becomes incarnate in believers.

To our surprise, we discover that Jesus makes us God's "children." Weren't we already? Are we not, by virtue of being created by God, already children by inheritance? As a consequence of the "Big Bang," are we not all of one substance with the universe? Do we not "belong" here, and isn't everything "of God" and of one reality in God? So why do we discover ourselves to be orphans, alienated from the universe and one another, estranged from the One who created us for relationship? What have we done to create this chasm that yawns at our feet?

Orphans. We are homeless runaways, easing the pain of separation and the anger of rebellion with chemicals and addictions and unfulfilling relationships with others who are separated from us by the same bottomless abysses.

And because we cannot bridge this gulf, because we cannot even give an account of who we are, God has thrown across a span: Jesus, in whom all the abysses collapse into relatedness, in whom alienation collapses into love, in whom our rebellion collapses into camaraderie, in whom our meaninglessness collapses into joy, purpose, and vocation.

Adopted. Not by choosing God but by being sought out and chosen by God. Unable to believe our good fortune, we need the Spirit to coach us to cry, "Daddy!" To our surprise, we become heirs, inheritors, of one substance with the universe, belonging to everything and everyone, *related*—provided, of course, that we bear the cost of becoming reconcilers and abyss-crossers ourselves.

Prayer: **All praise to you, O God, for Jesus Christ who bridges troubled waters so that your love may reach us. Amen.**

GOD'S GIFTS TO GOD'S PEOPLE

June 1–7, 1998
Monday, June 1

Carol A. Wehrheim✤
Read Proverbs 8:1-4.

In congregational life, the pace often slows now, this week after Pentecost. Summer usually brings a different tempo. Perhaps you have a smidgen more time to ponder these readings, whether you are preparing a sermon, a church school lesson, or yourself for worshiping God on Sunday morning. Read the Proverbs passage, allowing it to play in your mind like a video.

What image do you have of wisdom, wisdom, who stands in the middle of the public square and cries out? Her cry is to "all that live." Life given by the breath of God? Life taken by depriving others? Life eked out day by day?

As you begin this week, ponder the reason that wisdom is addressing you. How is it that you live? No quick, facile answers now. Dig deeply into the corners of your living to ponder what it is that gives you life. Why would wisdom be calling out to you? What is she offering?

Prayer: O God of wisdom, you have known us from our earliest beginnings, yet you allow us to find our way to you. Grant us the courage to listen to wisdom and the understanding to comprehend all the truth that she has for us. Amen.

✤Writer and editor; member of Nassau Presbyterian Church (U.S.A.); Princeton, New Jersey.

Tuesday, June 2   Read Proverbs 8:22-31.

Blithely we refer to the two creation stories in Genesis and forget that scripture tells and celebrates the work of the creating God elsewhere in the Bible. These verses (22-23) from Proverbs begin with wisdom's clear message that she was the first of all God's creation. Sounding just a bit like a firstborn, she emphasizes the honor of being the first product of God's creative acts.

Wisdom follows this declaration in verses 24-29 by describing the mighty creative acts that brought forth this world and by reminding us that she bore witness to creation. These few verses capture the grandeur and scope of this creation of the world.

Finally in verses 30-31, wisdom extols the joy of being that which gave God great joy and of rejoicing with God in the wonder of God's creation. This is not a somber God but one who is exuberant and filled with joy. At the end of this passage, we human beings are noted. We too are a source of delight for God and for wisdom.

Read these verses aloud. Notice how they tumble rapidly from your mouth. Wisdom can barely contain herself as she makes the point that you must pay attention to the wisdom and understanding she brings. And what is that wisdom? God is creator, and God is with us from the beginning. How can you rejoice in that knowledge this week?

Prayer: **God of great joy, show us the way to rejoice in your love and to delight in your creation. May we hear all you would have us know. Amen.**

165

Wednesday, June 3   Read Psalm 8.

Psalm 8 is the first song of praise in the psalter and is the only psalm in the whole collection that addresses God in the second person throughout. The opening and closing verses of Psalm 8 recall the great majesty and splendor of God the Almighty: "O Lord, our Sovereign, how majestic is your name in all the earth!" God is sovereign over all. Within this framework, humanity finds its identity. The psalmist had no trouble remembering the one true God.

As with the Proverbs selection, this psalm presents the Creator God. God's creation is orderly, giving us confidence in its maker. God's creation is beyond our ken, making us feel secure as a part of it. Yet as great as that creation is, it is minuscule compared to its creator.

After establishing the greatness of God, Psalm 8 goes on in its middle and longest portion to focus on humankind, with verse 5 as the centerpiece. We discover that we have royal status. Yet even in verses 3-8, God is the primary actor. In *The Message of the Psalms* (Augsburg Fortress, 1984, pages 37–38), Walter Brueggemann calls attention to the way the first and last verses envelope or surround the middle. It reminds one of an apple turnover: The filling is tasty, but the flaky crust provides the shape and boundaries. Focusing on the middle verses alone misses the point of this psalm. Without the knowledge of the majesty of God, humankind flounders. We are both God's creation and God's delight.

Prayer: **Majestic God, as you delight in us, your splendor overwhelms us. Lead us in your way so that we know your presence always and sing your praises. Amen.**

Thursday, June 4   Read Psalm 8:2-8.

When did you last look up to a starry night and feel the insignificance that this psalmist describes? If you live in a sparsely populated area, you may take this view for granted. One starry winter night, I was dazzled by the multitude of stars in a country sky. Even on a clear night the city lights eclipse most of the lights where I live—or is it the pollution that never quite disappears?

This description of the place of humankind suggests that Psalm 8 was constructed in the royal court. While the psalmist extols the place of humankind in the order of God's creation, can we today sit back proudly in this seat of honor? No place of honor is without responsibility, not for us or for the king of Israel. As those who have dominion over the rest of creation, we have heavy obligations. As the monarch is responsible for the realm, we are responsible for "the beasts of the field, the birds of the air, and the fish of the sea." "Crowned with glory and honor," we are the caretakers of the works of God's hands.

As you travel about your community, check out how the beasts, birds, and fish are doing. Is pollution of the waters killing the fish? Is development of land destroying the habitat of the birds and the beasts? How are the works of God's hands being given the glory and honor with which God has crowned human beings?

Prayer: **God of all creation, praise and honor to you. Awaken us to the task of caring for your world. Amen.**

Friday, June 5   Read John 16:12-15.

In John 16, Jesus is talking with his disciples for one of the last times on earth. Verses 12-15 come from his fifth and final teaching about the Spirit (the other teachings being found in 14:16-17; 14:25-26; 15:25; and 16:7-11). In verse 4, he explains that it was not necessary for him to tell them these things before because he was with them. Now he is about to go from them, and they must know what he knows.

While Jesus speaks these words to the disciples before the Ascension, the speech is also from Christ to the church in the world. These words assure us that we too will receive the gift of the Spirit.

An important gift of the Spirit is truth. For "the Spirit of truth…will guide you into all truth…and he will declare to you the things that are to come." No doubt, Christians of every age have needed this gift of discernment brought from the Spirit, but surely we need it in our time. This discernment makes it possible for the church to be a community of faith that holds both memory and hope, for the Spirit is the ongoing teacher of the church. The Spirit will declare or teach us all that is of Christ, and that word is from the Creator and Godhead.

Many claim possession of the Spirit, of course, and in time are found wanting. We, human that we are, dare assert such a claim only with hesitancy. Yet we are assured that the Spirit is among us, working and teaching.

Prayer: **Holy God, giver of the Spirit of truth, open our hearts to your touch, our ears to your word, and our minds to your ways. Come, Holy Spirit, come. Amen.**

Saturday, June 6   Read Romans 5:1-5.

What is it with Paul? Earlier in the Letter to the Romans (2:17, 23), he admonished them for boasting about the way they carried out the law of God. Now he is entreating them to boast of their relationship to God. Well, perhaps that is not quite what he is saying, but our culture does not look favorably upon boasting. A little too much boasting sounds fishy to us. We tend to think that perhaps there is nothing behind the words.

Romans 1–4 pretty much tells it like it is, mincing few words: Do not judge others. Live by the law and die by the law. In these few verses that open chapter 5, Paul reminds the Roman followers that being justified by faith, they have peace with God through Jesus Christ. Therefore, for the Romans and for us, it is not through our doing that we are reconciled with God but rather through our faith in Jesus Christ.

However, we may boast in the hope that we have from God. We may boast in the sufferings we endure, not because we are enduring them but because God is with us and because we are assured that suffering will eventually call us back to the hope that we know through God's love. These three gifts: peace, hope and love are from God. We do nothing to earn them.

So yes, let us boast of our hope, our peace, and our love. Let us boast because the Holy Spirit fills us. Let us boast boldly!

Prayer: **O Giver of love, hope, and peace, open our mouths to boast of you. Rid our minds of all that does not praise you. May our suffering only serve to bring us closer to you. Amen.**

Sunday, June 7   Read Romans 5:1-5.

On this Trinity Sunday, let us consider not the persons of the Trinity but the three gifts from God that Paul describes to the Roman Christians. What do they mean to us as we go about our lives?

Love. Her husband of barely a year had died minutes before. As I hugged her, she whispered in my ear, "I don't understand this God of yours." Neither did I, but God's love was surrounding the two of us as we grieved. And it has done so ever since. Our love for those who suffer and don't understand is the strongest witness we can give toward opening the way for them to know God.

Hope. "He is drinking again," she said with tears in the corners of her eyes. Knowing what she was experiencing, I could only sit with her confident in my hope—hope based not on some desperate wish for sobriety for her husband, though surely that was our prayer, but hope based on the assurance that God would not desert either of them.

Peace. "Why should I go to church school? I don't even believe in God." The sixth-grade boy waited for my reaction. Getting nothing but a clear expectation that he was to head for the church school class, he went in that direction. One day I pray that he too will be at peace with God.

Love, hope, peace—all gifts from God, gifts that God gives freely. How have these gifts been realized in your life and congregation?

Prayer: **Gracious Giver, make us ready to receive your love, hope, and peace. Pour these gifts into our hearts through the Holy Spirit. Amen.**

In Relationship with God

June 8–14, 1998   Mary Lou Wagner✤
Monday, June 8   Read 1 Kings 21:1-4.

I will not give you my ancestral inheritance.

King Ahab of Israel asked Naboth to sell him a vineyard next to the palace. Naboth said, "No." Ahab did not ask why. He knew why! According to well-established legal and religious laws and customs, ancestral land must remain in the family forever. This was God-given land, a place to which future generations could return to remember and celebrate who and whose they were (Leviticus 25). Ahab understood the reason; but because he did not get what he wanted, he went home and pouted.

What a humorous picture! Visualize this grown man in bed with his crown, face to the wall because his powerful position was not enough to get him something he knew he should not have. Visualize Naboth telling his family of his refusal of the most powerful authority figure in their land and of the possible consequences of this bold refusal.

Ahab chose to ignore God's laws and then became angry because he knew Naboth was right. Naboth chose to acknowledge and obey God regardless of the consequences.

Suggestion for meditation: **What is God saying to me in this passage about the use of power, authority, and possessions? In what ways is God trying to lead me into deeper relationships with God and neighbor?**

Prayer: **O God, help me make decisions that will honor and glorify you. Amen.**

✤Layperson at Fairview United Methodist Church, Dayton, Ohio; participant in The Upper Room's two-year Academy for Spiritual Formation.

171

Tuesday, June 9   Read 1 Kings 21:5-15.

Why are you so depressed that you will not eat?

Now Jezebel enters the scene, finds her husband despondent, and asks a natural question, "Why are you so depressed?" He then relates the story of his failed negotiations with Naboth over the garden plot.

However, in Ahab's telling of the situation he omits Naboth's reason for not selling. Notice that Ahab does not actually lie. He just leaves out the most important part. This omission makes Naboth seem unreasonable.

Now Jezebel was not known for her reverence to God and God's laws, so this information probably would have made little difference to her. But in leaving out the real reason, Ahab rationalizes his behavior and sets himself up as a victim of injustice.

This discussion adds a new dynamic to the story. Jezebel decides to step in and solve the dilemma. She devises a plan to have Naboth falsely accused and convicted of cursing God. As a result of this trickery, Naboth is stoned to death.

King Ahab is not visible in this part of the story (vv. 8-14). Jezebel does the dirty work, and Ahab consents either by his silence or his ignorance, or both.

Suggestion for meditation: **How often do I fail to take responsibility for my own decisions and problems? How often do I fail to deal with the real issue of "unfinished business" in my relationships with God and neighbor? How often do I leave out the most important part in searching for a solution to a problem?**

Prayer: **O God, help me see the places in my being that need to be cleansed and healed by your loving spirit. Amen.**

Wednesday, June 10   Read 1 Kings 21:15-21*a*.

Have you found me, O my enemy?

King Ahab and the prophet Elijah were not strangers. Elijah had confronted Ahab on other occasions. Finding the king in Naboth's vineyard, Elijah delivers two messages from the Lord. First, to declare Ahab's sins: murder and theft. Second, to warn of punishment by a terrible death.

Elijah delivers these messages with energy, projecting his own anger at Ahab, as well that of the Lord's. Ahab actually listens to what Elijah has to say, which leads to his repentance and confession. The Lord hears and grants him a reprieve.

When I was a little girl my parents and I lived in a house that had wonderful hiding places. I found and used them all. My favorite spot was at the back of my mother's long, narrow closet. It was very dark in there; the clothes hanging down around me shielded me from all light. I could not see out and no one could see in. I went there when I was sad or when I knew I had done something wrong.

Yet my mother knew where I was and always found me. She usually delayed the end result, walking through the house, calling my name and looking under beds and tables. Sometimes I could take it no longer and emerged blinking in the light, running into her arms. Sometimes she had to join me in the closet to hash out the reason for my disappearance.

God is always seeking our attention, watching and waiting for us to want to be found. When we are willing to let God find us, we can say, "Have you found me, O my Friend?"

Suggestion for meditation: **What part of my life am I hiding from God? Why am I afraid to open all of my life to God?**

Prayer: **O God, my friend and my healer, help me be willing to let you find me and allow you to heal our relationship. Amen.**

Thursday, June 11   Read Psalm 5:1-8.

Lead me, O Lord, in your righteousness.

This psalm of lament and petition for help surely could reflect the thoughts of Naboth, who, finding himself falsely accused, became the victim of violence (1 Kings 21:5-8). Like Naboth we can easily name external enemies: those who abuse, kill, are deceitful, or for some reason do not agree with us. We recognize internal enemies less easily and often acknowledge them with much pain.

Several years ago a physician friend realized that the relationship with his colleagues was slowly but definitely deteriorating. It became stressful to work in a hostile environment that had once been amiable. After seeking legal advice, he was told that his "weakness" in the medical practice was that he took too much time with each patient. Innuendos, exclusion from meetings, decisions made on his day off turned his work life into a living hell. He no longer wanted to go to work.

The physician found another practice farther from home and with less income. Relieved to be separated from his mean-spirited former partners, he thought his worst times were over. The new external situation was pleasant and affirming. But as he adjusted to his new schedule—more hours, less pay, less time with his family, long hours commuting—the internal enemies of doubt, fear, discouragement, and bitterness threatened to take hold. He and his family continued to pray for strength, forgiveness, and peace: "Lead me, O Lord, in your righteousness."

Suggestion for meditation: **Who are my enemies? What are my weaknesses in these relationships? What inner enemies are threatening to destroy my relationship with God and people?**

Prayer: **O God, help me be willing to let you do the leading, for your way and your timing are perfect. Amen.**

Friday, June 12   Read Galatians 2:15-21.

It is not longer I who live but Christ who lives in me.

"And what do you do?" said the person to whom I had just been introduced. I hesitated in answering. I knew what she meant—"What is your income-producing job?"—but I was not comfortable with the question.

At that time I was working part-time as a spiritual counselor at a rehabilitation center for head-injured persons—part-time because I was in the middle of chemotherapy for breast cancer. Between my job and my treatments, I was too exhausted to "do" anything. I finally answered, telling her briefly about my job.

Later I reflected on my answer and began to focus on my discomfort with the *do* and *doing* part of the question. Compared to previous work experience, I was not being very productive. Did this physical downtime make me less of a person? If and when I quit my job and concluded my treatments, I would still be me. What does being "me" mean?

For the Christian, the answer rests in our baptism. We are baptized into Christ, and we belong to Christ as redeemed and forgiven children of God. This is a spiritual reality regardless of what we do or do not do for a living.

At times, the apostle Paul found himself gainfully employed; other times he did not. Yet he could still affirm boldly, "It is no longer I who live, but it is Christ who lives in me." His authentic humanness was rooted in Christ, not in other people's value systems. When meeting a stranger, consider the following as a conversation-starter: "Tell me about who you are"—rather than "Tell me what you do."

Suggestion for meditation: **Who am I? Who is God calling me to become?**

Prayer: **O God, help me remember to be your child in all phases and situations of my life. Amen.**

Saturday, June 13   Read Luke 7:36-50.

Weeping [she] began to bathe his feet with her tears and to dry them with her hair.

In this wonderfully detailed account of Jesus' visit with Simon the Pharisee, we get a good look at Jesus the rule-breaker. A weeping, gift-bearing woman, known to be a prostitute, interrupts Jesus' conversation with his host. She does not just greet him, leave her gift, and go. She kneels behind Jesus, washing his feet with her tears and drying them with her hair.

Simon is offended, both by this party crasher's actions and by Jesus' calm acceptance of her behavior. For Simon, the whole scene is inappropriate and politically incorrect. However, Jesus does not share Simon's view. Jesus proceeds to tell him about the woman's response of gratitude and relief that comes from being accepted and loved.

Then Jesus breaks another rule. He forgives the woman. And now Simon's guests express their displeasure with Jesus: "Who is this who even forgives sins?" Forgiveness comes when we recognize our personal sin and also the forgiver Jesus, the Christ, Son of God, who wants us to lead lives of grace and joy.

Forgiveness comes when we least expect it and in many forms. We often miss it because our own set of exclusive and unbending rules blinds us to other ways of seeing and being. Sometimes we miss God's grace because we fail to see the love and gratitude of Jesus in others.

Suggestion for meditation: **Recall a time when you missed the grace and forgiveness of the moment. How does your rigid adherence to the rules of culture make you insensitive to the needs of others? What hinders you from living a life of gratitude and freedom in Christ?**

Prayer: **O God, help me recognize the many opportunities you give me to accept your forgiveness. Amen.**

Sunday, June 14   Read Luke 8:1-3.

The twelve were with him, as well as some women...who provided for them out of their resources.

Jesus is on a walking tour "proclaiming and bringing the good news of the kingdom of God." The women accompanying him are persons he has helped and healed. With grateful hearts they respond by serving in any way they can, even sharing their own resources. They make themselves available in his ministry.

All of us are on a spiritual journey in relationship with God, Jesus being our teacher and guide. Out of this relationship we make ourselves available in ministry using all of our resources. Proclaiming and bringing the good news is a lifetime commitment to a Christ-centered lifestyle. This commitment involves our sharing the resources of who we are and what we have with those who need us.

One of my friends, an effective teacher in a vocational school, is a competent and gifted cosmetologist. A high percentage of her students pass the exams for certification on the first try. However, proof of her effectiveness lies not only in the academic success stories but in the lifestyle changes that happen again and again.

Spending three to four hours daily with this sensitive, caring, authentic Christian woman motivates these young persons to search for the reason behind a life lived in patience, understanding, and stability. My friend's main resource is the strength she receives from her awareness of God's presence—an awareness she gives to her students.

Suggestion for meditation: **What are my personal resources? Of all my resources, which ones am I giving to Christ for use in ministry and which ones am I withholding?**

Prayer: **O God, make me aware of your presence every minute. Out of a grateful heart, help me share generously the resources you have given. Amen.**

JOURNEY TOWARD WHOLENESS

June 15–21, 1998   **Martin Thielen**✤
Monday, June 15   Read 1 Kings 19:1-4.

A man was leaving for church one Sunday morning. His neighbor, who prided himself on his self-sufficiency and independence, asked him, "Where are you going?"

"To church," the man replied.

The neighbor said, "Church is for people who can't walk on their own two feet."

"Perhaps so," said the man, "but who's not stumbling?"

The characters in this week's readings are all stumbling. Elijah, burned out and depressed, told God he wanted to die. The psalmist, full of despair, wondered why God had abandoned him. The Gerasene demoniac, cut off from his community, lived alone among the tombs. Who's not stumbling?

Everybody stumbles at one time or another. Like Elijah in today's reading, sometimes we find ourselves in the wilderness, frightened and discouraged. Thankfully, despair is not the final word. Elijah, along with the psalmist and the Gerasene demoniac, take concrete steps toward renewal. This week we will walk with them on their journey toward wholeness.

A preschooler had worked hard to make a coffee mug for his father. The day finally came for him to take his gift home. In the excitement of the moment he slipped and fell; the mug broke into pieces. Devastated, he dropped to the floor and cried. After the sobbing eased and tears had been wiped away, his mother suggested, "Let's pick up the pieces and see what we can make with what's left." God is in the business of picking up the pieces of our life and making something with what's left.

Prayer: **Lord, I stumble in many ways. Please guide me toward wholeness. Amen.**

✤Pastor of Monterey United Methodist Church; Monterey, Tennessee.

Tuesday, June 16   Read 1 Kings 19:4, 9-10;
                                        Psalm 42.

Andy and Carol had waited for this moment for over a decade. After years of disappointment and endless medical procedures, Carol finally gave birth to their child. The joy of birth gave way to the trauma of complications. Forced to leave the delivery room, Andy found himself in the hospital chapel, praying for his newborn son. However, as he prayed, something snapped. Andy was mad, and he was mad at God. "How can you do this to us?" screamed Andy. "After all these years of waiting and praying, you finally give us a child. And now, as soon as he arrives, it looks like you're going to take him away!"

Andy and Carol's son survived and eventually thrived. And so did Andy's prayer life. That day in the hospital chapel, Andy learned that it was okay to share his deepest frustrations and anger with God.

Elijah does not hesitate to share his disappointments with God. In verse 4 he says, "It is enough; now, O Lord, take away my life." Later, in verse 10, Elijah complains to God, "I have been very zealous for the Lord...and they are seeking my life, to take it away."

The psalmist, like Elijah, also shares his deepest frustrations with God. "My tears have been my food day and night, while people say to me continually, 'Where is your God?'" He later states, "I say to God, my rock, 'Why have you forgotten me?'"

Our journey toward wholeness begins by honestly admitting our brokenness and pain to God. Do not attempt to sanitize your prayers. Openly share your doubts, fears, anger, and frustrations with the Lord. God can take it!

Prayer: **Lord, sometimes I feel abandoned by you. Thank you for understanding how I feel. Help me become more aware of your love, strength, and presence. Amen.**

179

Wednesday, June 17   Read 1 Kings 19:4-8.

A member of my congregation felt distant from God. She had trouble praying. She also was not sleeping well and had lost her appetite. She dropped by my office to talk about her spiritual life and to request prayer for healing. I listened to her story, asked some questions, and offered a prayer on her behalf. She seemed grateful for my concern. However, she acted surprised when I gently insisted she see her doctor and have a complete physical exam. She set an appointment before she left my office. A few weeks later she told me her doctor diagnosed her as clinically depressed. After a few months of medication, she once again felt close to God.

Taking care of our physical body is an important spiritual issue. We see that clearly in today's reading. This passage finds Elijah deeply discouraged. He is so depressed that he does not even want to live. Notice what God does *not* do: God does not preach a sermon to Elijah. God does not encourage Elijah to pray or go to church. God does not send Elijah to a counselor.

What does God do? God restores Elijah's physical body. Elijah sleeps, then eats, then sleeps again, then eats again. Finally, God sends Elijah on a long walk. Elijah's journey toward wholeness includes adequate sleep, nourishing food and drink, and invigorating exercise. Only after his physical needs are met does God deal with other, more spiritual issues.

Do you feel burned out? The root problem may not be emotional or spiritual but physical. Any journey toward wholeness includes adequate sleep, balanced diet, and regular exercise. The Bible teaches us that our bodies are the temple of God. How are you treating God's temple?

Prayer: **Help me, Lord, to be a good steward of my physical body, so I can better serve you and others. Amen.**

Thursday, June 18   Read 1 Kings 19:9-15*a*;
                                         Psalm 43.

Today's reading finds Elijah in a cave at Mount Horeb, spending time in quiet solitude. During this time of solitude, Elijah encounters the living Lord. Probably to his surprise, Elijah discovers God's presence not in the mighty wind, powerful earthquake, or raging fire on the mountain. Rather, Elijah experiences God in the context of silence, where God speaks to him in a "still small voice" (KJV).

We live in a noisy, frantic, and busy world. Few opportunities exist for silence, reflection, and prayer. However, times of solitude when we can "be still, and know that I am God" (Ps. 46:10) are absolutely essential. We cannot be whole without such times of silence. Even Jesus, the son of God, needed regular times of solitude to think and pray. Today's culture would do well to heed the words of the prophet Habakkuk, "The Lord is in his holy temple; let all the earth keep silence before him" (2:20).

The older I get, the more important silence and solitude become to me. I believe that every person can carve out times of silence in his or her daily schedule. Reading *The Upper Room Disciplines* is one way to accomplish this goal. Other possibilities include walking, woodworking, or gardening. For me, journaling has become an important time of solitude. It provides a daily opportunity to reflect on the events of the day and upon my relationship with God. I record events, thoughts, feelings, insights, and prayers. Whatever method of reflection you use, do not neglect to schedule times of solitude. It is an important step in your journey toward wholeness.

Prayer: **Forgive me, Lord, for being too busy to think and pray. Help me make time every day to "be still and know that [you are] God." Amen.**

Friday, June 19   Read Psalm 42:1-4;
                                             Galatians 3:26-28.

Yesterday's reading reminded us of the importance of solitude. Yet in our journey toward wholeness, we also need other people, especially the community of faith. Even Elijah enlisted the help of others. (See 1 Kings 19:15*b*-21.)

Today's readings affirm our need for relationships. Even in despair, the psalmist longed to worship God with others. Verse 4 says, "I went with the throng, and led them in procession to the house of God,...a multitude keeping festival." Gathering with fellow believers for praise, prayer, word, and sacrament is crucial to our spiritual well-being.

Today's reading from Galatians reminds us that we are not solitary believers but "children of God...one in Jesus Christ." There is no such thing as a "lone ranger" Christian. We always venture forth on our journey toward wholeness with others.

A man sat on a beach and watched two children play in the sand. They were hard at work by the water's edge, building an elaborate sand castle with gates, towers, and moats. Just as they finished their project, a big wave reduced the sand castle to a heap of wet sand. He expected the children to burst into tears, but they didn't. Instead they held each other's hands, laughed a big belly laugh, and sat down to build another castle.

The man reflected that all the things in our lives—all the complicated structures we spend so much time and energy creating—are built on sand. Only our relationships with other people endure. Sooner or later, a wave will come along and knock down what we have worked so hard to build. When that happens, only the person who has hold of somebody's hand will be able to laugh and rebuild.

Prayer: **Thank you, Lord, for the important people in my life. Remind me constantly that relationships—with you and others— matter most. Amen.**

Saturday, June 20   Read Galatians 3:23-39.

Over the past few days we have considered several important strategies for seeking wholeness. However, these alone are not enough. Ultimately, authentic wholeness comes from God. A careful examination of 1 Kings 19 reveals that Elijah's renewal came primarily through his encounter with God. Therefore, any journey toward wholeness must include spiritual dimensions.

Today's passage says, "For in Christ Jesus you are all children of God through faith. As many of you as were baptized into Christ have clothed yourselves with Christ." Through our baptism, God adopts us as God's children. And as God's children, God invites us to participate in a lifelong journey toward wholeness. To be sure, wholeness does not come all at once, nor is it finally completed in this lifetime. However, God gives us love, grace, and strength to continue the journey, even when we can only stumble along, incomplete and broken. When we trip and stumble because of sin, God stands ready to forgive us. This kind of love, acceptance and forgiveness is our birthright as baptized children of God and is the secret of authentic wholeness.

Several years ago I heard an Olympic diver being interviewed. The reporter asked her how she handled the incredible stress as she stood on the platform and prepared to dive off. She said, "On the platform, right before I dive, I always say to myself, *If I blow this, my mother will still love me.*" Even when we stumble on our journey, even when we feel more broken than whole, God still loves us. Thanks be to God!

Prayer: **Without you, Lord, I am incomplete. Thank you for claiming me as your child. Help me to live like the child of God that I am. Amen.**

Sunday, June 21   Read 1 Kings 19:15*a*;
                                       Luke 8:26-39.

Over the past week we have examined several important steps in the journey toward wholeness. These steps include acknowledging our pain, taking care of our body, scheduling times of solitude, relating to other people, and becoming children of God. All of these strategies are important, but our effort to achieve wholeness is not to be an end in itself. Faithful Christians seek wholeness in order to better serve God and neighbor.

That was certainly the case with Elijah. God restored him in order to send him back into service. It is no accident that our text ends with God's saying to Elijah, "Go...." We see the same principle in today's Gospel lesson. The Gerasene demoniac was a deeply disturbed person. However, through the grace and power of Jesus Christ, the demoniac was made whole. After healing him, Jesus commissioned him to "return to your home, and declare how much God has done for you." Jesus made him whole—not only for his own benefit but for the benefit of others. In the Bible, people are always saved to serve.

Although we all need times of healing and restoration, seeking personal wholeness can become an obsession. That kind of self-absorption is sinful. Seeking wholeness for its own sake is never God's plan for us; we seek wholeness in order to better serve the kingdom of God.

We know, of course, that we will never be completely whole in this life. However, we must not let our brokenness keep us from serving God and neighbor. Even the great patriarch Jacob stumbled. But then, who's *not* stumbling?

Prayer: Dear Lord, in my wholeness and in my brokenness help me faithfully serve you and others, through Jesus Christ my Lord. Amen.

REALIZING GOD'S POWER

June 22–28, 1998   **Marshall Shelley**♣
Monday, June 22   Read 2 Kings 2:1-2, 6-14.

For a "human being like us" (James 5:17), Elijah's life was pretty eventful and his departure even more spectacular. He had confronted evil kings and survived. He announced an upcoming three-and-a-half-year drought; he demonstrated the supernatural power of God during that time; and his prayer eventually ended the drought. Then he fled as a fugitive, knew despair, witnessed earthquake and fire, and he clearly heard God's still small voice.

Then, when his life was over, Elijah didn't die. He was taken up into heaven in a whirlwind with chariots of fire and horses ablaze with light.

Why such a dramatic exit?

We can't be sure, but we do know that Elijah would make a mysterious and supernatural reappearance on the Mount of Transfiguration with Moses during Jesus' life on earth. Thus, at least twice Elijah is seen amid supernatural light.

We may not know all the reasons. But one unmistakable fact was communicated to those who saw him at these times: There's more to life than a pale, earthly existence.

Before the resurrection of Jesus, people did not have as clear a sign that there was life beyond death. Elijah's dramatic departure—and his subsequent reappearance—clearly demonstrates that life extends beyond this life.

Refusing to limit our vision to this life has always been a mark of God's farsighted followers.

Prayer: **Lord God, give us eyes to see just how near your eternal life is to us in our daily walk. Amen.**

♣Vice president of *Christianity Today, Inc.* in Carol Stream, Illinois.

Tuesday, June 23   Read 2 Kings 2:1-2, 6-14.

Do you gain strength from solitude? Or do you get your energy from being with others? Some people, when facing stressful or emotionally intense times, want to be alone. Others in the same situations want to be with people.

Elijah may have been one of those people who preferred solitude. We know that during a severe famine he camped alone at Cherith; and after his intense confrontation with the prophets of Baal, he went into isolation.

His protégé Elisha seems to prefer company. During Elisha's ministry, he heads a school of prophets and spends most of his time with people.

In this passage, as Elijah approaches the end of his life, he asks Elisha to leave him. Is he again seeking solitude? Despite the direct request, Elisha repeatedly refuses to leave his master. He knows the end of his master's life is near. Can he not imagine a person facing death alone?

Elijah asks what he can do for Elisha, and the younger man asks for a double portion of his master's spirit. What is he asking for? Perhaps he is requesting all of Elijah's power and authority. More likely, he's asking to be Elijah's spiritual heir—the firstborn son received a "double portion" of the father's inheritance (Deut. 21:17), while the others received a single portion.

Either way, it's clear that Elisha recognizes God's unique use of his master, despite their different personalities. Elisha stands willing and eager to serve God.

Spiritual power comes from following God and those close to God. After Elijah's departure, Elisha picked up his mantle and struck the waters of the Jordan. The waters parted, allowing him to cross. His request had been granted: The power of Elijah and God was with him.

Prayer: **Lord God, make me determined to grab hold of your power and to spend the rest of my life in your service. Amen.**

186

Wednesday, June 24   Read Psalm 77:1-2, 11-20.

Have you ever lost sleep because something was troubling you? Perhaps a relationship was going sour, and you didn't know how to improve it. Perhaps you were dreading the events of the next day. Perhaps you were fearful that you wouldn't live up to expectations.

At some time, most of us know the sleeplessness and distress the psalmist describes: "At night I stretched out untiring hands and my soul refused to be comforted" (v. 2, NIV). Even Jesus knew at least one night like this in the Garden of Gethsemane.

What does the psalmist do with this distress? Crying out to God (v. 1) is the first step. God does not resent the cries of God's people—even their cries of frustration and anger. God invites them.

But beyond that, the psalmist remembers the deeds of the Lord. Two different kinds of deeds impress the troubled psalmist: First, he considers God's redemptive power—"With your mighty arm you redeemed your people" (v. 15, NIV). In times of distress, it's good to remember how God has worked in the past to bring good out of evil. God has used plague and pestilence to free people, brought deliverance to the oppressed, and given strength to endure when physical deliverance did not come. Healing takes many forms, including, ultimately, the death and resurrection of Christ, through whom we receive eternal life.

Second, the psalmist considers God's power over nature—"the waters saw you and writhed; the very depths were convulsed" (v. 16, NIV). What is it about torrents of rain, teeth-rattling thunder, tree-splitting lightning, and tremors and earthquakes that puts distress to rest? Like Job, the psalmist finds in the irresistible whirlwind the comfort of knowing our smallness compared to God's almighty strength.

Prayer: **Creator God, help me give my fears to the winds, to be borne away by your almighty and redemptive power. Amen.**

Thursday, June 25   Read Galatians 5:1, 13-25.

Freedom isn't free; it always has a price. Fifty-five years ago, a generation learned that freedom meant the sacrifice of lives to stop Hitler's madness and cruelty. More recently, another generation learned that freedom can lead to self-indulgence, self-absorption, and self-destruction.

Both generations paid a price. The difference? The earlier generation understood the price they were paying for their freedom at the time they were paying it. The more recent generation doesn't realize the price of freedom until it's too late.

We may assume freedom means doing whatever we want. But if we "use [our] freedom to indulge the sinful nature," it often leads to addictions, damaged relationships, and enslaving habits. Self-centered freedom means only that a person serves himself or herself. And that can be a dictator more capricious and foolish than any foreign despot. "Watch out or you will be destroyed by each other."

Christ frees us for something more than selfishness. Christ frees us and empowers us to love, to serve one another. We are free to be selfless.

No one is ever free from being a servant; it's just a matter of whom you serve. Joshua said it well: "Choose for yourselves this day whom you will serve....As for me and my household, we will serve the Lord" (Josh. 24:15, NIV). Ultimately, choosing whom you will serve may be the only true choice you have.

Some people reject God's authority because they want to be their own boss. Others pursue God because they know true freedom can't be found anywhere else. Choosing to serve God is not a loss of freedom; it's choosing the better master.

Prayer: **Normally I see only with eyes that seek personal gain. Free me, Lord. Give me eyes to see how I can honor you. Amen.**

Friday, June 26   Galatians 5:1, 13-25.

"Express yourself."

"Be genuine."

"Let people see who you really are."

Such advice is so common today that it's dangerous to question it. But if our genuine self is twisted, sick, or evil, we must question that common thinking. One wag put it humorously: "About the worst advice you can give some people is to 'be yourself.'"

There's nothing wrong with authenticity. What's wrong is the assumption that whatever I am right now is okay, that whatever I am right now is what I should be. In this passage, the apostle Paul points out that natural instincts aren't always good. At least two forces are at work inside us: the desires of the sinful nature and the work of God's spirit.

Thus, any time you express yourself in word or action, the "genuine" you that's revealed may be your sinful nature or the spirit of God working within. The sinful nature shows up in jealousy, arrogance, sexual immorality, rage, and selfish ambition (vv. 19-20). And if this is the fruit of your life, you "will not inherit the kingdom of God."

On the other hand, if your life produces the fruit of the Spirit—love, joy, peace, patience, kindness, goodness, faithfulness, gentleness, and self-control—it's convincing evidence that you are living by God's spirit.

Before you "express yourself," ask yourself which of the forces your words or actions reveal. Which pattern do they reinforce? Even with the fruit of the Spirit ripening, remain vigilant—spiritual fruit growers can become conceited, provoking and envying one another (v. 26).

Prayer: **Lord, sharpen my instincts so that they are your instincts, so that my life displays the fruit of your Spirit. Amen.**

Saturday, June 27   Read Luke 9:51-62.

For some, there's nothing more maddening than to offer compassion, kindness, or generosity and to have it belittled.

Perhaps you gave a quarter to a panhandler, and he shouted after you, "Is that all?" Perhaps you took a Saturday morning to cut the lawn of a widow who lives nearby, but when you were done, she criticized the way you trimmed around the shrubs. Perhaps you arranged an outing for some children and instead of gratitude all you heard was a string of complaints: "It's too hot." Or what particularly stings: "This is boring."

Suddenly anger replaces your noble feelings of generosity. Let the ingrates do without! It'll be a long time before they get the benefit of your generosity again!

This is a mild form of what James and John felt. Traveling with Jesus, they had nobly overcome their racial prejudice to travel through Samaria, a land of mixed-race people. They were showing they weren't bigoted like other Jews who avoided even setting foot in Samaritan land.

But the Samaritans didn't see this visit as an honor. The villagers snubbed the offer of friendship from Jesus and his disciples. And James and John were incensed. Their feelings of charity turned into feelings of outrage. They were ready to torch the town.

Perhaps recalling Elijah's treatment of the wicked priests of Baal (2 Kings 1), the disciples asked Jesus, "Do you want us to call fire down from heaven to destroy them?" Jesus rebukes them. Despite the snub, this would have been a misuse of power. Christ's power is not to be used to destroy.

Sometimes the truly praiseworthy act is not the initial generosity; it's absorbing the pain of rejection.

Prayer: **Lord, give me the grace to absorb the pain that others cause me and to continue to show your love joyfully. Amen.**

Sunday, June 28   Read Luke 9:51-62.

One of the most telling signs of Jesus' power was his ability to speak the truth—even when the truth was going to be hard for people to accept. When it came to inviting people to follow him, he didn't recruit with an appealing sales pitch. He never put a spin on the situation: "Discipleship—It's not just a job; it's an adventure." He never tried to enlist followers by pointing out the generous compensation package (even though the retirement plan is "out of this world").

No, Jesus seems to take the opposite approach, emphasizing the costs of following him. Discipleship will be a costly relationship. And he is direct and clear about that.

One man volunteers to follow him and makes an impressive promise: "I will follow you wherever you go." Instead of rushing to sign up such an eager recruit, Jesus reviews the demanding lifestyle that comes with being his follower.

Another man says he's willing to follow Jesus but only after he's attended to his father's burial. Was the father dead and awaiting burial? Or was the son intending to wait for his father's eventual death so he could follow Jesus without his father's criticisms of his son's commitments? Whatever the situation, Jesus doesn't accept it as an excuse. Serving Jesus takes precedence.

The third man also claims family obligations that Jesus rejects. Perhaps Jesus recognizes that this is the crucial moment in these men's lives—that if they put off the commitment today, then they will find another excuse tomorrow. They would never get around to breaking with their habits to follow Christ.

Following Jesus is not for sissies—or procrastinators. Jesus refuses to be a convenient addition to our life. If he is to be Lord at all, he must be Lord of all.

Prayer: **Lord, yes. I am yours. Right now. So be it.**

HEALING AND WHOLENESS

June 29—July 5, 1998   **Charles V. Bryant**♣
Monday, June 29   Read 2 Kings 5:1-7.

Let's begin this week with a confession. Everyone has a type of leprosy; maybe not Naaman's kind, but something that is dreadfully wrong. We may not even realize it now, but someday we will. "Cancer? Oh, no! It can't be. Not me!" someone cries. "Oh, no! You can't mean me," another says to the boss who's downsizing the staff. "You mean you're leaving me?" a spouse cries with shock. And so all around us, maybe even with us, in different shapes, sizes, forms, intensities, and colors—something's dreadfully wrong.

Today's reading offers an assurance of healing and wholeness, especially if we're in touch with God. Even though, for the moment, God seems far away and we're out of touch, let's receive comfort from the knowledge that God is lovingly focused on us and near. We're never out of divine sight. God's attention and compassion add up to the hope of being whole again.

Let's commit this week to letting God work out the details of grace toward us. At first, Naaman didn't know that his own household contained an important "insignificant" person, whom God planted as a messenger and as a means of healing hope. Then to Naaman came an awareness that comes from being open to God. Let's stay open to God's way of healing. In tomorrow's reading we'll see that God's ways of healing and wholeness are sometimes strange but effective.

Suggestion for meditation: **Let's not ask God why, what, when, or how—simply be aware of every "insignificant" thing or person as a possible means of our healing and wholeness.**

♣United Methodist clergy; author; national and interdenominational workshop leader on spiritual gifts.

Tuesday, June 30   Read 2 Kings 5:8-14.

A newspaper quoted Mickey Mantle, a baseball Hall of Fame member, as saying something to this effect after receiving a liver transplant: "If I'd known that I'd live this long, I would've taken better care of my body." Hindsight is clear; foresight can be too. Elisha teaches us that in our reading.

Because of Elisha's faith, he can tell Naaman to dip himself a ridiculous number of times in a muddy river and his future will be different. This approach seems ludicrous to Naaman, the leper. He wants a "magic bullet" type of cure. He wants to go to Johns Hopkins Medical Center, the world's number one hospital, to see the best and most popular doctors. He obviously has enough money (see v. 5), so that the cost of such a cure is not a problem.

Where do you need healing? What is God saying to you in your misery just now? To seek out the most famous healers or counselors? Maybe. But listening to God's invitation to healing and wholeness may take you into the backyard to climb a tree or plant a flower or mow your grass or rake leaves. It may take you to a riverbank or a rugged mountain—maybe even to carry an ugly, heavy cross. (See Luke 9:23.)

Look at it like this: It wasn't the muddy water of the River Jordan that healed Naaman's leprosy. Lots of things did it. Some you know: his boss, his wife, his wife's maid, the king of Israel, Elisha the prophet, water, and mud. But his healing and wholeness came in his response of obedience to the prophet.

Suggestion for meditation: **Ultimately, healing and wholeness come from what is inside, not outside. Meditate on the things you must do from the inside, especially obey.**

Wednesday, July 1   Read Psalm 30.

At age thirteen, I ran away from home. My worst experience did not involve being hungry, broke, homeless, friendless, lost, and cold. For me, the worst experience was that I couldn't remember what my mother looked like! I couldn't visualize her face. This devastated me. After several days, while digging in my backpack, desperately searching for a crumb to eat, I found a picture of her in my billfold—the only thing in it. Seeing her face turned me back toward home.

Our psalmist wasn't hungry, broke, or lost in the woods. She or he simply and painfully couldn't see God's face in the midst of prosperity: "Thou didst hide thy face, I was dismayed" (v. 7, RSV).

Some of us hold the notion that prosperity, success, or health proves the presence and favor of God. Unlike Job, our writer didn't lose material wealth, family, or health—only God's face. Apparently the dismay from this loss was more mental than physical.

Fortunately the psalmist was honest enough to examine true values in life and discovered with Saint Augustine that "our hearts are restless till they rest in thee."

Take a look at yourself. Can you give thanks to God in all circumstances (1 Thess. 5:18)? Have you lost sight of God's presence in sickness or in health, in success or in hardship? Can you thank God for good and bad times, for losses and gains, for sadness and happiness? If you can see the face of God wherever you are and in all situations, you're on your way to wholeness (John 10:10).

Prayer: **God, please don't let me forget who you are and what you look like. Ever lead me toward home. Amen.**

194

Thursday, July 2   Read Galatians 6:1-6.

In Christ, all things come together—God and the world (2 Cor. 5:19), the church and the world (Matt. 16:15-18), the church and its members (Eph. 5:29-30), sinners and saints (Rom. 3:23-24), and the spirit and flesh (1 Cor. 6:19). Therefore, Christ is our wholeness.

An important feature of today's reading is how to restore health or wholeness to the whole body. We know that when any part of the human body is sick, the whole body suffers. Using the physical body as a metaphor, Paul teaches us the same about our spiritual togetherness in Christ. Our reading emphasizes the importance of a health check of the body of Christ.

How gently we treat an ill part of the human body! We wouldn't dare slap a head that aches, a leg that is broken, or a nose that bleeds. The whole body quickly, thoroughly, and gently focuses attention on the ill part. Paul says that as Christians we need to focus "gentle" attention on another who may be behaving inappropriately (6:10).

Gentleness is a fruit of the Spirit (Gal. 5:23). A healthy Christian (the spiritual person) can only deal with a wayward sister or brother in "the spirit of gentleness." Few things are more healing than a gentle word or act.

Suggestion for meditation: **As you want others to speak and act kindly toward you, do so to them.**

Prayer: **O Christ, you who bring healing and health to the world, be present and visible in our words and actions today. Amen.**

Friday, July 3   Read Galatians 6:7-16.

The young wife of a farmer friend proudly showed me her first personal garden patch. She said she wanted to show her husband that she too could grow something. Several weeks later, I visited and found her sad and crying. Her half-acre of squash turned out to be the largest crop of gourds (the inedible variety) in the county! "Whatsoever a man [or woman!] sows, that he [or she] will also reap" (v. 7, RSV).

Our reading tells us that we are flesh and spirit—soul and body. To neglect either is to suffer in both aspects. If we harm the body, we reap physical illness. If we neglect the Spirit, we reap spiritual illness. This is the law of wholeness. We work it in tandem—flesh and spirit, or we're sick and in need of healing. For this reason, Jesus declared spiritual forgiveness first to a paralytic instead of physical healing (Matt. 9:2). Spirit and body mutually affect each other.

Another aspect to this flesh and spirit dichotomy is the social, which Paul addresses in verse 10. While we reap personal harm out of personal evil, others also reap harmful results from the evil we do.

The solution to personal and social evil is to "do good to all." This healing leads to wholeness.

Suggestion for meditation: **"Whatever is true, whatever is honorable, whatever is just,...whatever is gracious,...think about these things" (Phil. 4:8).**

Saturday, July 4   Read Luke 10:1-11.

We have heard that peace is more than the absence of war. I would add that peace requires a preventive measure so that we rid ourselves of the causes of war. Likewise, health is more than the absence of sickness. It includes prevention by getting rid of things that cause illness and accepting that which guarantees health. Jesus sent out messengers to declare ultimate healing and wholeness for individuals and nations: "The kingdom of God has come near."

Many illnesses recur only because the patients do not change their attitude and behavior. "Wars and rumors of wars" (Mark 13:7) prevail only because individuals and nations do not accept the ultimate cure and prevention of war—God.

Today we celebrate the Fourth of July, which is only a *when* on the calendar. What about the *what* or *why*? Well, it is a holiday that celebrates peace and freedom. But isn't it true that we have lost much of the *what* and most of the *why*? The *what* and *why* come in the same package with the *when*. It's a triple dose; one doesn't make sense or help without the others.

Our reading describes three aspects of ultimate health and peace:
- remaining in the care of faithful providers and obedient recipients (vv. 5-7);
- getting rid of things that cause illness or conflict (v. 9);
- accepting the ultimate peace and health giver—God (v. 9*b*).

A genuine celebration of the Fourth of July remembers the Declaration of Independence. Likewise, a genuine celebration of health and wholeness remembers God as the primary source of all peace and health.

Suggestion for meditation: **A kingdom has a king; God brings wholeness—peace and health.**

Sunday, July 5   Read Luke 10:16-20.

"The seventy returned with joy." What a picture! Most American church members celebrated the Fourth yesterday (Saturday). Did they return today (Sunday) to the place of worship *with joy*? What is joy?

Joy is the essence of fulfillment, fullness—wholeness. You remember the psalmist's "joy with the morning" (Ps. 30:5)? Well, it also may be joy in the *mourning*. You see, joy, as the essence of wholeness, doesn't depend upon the absence of illness or war. It is more than that. Joy isn't even the absence of sickness, pain, or suffering. It is more than that.

When the messengers *returned with joy*, they remembered and celebrated God's powerful presence even when they thought they were on their own, alone. When they rattled on about their successes, our Lord reminded them of something more important than personal piety and power. More important than all other things is our immediate, intimate, and ultimate relationship to God. (Read verse 20.)

To know God, to experience God, to believe God unreservedly is to believe in the One who created all things (John 1:3). This includes healing or its absence, success or failure, pain or pleasure. The sum of the "all things" is an "unutterable and exalted joy" (1 Pet. 1:8, RSV). For this reason, Paul could say, "For I know whom I have believed, and I am sure that he is able to guard until that Day what has been entrusted to me" (2 Tim. 1:12, RSV).

Suggestion for meditation: **All things, healing or nonhealing, move us toward God. God in Christ (2 Cor. 5:17) is our wholeness, fulfillment, perfection, and joy.**

ARE YOU LISTENING?

July 6–12, 1998   Mel Johnson✤
Monday, July 6   Read Amos 7:7-17.

In hardware-store language, a plumb line is a cord with a weight at one end, and one uses it to determine the verticality of a wall. It serves as a standard of measurement. My father, who was fifty-five when I was born, was a great frequenter of hardware stores, often looking for tools, gadgets, and whatever else was new on the market. One of my dearest memories is of him seated at his desk, drawing a barn with a straightedge ruler and mechanical pencil—scaled to a fraction of an inch, accurately measured.

This passage speaks about measurement. We, as God's children, fall short again and again. We miss the mark when it comes to God's standards. We miss opportunities and surprises and calls. But Amos didn't miss the mark. He heard the call and responded. A shepherd at heart but a prophet by call, Amos traveled into the center of action. There Amaziah, a man of a king, confronted Amos, a man of God.

I long to be a woman of God when meeting life's opportunities, possibilities and challenges. I try to keep my standards consistent with what I know about God and God's expectations of my response. Today let us consider God's standards, God's measurement. What does God want of each of us in these moments? In what ways do we hear God's call for this day?

Prayer: **Gracious God, we are grateful for the message of Amos that challenges our complacency. Come to us as we listen. Bless us and renew us with words of encouragement. Help us to know deep within that you are always with us. Amen.**

✤Adult studies and journaling teacher; retreat leader and writer; member of Community United Methodist Church; Elm Grove, Wisconsin.

Tuesday, July 7   Read Psalm 82.

One of the places I volunteer is The Gathering, a meal program at an inner-city Milwaukee Episcopal church. Sometimes I go with the mindset that I am helping others. Then the volunteer orientation begins, familiar but ever new. The leader speaks words that I need to hear every time, words that remind me to welcome each guest as if this were my home, to serve with love, to listen with compassion. In my serving, I find myself being served in words exchanged, smiles and hugs given freely, laughter shared. For a short time, I get a small glimpse of the world God intended.

Psalm 82 speaks to us about this world that God intended, about gods and God, about putting an end to any form of injustice and separation. As late twentieth-century Christians, we find it difficult to imagine a worldview such as this psalm describes—a worldview that considered mountains to be foundations of the earth, foundations that held up the sky and held back the waters.

In ancient times the shaking of the earth's foundations threatened all creation. Our worldview has changed, but God's view has not changed. Now, as then, there is one God—a God of compassion, a God who despises injustice and separation, a God who loves kindness and righteousness. God needs each of us to bring that worldview of justice into being. Like the psalmist, may we too pray, "Rise up, O God, judge the earth; for all the nations belong to you!"

And may we offer to do our part.

Suggestion for meditation: **In your quiet time today ask God to show you where you can be an instrument of justice and compassion. Then be open to being led, giving God the glory.**

Wednesday, July 8   Read Luke 10:25-29.

For four years Harley resided in a health care center. Stricken with Parkinson's disease, confined to a wheelchair, eyes closed much of the time, head bent down, he sat day after day. Harley's world became reduced to listening. I visited him several times a week during those years, fed him occasionally, and spoke constantly. I talked to him about sports, about our church, about his family and ours, about anything that entered my mind. Sometimes he would chuckle, sometimes he would add a word or two. I found myself saying things that I have never said to anyone before or since. Jesus said, "Whoever listens." Harley became for me a beloved listening friend.

Listening has to do with giving and receiving. It is hard to do. Our agendas—work to do, calls to make—fill our lives, minds and hearts. We even know how to listen with our ears while our minds are thinking of something else. But our wandering eyes and our unwelcoming body language give us away. Oftentimes we come to prayer more ready to speak than to listen.

The lawyer rises in his self-importance. To whom is he listening? Who does he hope will listen? He comes with his own agenda and all the right answers. But Jesus invites him to hear and to think in a new way. Will the lawyer listen?

"But wanting to justify himself," the lawyer pushes on. How does our need for self-justification interfere with our listening?

We all long to be listened to. God does too. And God is patient. And God does speak—in the rustling grass, rain on the roof, blowing breezes, morning bird songs, the voice of a friend, a letter in the mailbox. All of creation reveals God's nature. At its deepest level, listening is soul responding to soul. Listen. God is speaking.

Prayer: **Generous God, thank you for listening to us attentively, expectantly, and compassionately. Bless us this day with these gifts that we might be your listening people. Amen.**

Thursday, July 9   Read Colossians 1:1-8.

Several years ago I went on a retreat with writer and friend Macrina Wiederkehr. She had just published her second book, and her written words had been finding their way into my heart. On the retreat she read aloud from her book again and again. I had not had someone read to me since I was a child. It was a powerful experience. The power was such that a friend and I now share books, taking turns reading aloud.

The writer of Colossians intended that his letters be read aloud. In verses 3-8, he uses the word *heard* three times. The writer expresses thanks to the community of saints and faithful at Colossae for their willingness to listen. Unlike Amos whose words fell on deaf ears, these words reached a receptive people. We have a sense of so much possibility.

With encouragement, the Colossians listened and responded. The writer affirmed their faith and their love, which were based on the love and promise of Jesus Christ. This faith took root, grew, and bore fruit from "the day you heard it and truly comprehended the grace of God."

Grace—God's unmerited favor. It is a mystery. God's grace. I will never fully understand the mystery of God's grace. Nor do I want to. Grace helps bear fruit in me and through me, and I am grateful.

Today think about the fruit our lives bear, about the ways we help others bear fruit in their lives. The writer of Colossians affirmed this fruit-bearing potential in the people at Colossae. Who needs this affirmation from you to grow and become more? Read this letter aloud and receive it as God's gift to you.

Prayer: **God of grace and glory, listening ear and loving friend, thank you for all the ways you encourage and affirm us. Bless us this day as we go forth to be your blessing. Amen.**

Friday, July 10   Read Colossians 1:9-14.

Decisive by nature and even impulsive at times, I occasionally say yes to something without thinking it through. Some time ago as a new volunteer in a large Milwaukee service organization I was asked to be the thrift shop chairperson for a year. Flattered to be asked and afraid to say no, I spent the year struggling with budgets, staff, hundreds of volunteers, and the shop itself. I struggled because I was the wrong person for the task. Business and finances were strictly at odds with my foreign language teaching major. I had followed my will and desires, not God's. I had not listened!

These verses are a prayer for Christians then and now. The writer reassures the people at Colossae that persons are praying for them without ceasing. The prayer request is that all will be filled with the knowledge of God's will for their lives.

These words touch my heart as I think about those persons known and unknown who pray for me. Daily I thank God for them. Sometimes I send notes to persons I know—notes of gratitude with words of encouragement for their own journeys. In this connectedness I draw closer to God and to others. Together we can do great things. Together we can endure much. God has given us to one another to be the body of Christ in the midst of all of life.

Prayer: **Loving God, these prayerful words of Colossians invite us into a closer relationship with you and one another. Help us measure our choices today against what we know about your will. In the name and in the spirit of the living Christ. Amen.**

Saturday, July 11   Read Luke 10:25-37.

My husband, David, was in Vietnam in the mid-sixties. Fresh out of college, married and with a young daughter, he received a commission and went overseas to fulfill his ROTC active duty army commitment. Sometimes in a helicopter, sometimes on foot patrol with just a few men, other times with an infantry company, his role as a forward observer was to call in artillery fire. Many avoided serving during these years of such great conflict at home and abroad. But David had made a commitment to serve, and he honored that commitment. I learned a lot from him about responding when need arises, about being faithful to a commitment.

In this passage, the lawyer is testing Jesus. The lawyer questions him about eternal life, hoping for the traditional response: that one obtains eternal life through obedience to the law. Jesus counters with a question; the lawyer responds. I sense a bit of smugness in the lawyer at this point, and he can't resist asking one more question: "And who is my neighbor?" Now comes the hard part: Everyone is our neighbor. The priest and the Levite knew the demands of God's law; the Samaritan gave spirit to the law.

Listen. God is speaking: Everyone is our neighbor. Everyone is worthy of our love and compassion. The small world of Jesus' day has given way to one giant complex world. Now more than ever we need—and need to be—neighbors. When that happens, God is revealed, and we come to know that we are more alike than we are different. Let us listen for God, and let us cherish and honor our differences.

Prayer: **Merciful God, help us listen for your still small voice that empowers us to love our neighbors as ourselves. Amen.**

Sunday, July 12   Read Luke 10:25-37.

Years ago when I was new at adult church school teaching, a woman in my class threatened to destroy the class with her nonstop monopolizing of the hours. She challenged me over and over again—not in a questioning manner like the lawyer in today's reading but rather by having something to say on *every* topic. In an effort to hold the class together, I wrote her a letter in which I described how her behavior interfered with the class. She called and thanked me. She listened to my pen and ink in a way that she had not listened to my spoken words in class.

Jesus is my encourager in using a variety of ways to make a point. He questions; he answers; he speaks in parables; he writes in the sand. Jesus intended this parable to challenge an accepted way of thinking—that of adhering to the law. With Jesus, love and compassion enter our world like rays of sunshine after a thunderstorm. Loving service knows no barriers. A despised Samaritan reveals God's selfless love, a love that results in eternal life.

Our week's scriptures have led us through messages of those who listened, heard, and even questioned. Some of us have spent our days being, doing, loving, affirming, encouraging, and challenging others. Others of us have been the recipients. Sunday invites us to rest, to receive, and to think about the source of our empowerment—about how we have listened, about how we have followed.

Listen again to Jesus' words: "Go and do likewise." The power is there. Take it.

Prayer: **All-inclusive God, you love each of us in a special way, reminding us that each is unique and chosen but not exclusive. Create in us a desire to embody that kind of love in your world. Amen.**

HOLDING IT ALL TOGETHER

July 13–19, 1998   **Charles M. (Chuck) Olsen**✤
Monday, July 13   Read Colossians 1:15-17.

God's big plan

God has a big plan! It is to unite *everything* in Jesus Christ—things in heaven and things on earth. That's a tall order, considering the diversity and animosity that exists within and among our worldviews and cultures. But the writer of Colossians reaffirms an assertion stated in Ephesians—all things are to be united in Christ: "In him all things hold together." All things cohere in Christ. He is the "spiritual glue" that can keep our world from flying apart.

Vision is everything. Discernment of God's will and yearning for the world, for the church, and for us individually aligns with a central, core vision. For the prophets it was the "shalom" of God. That central vision exposed any injustice or idolatry. For Jesus it was the kingdom of God. He could teach, tell stories, and face his own temptations with that as a reference point. Now this writer offers a vision—of God's uniting everything in the Christ who alone can reconcile all things to himself and hold everything together.

You want to know what God is like? Or up to? Look at Christ. He is God's image. "*In him* all things...were created" (italics added). Now "*in him* all things hold together." This week we will take a close look at "all things" through the lens of our lectionary readings.

Suggestion for meditation: List all the extremes that your life or world presents you. Then hold and release them one by one to Christ, the "image of the invisible God."

✤Director, Worshipful Work: Center for Transforming Religious Leadership; Heartland Presbyterian Center; Kansas City, Missouri.

Tuesday, July 14   Read Psalm 52.

The righteous and the evildoers

I like to speculate that the psalmists wrote most of the psalms between 2:00 and 4:00 A.M.—a time when the psalmists were trying to find some resolution to the perplexing contradictions and mysteries of life. At least that is when my mind seems to work overtime.

Many of the psalms wrestle with the presence of evil—its possession of the human spirit and the apparent rewards of plotting, lying, deceiving, and all-consuming lifestyles. But the resolution comes when the psalmist places behavior in the light of God's presence. That light exposes misplaced trust and vindicates the righteous.

How does Christ bring together the righteous and the evildoers? How can they find unity in him? He came into the presence of evil, faced all it could throw at him, and embraced it with divine, forgiving love. He became the bearer of evil and sin, taking the sting out of its hostility.

The Book of Revelation presents a picture of the final battles between the evil of the world and God's good. Its message is simple: In the end God will prevail, breaking the power of evil. Christ will reign!

Suggestion for meditation: With your eyes closed, relax into God's presence as you focus on your slow, deep breathing. Now attach "Lead us not into temptation" to each rising breath and "But deliver us from evil" to each falling breath. If recollections of temptations or the presence of evil come to mind, offer and release each to the love and presence of Christ.

Then pray with the psalmist: "I will thank you forever, because of what you have done. In the presence of the faithful I will proclaim your name, for it is good." Amen.

Wednesday, July 15   Read Amos 8:1-12.

Oppressor and victim

We are just doing our job, aren't we? We are taking advantage of the opportunities set before us. We have the "edge" that every good business person relishes. The name of the game is profit. So what if a few people get hurt in the process? After all, they had their chance. So what if the rules work in our favor? The object is to win—even if it means putting someone else out of business.

Not so, according to the politics, economics, and theology of the prophet Amos. He cries out against oppressors who trample the needy and bring ruin to the poor—all in the name of business opportunity. With pride they cheat the poor and deny them any fruits of a compassionate economic system. With singing in their feasts they unwittingly starve themselves from any bread that comes from the word of God.

How could Jesus bring together both oppressor and victim? He told the truth. He held the mirrors of parables and stories before people so they could see themselves in a new light—the light of the kingdom of God. He integrated love and justice within his being in such a way that it became possible for people to change and be transformed.

Persons being ordained in the Presbyterian church are asked if they will follow the love and justice of Jesus Christ in their ministry. The love and justice of Jesus—yes, that's the clue for Amos, the church, all systems of our world, and for you and me!

Suggestion for meditation: **Phrase a prayer that people on the edge (victims, marginalized, powerless, and poor) might pray. Then pray the prayer.**

Thursday, July 16   Read Luke 10:38-42.

Introverts and extroverts

If Mary and Martha were to take the Myers-Briggs personality preference inventory, they certainly would score in opposite quadrants—because they were opposites! One was an introverted, feeling-type person. The other was an extroverted, judging type.

And how could Jesus ever "win" in this situation? He loves both Martha and Mary and has the unique capacity to meet each right where she is. If we fast-forward the story of their relationship to Jesus to the death of their brother, Lazarus, we will see each of them approach the tardy Jesus with the very same statement: "If you had been here, my brother would not have died" (John 11:21). Martha speaks it as in-your-face confrontation. Jesus responds with a theological discussion, which Martha needs. Mary waters the statement with tears of grief. (Read John 11:32.) Jesus responds with his own tears, which Mary needs.

The capacity to love and embrace all personality types and unite them into one body is Jesus' gracious gift to us. In him all things hold together—and that includes people. Bonhoeffer observes that the "wish dreams" we all bring to community must dissolve in disillusionment. Only when we have become disillusioned with the possibility that we can make community happen via our own affinity for one another can the gift of community in Christ break upon us. We rub one another wrong. The bond of unity can come only through the grace of our Lord Jesus Christ.

Suggestion for meditation: **What is your personality type? Who else in the Bible seems to have the same personality? In solitude reflect upon God's or Jesus' attitude and/or behavior to that blessed person! And what will be your response?**

Friday, July 17   Read Luke 10:38-42.

Spiritual coherence

Parker Palmer reveals his own internal quandary in his book *The Active Life*. As a Quaker, he was inclined toward a life of solitude and lived for a brief time in a monastic community to test this bent. But he was also an activist and realized that the cloistered life would deny this other bent. Palmer's description of his struggle is helpful, because it touches the nerve that has been sensitized by our own struggles.

Both Mary and Martha reside within us. We are prone to both being and doing—the contemplative and the active. The trick is to find the balance. We invent structures that embrace both work and Sabbath rest but have a hard time maintaining them. How many times have we said to ourselves, *We ought to rest . . . take a vacation . . . go on a retreat . . . maintain a daily holy space* but find it crowded out by all the things we need to do?

With the fragmentation of contemporary life and "many things" that worry and distract people, one gift that religious leaders could offer would be a model of a life that finds balance between being and doing. Jesus certainly modeled it for us. But that will not come naturally or by default; we must choose it. Mary chose to sit and listen. That was the better part for that time and place. Timing is everything, or so they say. So choose.

Suggestion for meditation: After rereading the text, make two lists of opportunities in the next month—one for "sitting and listening" and one for "doing and speaking." From each list, choose five and prioritize them. What might Mary have to say to you about your list? What might Martha add?

Saturday, July 18   Read Colossians 1:21-28.

Outsiders and insiders

When the writer suggests that Christ was out to reconcile all things unto himself, he was not talking blue sky. He had specific groups of people in mind—Jews and Gentiles, slave and free, female and male. The religious power elite, or insiders, placed certain people (outsiders) beyond the fixed boundaries of God's grace. But neither they nor we can limit Christ's love and grace. The Holy Spirit worked in obvious ways—converting a Roman centurion, baptizing an "unclean" eunuch from Ethiopia, pouring the Spirit out upon Gentile Christians who had not engaged in Jewish rites, and allowing gifted women to lead in house communities.

Who are the people on the margins or outside the efforts and budgets of our churches? Can Christ's love somehow bring all together?

The church symbolizes God's big plan (to unite everything in Christ, who will hold it all together). The world needs a visible sign of what God is up to. The only place to find that sign is in a visible church. No matter how hard we preach, no matter how creative our programs, if the church fails to offer a symbol and sign of unlikely extremes coming together, the words and programs are empty and hollow.

Likewise, each follower is to be a sign as well. For Paul the sign was as a servant and steward of the mystery of faith. That mystery—often hidden today as it was yesterday—is that the outsiders have a place at the Lord's table. Christ will gather people from the East and from the West—from the highways and byways of life to insure that the banquet table is full!

Suggestion for meditation: **Arrange a list of your own great "cloud of witnesses"—those persons and groups who have served as signs of God's big plan. Offer thanksgiving to God for every aspect of their lives that embodied the sign of gospel.**

211

Sunday, July 19   Read Colossians 1:18-20.

Everything!

Having journeyed this week through the many extremes and polarities of modern life—and having seen that Christ embraces all—we now return to where we started, focusing on the all-sufficient Lord.

Christ is the firstborn of all creation, the head of the church, with all the fullness of God dwelling in him. When the extremities of the world blur our focus, we do well to return our attention to Christ. When Mary sat and fixed her gaze on Jesus, he blessed her and affirmed that she had chosen a better part. Worship and adoration are not a waste of time. All vision and service flow from that gaze.

Several years ago the Presbyterians convened a conference on "Jesus Christ." It did not have a specific functional, missional, programmatic, or utilitarian purpose. The planners recognized that the multifaceted agenda of the many diverse groups within the church did not provide opportunity for this single unifying gaze and focus. The surprisingly large attendance and the positive responses of those who came away underlined the need for frequent consideration of the essence of the One we have come to call Lord.

As a youngster, I remember my sense of awe in viewing the mobile that hung in the entrance of the Pittsburgh airport. The large, multishaped pieces of metal hung in perfect balance with a quiet, dynamic movement. I remember thinking, *If I had put that together, it would have been a pile of junk!* But it hung in perfect balance from a central cable in what for me has become a visual image of all things hanging together in Christ!

Suggestion for meditation: **As you relax with deep, slow breathing, attach a name or attribute for Jesus to the rise and fall of each breath. When no more names or attributes surface, close with the Lord's Prayer.**

GOD'S RESTORING AND ABIDING LOVE

July 20–26, 1998   **Roela Victoria Rivera**✤
Monday, July 20   Read Hosea 1:2-10.

This week's theme, "God's Restoring and Abiding Love," reflects God's relationship to sinful people. It exposes the exceeding hatefulness of sin to magnify the power of God's love to redeem.

We begin with the story of the prodigal wife as a counterpart of the other Galilean tale of the prodigal son. The Lord asks Hosea to marry an unfaithful woman. Hosea comes to understand Israel's relationship to God in the context of his relationship to Gomer. God was faithful and full of affection, showering God's "wife," the people of Israel, with all goodness and favor. The people of Israel became faithless and turned their back on God. In much the same way, Gomer, after bearing their third child, leaves home. Gripped with deep anguish and shame, Hosea disowns his third child, naming him "Not my people."

Hosea's anguish gives way to deep sympathy and compassion; his anger turns to lovingkindness (KJV). Now Hosea's lovingkindness becomes a key to understanding God's lovingkindness. Hosea redeems Gomer just as God redeems Israel.

Today, as in the past, unfaithfulness results in broken relationships and dysfunctional homes, social ills and tragedies. Yet we too can receive God's restoring love when we reclaim our relationship as "children of the living God."

Prayer: **Lord, we give you thanks that in spite of our unfaithfulness, you continue to shower us with your restoring and abiding love. Amen.**

✤Director of Studies, Scarritt-Bennett Center; Nashville, Tennessee; diaconal minister; member, General Commission on Communication, United Methodist Church; Communication Arts instructor; creative artist and writer-editor.

Tuesday, July 21   Read Psalm 85:1-7.

When our family moved to Nashville from the Philippines by way of California, our own mixed feelings about the move confronted us. We felt deep anxiety about what lay ahead of us in a new environment with new people, new challenges, and new expectations. The transition was not easy. But the prayers and support of our loved ones and new friends transformed our anxiety to trust and excitement. The new dimension in our careers and faith ministry excited us.

The outstanding peculiarity of verses 1-7 is the sudden transition of feeling. The people begin with exuberant thanksgiving for the restoration of Israel from desolation to prosperity and for the forgiveness of their wrongdoings. Then—without warning in seemingly unexpected circumstances—the psalmist complains about God's continued wrath and makes entreaties for restoration.

To the Israelites, the period of their return from Exile brought conflicting emotions—from gratitude for God's mercy to discouragement in view of ruined cities, fallen Temple, mourning people, and powerful enemies.

While restoration is the sign of forgiveness and hope, the Israelites, like many of us today, still live in vexation and helplessness because of the great responsibility that lies before them. A lot of work has to be done; freedom is coupled with responsibility, and it is often a long process.

Some of us, like the Israelites, fear moving on, perhaps because of meager resources, lukewarm acceptance, and strange reactions from people around us. In our weakness, we turn to God for strength. God's restoring and abiding love is the whole fullness of God's delivering grace.

Prayer: **Thank you, God, for understanding our feelings, and thank you for being always there whenever we need you! Amen.**

Wednesday, July 22   Read Psalm 85:8-13.

The Filipino people have a long, colorful history of faith, culture, and tradition. Amidst the powerful influence of external forces and internal upheavals, they have stood unperturbed. Like the resilient bamboo, they have swayed gracefully and bravely against the current of the wind of time and the harsh realities and exigencies of life.

Psalm 85 (vv. 8-13) brings solid hopes and bright expectations—based upon divine promises—to bear on present discouragements and seemingly trying moments. The psalmist demonstrates faithfulness to God's promise of salvation, peace, and righteousness.

The Filipino people, like the psalmist, have kept their faith and turned to God for their salvation. Their faith has saved them and restored their identity as a people. Their desolate journey through centuries of colonial rule only proved Filipino resiliency, valor, and bravery. Their experience of extreme poverty and injustice gave rise to people power. Their frequent encounters with natural calamities and disasters showed their extraordinary patience and resilient attitude. Their suffering in the economic, social, and political arenas of life—exploitation and oppression, desecration and destitution, injustice and corruption—challenged them to rise with human dignity and honor!

God has promised peace and righteousness to those who fear God and are faithful. Today, the Filipino people enjoy freedom and responsibility. Together they are working hard to restore their land. They are rising from economic desolation to economic prosperity. They keep their faith in their hearts and remain the only predominantly Christian nation in Asia.

Prayer: **With grateful hearts, we thank you, O Lord, for your words of assurance that your promise of peace and righteousness will always be with us. Amen.**

Thursday, July 23   Read Colossians 2:6-15.

True Christian circumcision

Earthly desires have wrecked many lives and broken many relationships. People have sacrificed fortunes and fame, health and career. Creative talent and skill have been wasted because of imperious lust. Today, as in the past, morality is at stake.

Today's writer invites the Colossians to attain the fullness of life in Christ. The writer's words speak to us today. We are to "continue to live [our] lives in [Christ], rooted and built up in him and established in the faith."

To attain a full life, the writer teaches the necessity of circumcision—not by an outward rite but by the cleansing of the heart. This Christian circumcision is "made without hands" by the Spirit. It is not a rite but a reality. It consists in the "putting off the body of the sins of the flesh" and being renewed in the Spirit. We are "of Christ." Our faith in Christ offers us a new life that delivers us from the dominion of earthly things.

This idea of ethical circumcision is common in the Hebrew Scriptures: "The Lord thy God will circumcise thine heart...to love thy God with thine heart" (Deut. 30:6, KJV). True Christian circumcision involves the inward change. Faith and baptism unite us to the transforming Christ.

Baptism is associated in time with inward change. Baptism effects the change, and it accompanies the change. It is more than circumcision, as is the dying of the old self by union with Christ and the rising again by participation in his resurrected life. We must die to sin that we may live to righteousness. We must die to self, that we may live to God.

Prayer: **We are truly blessed, O Lord, that you extend your restoring love to us through baptism and Christian circumcision to make us new again. Amen.**

Friday, July 24   Read Colossians 2:6-7.

Fullness of life in Christ

Abu Ali is facing a death penalty. He has been on death row for almost twelve years now in a maximum security institution. He was convicted of murdering a drug dealer who abused young girls. With his conviction, the world turned upside down for him.

In prison, Ali struggled with himself, trying to make sense of everything. With no one to turn to, with no one to love and no one to love him, he felt forsaken. Almost at the breaking point, he turned to God. He felt God's forgiveness, which transformed his life and made him whole again. This experience inspired Ali to begin studying God's word.

A missionary woman heard about Ali. She visited him in prison regularly and offered him her listening ears. She opened her hands and heart to him. Through her compassionate words and sincere intentions, she touched his life by sharing God's love, peace, and righteousness.

A Muslim by birth, Ali now considers himself a Christian. He has received the fullness of life in God. The writer of Colossians reminds us to continue to live our lives in Christ, just as we were taught. Through union with Christ, we participate in the fullness of life with Christ. It flows like the water of life and will fill us with wisdom, strength, beauty, courage, and patience. Out of it will come whatsoever things are lovely, whatsoever things are true and good.

Ali has found Christ. His life has been made whole again. He is now writing a book dedicated to the young. He himself will become a teacher, inspiring others to lead a good and righteous life with Christ!

Prayer: **In the midst of uncertainties and brokenness, you come to us, O Christ. You make us whole and fresh again. Thank you for the fullness of your love and mercy. Amen.**

Saturday, July 25   Read Luke 11:1-4.

Teaching on prayer

One night after Jesus' time of prayer, one of the disciples asked that he teach them how to pray. Jesus responded with these words:

> Father, hallowed be your name.
> Your kingdom come.
> Give us each day our daily bread.
> And forgive us our sins,
> for we ourselves forgive everyone indebted to us.
> And do not bring us to the time of trial.

Since that time, "The Lord's Prayer" has been prayed in many languages, in many situations, in many lands. We never weary of repeating it and lodging the heavenly words deep within the world's heart. We pray it in the realm of our senses, from the bottom of our hearts.

While Luke gives us an abbreviated form of the prayer recorded by Matthew (6:9-13), the two forms are identical in substance. Both forms serve as the divine model, laying down the lines on which our prayers should move.

The prayer consists of two marked divisions. The first one is general (pertaining to the conception and adoration of the Holy God), and the second one is particular and personal (continuing the first by outlining and making human petitions known to God).

Some persons recommend a prayer acronym: ACTS. A is for adoration of God; C is for confession of sin; T is for thanksgiving for everything; S is for supplication. Consider your prayer life in light of these aspects.

Prayer: Thank you, Jesus, for teaching us how to pray and for letting us know that you listen to our spoken, as well unspoken, prayers. Amen.

Sunday, July 26   Read Luke 11:5-13.

Pray with perseverance

When our family house was razed in 1989, my husband and I were in Jerusalem, Israel. In the sudden tragedy we lost not only our material possessions but also our priceless family heirlooms and creative treasures. In the midst of grief, we prayed in Gethsemane where Jesus prayed; somehow we had a sense of his deep anxiety and fearful agony. We realized how small our grief and losses were compared to his anxiety about betrayal and crucifixion! Then with tears of pain, we walked through the traditional stations of the cross. Again we realized how small our burden was compared to the heavy load of the cross of the world that Jesus bore when he painfully walked that same path.

We often pray in times of crises. We remember to come to God when the situation seems out of our control. But when we are in good shape, we forget many times to pray! Today's text focuses on the need for persistence in prayer, the need to continue in prayer through the good times and the bad.

For Jesus, prayer was habitual and necessary to his life—how he lived, moved, and spoke. The writer of First Thessalonians tells us to "pray without ceasing" (5:17)—to pray at all times, in times of need and sufficiency, in joy and in sorrow, in gain or loss, in times of triumph or the darkest hours of our lives.

Praying and waiting for an answer takes time. But God assures us of an answer. Some responses or blessings come quickly; other blessings come later, and we need to continually ask and wait. Sometimes, the long delay is but a test of faith and the blessing comes at the right time in God's own time.

Prayer: **We thank you, O Lord, for the knowledge that you are only a prayer away from us. Let your will be done in all that we ask in prayer. Amen.**

July 27—August 2, 1998   **Susan K. Wendorf**✚
Monday, July 27   Read Colossians 3:1-4.

I cannot remember when I didn't know where I lived—except maybe those early childhood years when, if I wandered too far down the street, I couldn't find my way back home without my older brother's help. Since reaching adulthood I've lived in more than a dozen dwellings in eight cities, and I'm happy to say I've always found my way home at the end of the day.

The author of Colossians encourages us to know where our *spiritual* home is as well as where our *physical* home is: "Set your minds on things that are above, not on things that are on earth." Having a solid spiritual home base is no less important for us than for the Colossian Christians, who were tempted to mix asceticism (the belief that rigorous self-denial gains salvation) and gnosticism (the belief that salvation requires access to secret knowledge) with their Christian faith. While our "-isms" may carry different names, they too threaten our faith. Like the first believers, we stand in need of grounding ourselves continually in the teachings of Christ.

Studying scripture; meditating on God's word; gathering with the community of faith for worship, prayer, dialogue, and debate—these are the building materials for our spiritual home. It is a lifelong process with new questions to address, new challenges to meet, new doubts to confront, new temptations to battle. When we know where we live, even if we start to wander, we can always find our way home to Christ, the center.

Suggestion for meditation: **Pray for spiritual stability; teach or take a class on Colossians.**

✚Family court counselor, freelance writer, and member of Dr. Martin Luther Church (ELCA); Oconomowoc, Wisconsin.

Tuesday, July 28   Read Hosea 11:1-11.

How many times could Israel "leave home" and still expect a warm welcome home upon return? How often could Israel, like Hosea's Gomer, whore after other Baals and still hope to find the visage of a smiling, open-armed God standing in the doorway of the once-promised land, promising again to forgive, if not also forget?

God's musing monologue in today's text is so like the emotional struggle a parent feels when a teenage child is out way past curfew: Do you punish for the sojourn or welcome upon the homecoming? Or a bit of both?

Lest we self-righteously jump into an indignant parent role, we do well to remember that we too have been the ones coming home late—probably more often than we care to admit. With shameless willfulness we, like Hosea's Israel, have run away to the gods of power, self-indulgence, prestige, riches, and irresponsibility. We have pitched our tents with the purveyors of false security and empty hope, severely trying God's sacred patience. We have done it before, and we'll surely do it again. If not today, then tomorrow; if not tomorrow, then next week. We only fool ourselves (certainly not God!) if we think we have nothing in common with those ancient targets of God's tirade.

Yet we need not fear the homecoming. God is eternally tolerant and endlessly understanding. God's steadfast love and forgiveness await us day after day, journey upon journey. No matter how far or how often we wander, God continues to welcome us home, being to us "like those who lift infants to their cheeks." What a powerful image! What a gracious God! Why would we ever want to leave home again?

Suggestion for meditation: **Pray for the strength to be faithful; work to provide a community shelter for teenage runaways.**

Wednesday, July 29   Read Psalm 107:1-9, 43.

There comes a time in each of our lives when we have to grow up: no more borrowing money from Mom and Dad, no more lame excuses for being late to work, no more taking the easy way out of a jam, no more abdicating responsibility for the direction our lives take. There comes a time when we have to leave the comfortable nests of our youth and establish our lives as adults. We have to do so physically, emotionally, psychologically, and spiritually.

Yes, spiritually! The psalmist recalls and recites God's faithfulness to an on-again, off-again community of believers, then concludes: "Let those who are wise give heed to these things, and consider the steadfast love of the Lord." Paul echoes this sentiment later when he writes, "Brothers and sisters, do not be children in your thinking; rather, be infants in evil, but in thinking be adults" (1 Cor. 14:20).

Growing up and leaving home is not an easy journey, physically or spiritually. As children, the world around us filled us with wonder and awe; we had simple thoughts and welcomed simple answers to questions far more complex than we could imagine. As we mature, we begin to discover that we have far more questions than answers, and a vast difference exists between having a "childlike" faith and a "childish" faith. Once we learn that fear—not doubt—is the opposite of faith, we can begin to examine and discard with faithful confidence the "pat answers" that easily satisfied the spiritual needs of our childhood. Then in wisdom, we can begin to "consider the steadfast love of the Lord," regardless of where our journeys take us.

Suggestion for meditation: **Pray for wisdom and insight; organize or support Christian day-care centers.**

Thursday, July 30   Read Luke 12:13-21.

Word was that the fish were biting in an area called The Eagle's Nest. Since I couldn't find walleyes in any of my usual places, I decided to motor over there, even though I had never before fished that part of the Chippewa Flowage, a 15,000-acre lake in northern Wisconsin. Before long I was lost. Every island I passed looked like the one before. I didn't even know if I were going in circles! After more than an hour of wandering, I remembered I had a compass in my tackle box. Working my way around islands, I steadily headed south until finally spotting a familiar landmark. In another fifteen minutes I was home. What a relief!

The rich fool in Jesus' parable wasn't so fortunate. He too had lost his bearings. Focusing on the acquisition and enjoyment of material things, he strayed far away from God's loving presence. He placed his trust in his own power to achieve and succeed and envisioned a long and carefree life of self-indulgence. Tragically he had no idea how lost he was, how in need he was of the compass of faith to direct him back to God's graceful presence.

The lesson of the parable is well taken, for who of us have not dreamed of a life of ease after a long day at work? Who of us have not wished for things we do not have, either for ourselves or for our loved ones? Who of us have not defended our decision to acquire this or that thing? Ah, it is so easy to get lost when all the islands look alike. Yet God continues to direct and redirect us, calling us in grace to hold the course, to keep our eyes and minds on the landmarks of faith, to hold fast to the riches of life lived in the peace and love of Christ. These gifts from God—grace, faith, peace, and love—are all we really need when it is time to go home.

Suggestion for meditation: **Pray for spiritual direction; listen closely to someone who is struggling with his or her faith.**

Friday, July 31   Read Colossians 3:5-11.

When my friends bought their first home, they decided to replace the living room carpeting before moving in. After their furniture was in place, they thought it looked shabby with the new carpeting, so they bought a new sofa and lamp tables. But then the dining room set didn't look right against the new living room furniture, so they went shopping again. I suspect only their budget prevented them from immediately redecorating the entire house as they compared one room with the next and the next and the next.

However, no budget prevents us from doing some spiritual home improvement as we grow in grace and faith. And from fornicating to lying, the Colossians' list of earthly ways that must be put to death is only the beginning—the big pieces of furniture, as it were. Next come the more subtle, the more deeply ingrained behaviors that also impede our conforming to the image of our Creator. Things like prejudice, manipulation, self-righteousness, pride, mean-spiritedness, the desire to control—these are the thoughts and mind games that continue to plague our life in Christ long after we have dumped the more obvious offenses.

As Christians, we have taken up a new residence; our home is in Christ, where mismatched thoughts and behaviors are as glaringly out of place as would be a Tiffany lamp in a house without electricity· The battle to get rid of the old and move in the new begins from the moment we first encounter the presence of Christ within and continues until the day we close the door on this earthly life. Today is a good day to begin redecorating.

Suggestion for meditation: **Pray for spiritual honesty; become involved in rehabilitating houses for the poor.**

Saturday, August 1   Read Psalm 107:1-9.

The relieved pilgrims who sang this hymn of grateful praise to God apparently could not be faulted for their slipshod sojourn, for it appears they simply and innocently wandered off the beaten path. They found themselves in more trouble than they could handle. In effect, they were on their way from home to church, but the desert that lay between was almost their undoing. No wonder they raised their voices in thanksgiving for God's "wonderful works to humankind."

Giving thanks to God comes easily when a life has been saved or a severe illness healed, when a near tragedy is narrowly escaped or a stretch of unemployment ends with a job offer. Those are the big "deserts" in our lives, and crossing them safely leads us to break out with shouts of joy and thanksgiving to God.

But if you are like I, we would all do well to be more mindful of God's daily blessings too. The sun rises and sets every day, yet how often do we thank God for anything but the most beautiful sunrise or sunset? We may bring home a paycheck every two weeks—sometimes complaining more about work than feeling grateful to God for our jobs. In short, we too often take God's gifts for granted, as though we earned or deserved them, rather than having a "gratitude attitude" toward all of life. So consider this suggestion: wherever you are right now; whatever you see, from a light switch to a computer; whatever you hear, from a whining child to a Mozart sonata; whatever you feel, from the floor beneath your feet to a warm breeze—name it and thank God for it.

Suggestion for meditation: **Pray for a grateful spirit; share a particular blessing with someone else today.**

Sunday, August 2   Read Hosea 11:8-11.

Of all the places I have lived or visited—from Canada to Mexico, Connecticut to California—and the countless cities, towns, and villages in between, home is always best. For me, that is Wisconsin, U.S.A. It could have been anywhere on earth, but here is where I happened to be born into this world, and here is home. I have no desire or reason to live anywhere else, and no intention to. I know where I belong, and I am home to stay.

Hosea's prophecy of the eventual end to Israel's exile envisioned a grand homecoming, orchestrated by God with compassion and forgiveness. In spite of everything, God would bring them home to where they belonged, home to the Holy One in their midst.

We experience great comfort in being able to live in familiar surroundings—to speak the language of one's neighbors, greet the store clerk by name, find the telephone in the dark of night, or travel in the city without consulting a map. Being home evokes feelings of confident security, warmth, and satisfaction; as the old saying goes, there's just no place like it.

Being spiritually at home with God is a far more precious gift than house or homeland. God will not abandon us, no matter where we roam. God will not forget us, no matter how often we take ourselves into exile. God will not shut us out, no matter how late we come home. God knows where we belong: home, with the Holy One in our midst.

Suggestion for meditation: **Pray for contentment and inner peace; volunteer to help in a soup kitchen or homeless shelter.**

INWARD AND OUTWARD RELIGION

August 3–9, 1998   **Ted Campbell**✤
Monday, August 3   Read Isaiah 1:1, 10-17.

Christian faith cannot be a merely spiritual or "inward" faith, for it is intimately tied to the incarnation of God in Jesus Christ (John 1:14); to the story of God's people Israel; and to the whole creation, including the material creation. Our faith embraces both outward and inward religion.

Isaiah the prophet announces a central biblical theme in denouncing acts of piety unconnected to acts of mercy. His concern in this passage, we might say, is with two different kinds of outward religion: the outward religion of piety toward God, and the outward religion of love for one's neighbor. Isaiah announces that God will no longer tolerate Judah's sacrifices, incense, and solemn assemblies (1:10-13). The Lord will reject acts of individual piety unless the people of Judah will "cease to do evil, learn to do good; seek justice, rescue the oppressed, defend the orphan, plead for the widow" (1:16-17).

Do not jump to the conclusion that Isaiah advocated "works righteousness." Those who have regular contact with the outcasts of society today (in Isaiah, the oppressed, the orphan, the widow) find their own spirituality deeply affected by those to whom they minister. "What I found," they say consistently, "is that *they* minister to *me*." A spiritual discipline worthy of consideration is to covenant to place ourselves regularly in the presence of persons whose reliance on God must be acute and immediate.

Prayer: **Give us grace, O Lord, that we may glorify you in all of our being: in our inward thoughts and in our outward acts. Give us grace to be instruments of your mercy in our world that the whole world may give praise to you. Amen.**

✤An elder of The United Methodist Church, Professor of Church History at Wesley Theological Seminary in Washington, D.C.

Tuesday, August 4   Read Isaiah 1:18-20.

After Isaiah's condemnation of piety toward God without responsibility to one's neighbor (1:10-20), he announces God's judgment and God's mercy (1:18-20). This widely quoted passage is often misread by those whose English dialect is hobbled by the lack of a second-person plural. Correctly rendered, it should read, "Though *y'all's* sins are like scarlet, they shall be like snow" (1:18; author adaptation, emphasis added). The prophet's concern here is not with an individual's sins but with those of a community—Isaiah's own nation of Judah.

Part of our inward piety must be our concern for the sins of the communities for which we are responsible. This does not come easily to those of us who partake of baby boomer culture. Part of our formation was the illusion that we were not part of the "establishment," and we couldn't take responsibility for its massive failures. Even though we now own mortgages, raise families, and belong to professional guilds, we find it difficult to take responsibility for institutions and their shortcomings. These aren't *my* sins, they are the sins of...

No, I am afraid they are mine. The congregation of which I am a part, the institution for which I work, the denomination to which I belong, even the stores where I buy merchandise: I have to take responsibility for these institutions and (yes) their sins. We cannot bear the sins of the whole world, but Isaiah's announcement of corporate forgiveness comes as cheap grace unless we are willing to stand under judgment for the failures of the communities for which we are responsible.

Prayer: Give me grace, O God, to take responsibility for the communities in which I participate. Let me feel that their failures and sins are my own, and let me feel the grace of forgiveness calling our communities to corporate conversion. Amen.

Wednesday, August 5   Read Psalm 50:1-8, 22-23.

Isaiah condemned the outward praise of God in sacrifices, incense, and assemblies when not joined to acts of mercy for the outcasts. The psalmist here condemns outward acts of praise when they are not linked to heartfelt thanksgiving:

Those who bring thanksgiving as their sacrifice honor me;
    to those who go the right way
    I will show the salvation of God (50:23).

Yesterday we considered how difficult it is to take responsibility for the failure of institutions or communities for which we are responsible. This psalm calls us to recognize a related problem: the problem that arises when we give ourselves too much credit for the good that individuals or communities do. Heartfelt *thanksgiving* implies that we are in debt to someone else for all that is good. We owe thanks to God. Psalms like this one became crucially important to Jews after the destruction of the second Temple, and they could no longer offer the traditional sacrifices there.

John Wesley's contemporary, Israel ben Eliezer, the "Baal Shem Tov" and founder of modern Hasidism, taught that true Judaism consists in three things: love for God, love for Torah (God's Law), and love for Israel (God's people). Jewish historian Bernard Weinryb compares Wesley and the Baal Shem Tov as advocates of a "religion of the heart." In both cases, neither rejected traditional outward forms of religion, but their religious revivals insisted that outward piety had to be linked to inward transformation. Our thanksgiving must consist not only in external words or acts but also in the heart's conviction that God alone is the author of all that is good.

Prayer: **Give us grace, O God, that we may give heartfelt thanks to you, acknowledging you as the source of every good gift. Amen.**

Thursday, August 6   Read Hebrews 11:1-3.

The central building on the campus of Southern Methodist University is beautifully domed Dallas Hall. At one time a garbage can on the S.M.U. campus had a lid that closely resembled the features of Dallas Hall. A debate raged in the campus newspaper: Was the garbage can lid designed as a copy of Dallas Hall, or was Dallas Hall designed after the garbage can lid? The debate ended when a member of the philosophy department pointed out that, according to Plato's understanding, we should think of both the garbage can lid and Dallas Hall as copies of an original idea in the mind of the Eternal.

The Epistle to the Hebrews reflects the ancient Platonic belief that all that exists in this visible world is a shadow or copy of the invisible, spiritual world. Here the author of the epistle claims that faith is a kind of spiritual sense that gives knowledge of the invisible world; it is the "conviction of things not seen" or of invisible things.

John Wesley consistently cited this passage (usually in Greek) to underscore his conviction that every human being has a kind of religious sensitivity that is the basis of inward religion. In this sense, every human being has some kind of faith, just as we all perceive the material world through our bodily senses.

Christ is "the true light, which enlightens everyone" (John 1:9). But if this is true, then we cannot think of Christian witness as offering something entirely unknown to the world. Part of our ministry must be our careful listening to the experiences that others have had of God.

Prayer: **Give us grace, O God, to perceive the eternal through the things that surround us. Give us grace to find the traces of your presence in every human being we encounter. Amen.**

Friday, August 7   Read Hebrews 11:8-16.

Part of inward religion is our vision of God's future. Faith is not only the "conviction of things not seen," it is also "the substance of things hoped for" (11:1, KJV), because the things hoped for are things that have not yet been seen. The author of the Epistle to the Hebrews goes on to illustrate this point in the rest of chapter 11 by giving examples of those who lived in hope of the unseen things that God had promised. Abraham and Sarah come first: Abraham set out for a place he had never seen; Sarah conceived a child in her old age, another event "not seen" beforehand.

On the one hand, our bodies and brains react against this idea: Synapses develop in our brains in such a way that old habits and old ways of thinking become familiar and comfortable, and we find it difficult to think beyond the things that we are accustomed to seeing. On the other hand, humans delight in breaking stereotypes and conventions. Part of the role that the visual arts play is to challenge the usual ways we think, to open up new connections and thoughts and possibilities for us. The visual arts help us to "see"—not that which is merely imaginary but that which has been "unseen" as yet.

Part of the regular discipline of the spiritual life, then, must be to envision new futures that God intends for us. We are not eternally stuck in a cycle: God is already out front with new hopes and dreams and ideas. The challenge of faith is to allow ourselves (regularly!) to be startled by God's surprising plans and to live according to that faith.

Prayer: **Give us grace, O God, to think new thoughts, dream new dreams, hope new hopes—even as you have thought and dreamed and hoped for us. And give us grace that we may live by your surprising vision. Amen.**

Saturday, August 8   Read Luke 12:32-34.

Religion has to do with whatever it is that we value above all else, whatever we value ultimately or finally. Our Lord states this in simple but challenging terms: We are to be careful about that which we value or "treasure," for "where your treasure is, there your heart will be also." Commenting on the first commandment, Martin Luther wrote, "That to which your heart clings and entrusts itself is, I say, really your God" (*Large Catechism*, commentary on the first commandment). This is why religious differences are always so sharp. Religious differences are not differences over indifferent matters (like chocolate or vanilla); they are differences over that which we value above all else.

The traditional term used by religious persons for this "ultimate valuing" is *worship*. As Christians, our worship of Jesus Christ distinguishes us. When we sing "Glory be to the Father and to the Son and to the Holy Ghost," we engage in the most distinctly Christian act, the worship of Christ. And although we may say these words week after week, we must ask whether our lives are in accord with them.

The discipline of inward religion calls us to question methodically whether in fact we value God in Christ above all else. Is it Christ to whom "your heart clings and entrusts itself"? Traditional spiritual disciplines (for example, the *Spiritual Exercises* of Saint Ignatius of Loyola) take us, as believers, through concrete acts by which we consider each aspect of our life in relation to Christ. Each act challenges us to consider whether we have valued something else above the final loyalty we profess to Christ.

Prayer: **Give us grace, O Christ, that we may be keenly aware of those things we have valued above you. Give us grace that we may place you above all things. Amen.**

Sunday, August 9   Read Luke 12:35-40.

At the conclusion of the film *E.T.*, some young boys carry a charming but homesick space alien along on their bicycles, intent on returning him to the mother ship. Thwarted by wicked authorities, one boy asks, "Can't he just *beam up* or something?" Another boy then delivers with an indignant snarl the best line of the film: "This is reality, stupid." Wonderful idea—that we could just "beam up" out of this world with all its complications and problems! But, "this is reality, stupid."

According to our Lord, we are to live consistently in the hope of Christ's final return. Some Christians, indeed, have taken this to mean that we are to live in such a heavenly manner that this wicked world is of no relevance.

In the early 1800s, evangelical Christians in the United States believed that Christ's return would culminate a long process of building the kingdom on earth. Consistent with this view of Christ's return, they set about reforming the structures of this world: opposing human slavery, advocating for the rights of women, encouraging temperance in the use of alcohol, reforming schools, etc. From the middle of the 1800s a new teaching about Christ's return prevailed, according to which Jesus would come back to "rapture" the church out of this world. Consistent with this understanding, evangelicals turned from social change and focused more and more on inward piety.

How we think about God's conclusion to human history affects what we do in the world today. One of the disciplines of the inward life is to live in such a way that we are constantly prepared for our Lord's return. Far from a call to neglect this world, I understand Jesus' words as a call to embody God's compassion in the world. After all, "this is reality!"

Prayer: **Give us grace, O God, so to live in this world that we may embody your compassion for all; and in so doing, we may always be prepared for your coming. Amen.**

To Belong to God

August 10–16, 1998
Monday, August 10

Norvene Vest✤
Read Isaiah 5:1-7.

Who is the vineyard? In this parable the vineyard is the house of Israel; that is, the people of God. Reading this passage in faith, we ourselves are the vineyard. God has created a rich, fertile soil of life for us and has sowed the choicest of vines within us, expecting fruitful yield. As God's vineyard, we have received abundant life to live, implanted with the vine of Christ's indwelling presence. Having prepared all, God watches us with expectant care.

It is difficult to take this parable seriously when awakening each morning to our usual routines and tasks. The joints ache a little, perhaps dreams were unsettling, and the day's troubles crowd the mind. We often feel inadequate even for the ordinary work of the day, much less for the great work that is God's.

Even as we sleepily brush teeth, the eyes of the Beloved are on us, empowering us for today's activity as cherished collaborators with God. Yet seldom are we fully aware of the powerful love with which God gives this day. Possibly the hardest discipline in being a Christian is remembering God's ongoing care for each one of us. God made us for joy, and we receive daily invitations to practice living in the faith that we really matter to God in every moment as it unfolds.

Suggestion for prayer: **Begin this day asking to notice how God will love you today. End the day recalling how God has loved you.**

✤Author and spiritual director; an Episcopal laywoman, specializing in adult Christian formation.

Tuesday, August 11   Read Psalm 80:1-3, 19.

The psalmist implores God for help, as we do. And the God addressed has a face that can shine and sits on a throne supported by angelic-looking creatures. These wonderfully human images invite delighted recognition, but do they help or hinder our relationship with God? As we live daily into love of God, who is God for us?

Throughout scripture we find images of God and of Jesus Christ not only as human but also as creaturely; for example, the mother hen longing to tuck wayward Jerusalem under her wings (Luke 13:34). Using human characteristics to describe God does help us understand God's personhood. For example, "ears" had an important role in early Hebrew society—knowledge was transmitted orally more often than in writing. The Hebrews knew how to listen carefully and precisely, and the ear for them effectively symbolized God's attentiveness. Likewise the "face" symbolized intimate presence; "shine" signified special blessing. (See Exod. 34:29.)

But scripture writers likewise had a keen awareness that all images tend to limit our appreciation of God's greatness; we are not to take language literally. God is by nature a great mystery, utterly beyond any idea the human imagination can conceive. We use images to help us reach toward God, but we are meant to love *God* more than we love our *ideas* of God.

It is often tempting even with human friends to think we know all about them, shutting off potential surprise and delight as well as growth in the relationship. By loving God, we commit ourselves to One both nearer than our breath and utterly beyond our reach.

Prayer: **How can I even pray to you who are beyond my knowing? Yet I know that you want my prayer. Speak in me, O God, beyond my speech, and help me love you truly in a way beyond my ability without you. Amen.**

In this parable, God's people are the vine, not the vineyard. We are the ones for whom God has acted in power, bringing us into the promised land. And we have been fruitful, filling the land to the sea and the River; our fidelity has been great. But God's promise does not unfold as we expect. Sometimes even the beloved vine is wounded and pulled apart by competing demands. Often even those most holy lament, "How can bad things happen to good people?"

Every life is like this cherished vine, occasionally reeling from harsh blows. In the face of large and small disasters, we are momentarily stopped. Has God "caused" this calamity? Why does God even "allow" apparent defeat of healthy growth and good purpose? Such issues evoke endless debate but no ultimate answers.

The deeper question, for the psalmist as for us, is the one of relationship: Is God with us? We need God's strength to flourish; are these difficulties a sign that God has abandoned us? When we feel vulnerable, alone, and weak, we wonder if we have done something wrong. But if we examine ourselves honestly and find no great sin, how can we explain God's apparent absence?

The psalmist deals with this deeper issue simply by continuing to pray, in effect insisting that our very vulnerability is a sign that we are meant for relationship. Our strength comes in union with God, and we do not cease to call upon God. Tears and struggle, doubt and complaint—all have a place in the essential action, which is to stay in relationship with God. We are a people whom God cannot abandon.

Suggestion for meditation: **In a quiet moment, let your awareness go deep in your body: Do you experience the presence or the absence of God right now? Pray to know that both presence and absence are simply different ways of experiencing God with us.**

Thursday, August 13   Read Hebrews 11:32-37.

What does it mean to be a friend of God? Look at the named "accomplishments" in these verses, ranging from quenching fire and putting armies to flight to being stoned to death and poverty-stricken. The writer commends both positive and negative outcomes because people of faith accomplish and experience both. These people are friends of God. The important element is the relationship, the commitment to serve and love God, rather than the success of the activity.

As we consider what we might expect of ourselves and others who live in faith, we may find it difficult to imagine that friends would receive such treatment. When a Christian suffers defeat, we may blame him or her; when a Christian succeeds, we seldom praise God. What does it mean to be a friend of God? In victory or loss, even in apparent absence of God's power and presence, the friendship of faith endures and remains steadfast.

Faith is conviction of things not seen. God's life and purpose are obscure to us, seen only occasionally and dimly. God is both like us—present and personal—and unlike us—so far beyond our imagining that we cannot control or predict what God will do. Echoing a child's prayer, we may wish instead for a God "with skin on." But in practice, life with God is uncontainable, always breaking the limits of our understanding. To be a friend of God is to learn to enjoy God's surprises, to be receptive to God's illusive reality. *Faith* is our word for friendship with God.

Suggestion for meditation: **Reflect on a time in the past when you experienced success and on another time when you felt failure. Can you now see God's presence in both situations? If not, talk with a spiritual friend to see if together you can discern God at work in your whole history.**

Friday, August 14   Read Hebrews 11:29–12:2.

A great cloud of witnesses teaches us about faith. We belong to a people of faith who trust in God's love even when the promises are not received. Our Judeo-Christian tradition takes human life and history seriously and therefore declines to pretend things are fine when they are not. Authentic faith doesn't hold off the suffering and grief that enter every life but experiences them to the full. But there is a difference between trouble experienced with faith and trouble experienced without faith. Somehow people of deep faith seem to grow from suffering, while the rest of us don't. What is the key to that difference?

The cloud of witnesses is united in following Jesus' model of suffering faith. His motive was the joy set before him; he was responding in love to the assurance of God's love. He endured; his action was not assertive mastery but rather sturdy persistence even to death. And Jesus joins his suffering to ours; he unites in his person the community of faithful people who strengthen one another in mutual care. Let us too take our part among this cloud of Christ's witnesses, acting with love, persevering, and living in unity with one another.

Prayer: **Help us remember, O God, that we are not alone in our desire to love and that, through Christ, you are even now creating something new in the midst of what must be endured. Amen.**

Saturday, August 15   Read Luke 12:49-53.

This Jesus is not meek and mild but is a man consumed with passion. He is under stress, in the grip of God's claims upon him. Jesus knows these claims will bring about his "baptism," which he senses will mean his own death. He sees that his faithfulness will bring division even in the most natural unions.

Hard language, this! How does it speak to us?

Throughout the week, we have considered what it means to belong to God. *Love, friendship, discipleship, faith*—all these terms point us again and again to the centrality of relationship with God at the core of our lives. God, the unfathomable Spirit, who is somehow utterly present within the very fabric of our daily round, seeks our unconditional response. No matter what the cost, no matter what the apparent result, we are to follow God. And yet God's call is often ambiguous and frequently against our instincts. Surely the son of God is meant to live and flourish, not die as a "criminal"! Surely the way of God is to bring harmony and not the breakdown of family ties! God's word is never easy to discern, seldom easy to obey. How can we do this?

God seeks a relationship with us, which grows in intimacy over time. Jesus understood the awfulness of his "baptism" only after thirty years of regular prayer, forty days of intense discernment, and three years of preaching and healing. We too are always invited only to take the next best step, staying constant in prayerful listening. The cumulative effect of divine intimacy over time may astonish us; certainly it will serve God.

Prayer: **Lord, help me listen and love you as fully as possible today. Amen.**

Sunday, August 16   Read Luke 12:54-56.

How do we interpret the present time? Are we able to see clearly what is happening around us with the eyes of Christ? As we have explored "signs" throughout the week, we have looked at a number of events that seem to be negative—the trampling of the beloved vine or the family divided against itself, only to discover that God draws growth and life from them. In contrast, signs that seem positive—the readiness of good soil in the vineyard or the faith of the ancient prophets—sometimes fail to reach fulfillment in human terms. It is clear that Jesus' interpretation demands a different understanding than the usual.

Living within a constant, receptive relationship with God is the key to genuine discernment. We are to relinquish the "easy way" of certainty about what God means and wants, becoming instead flexible people of fluid and permeable boundaries, open in compassion to all—even our enemies. Only in this way do we become genuine partners in God's unexpected and astonishing future.

Yet this openness is costly, exposing us to our own fiery baptism, and we do not have the strength for it unless the central core of our being is firmly rooted in God. And when we are so rooted, through constancy in prayer and receptivity of heart, we find ourselves amazingly responsive to the life-giving Word appearing now in our midst.

Prayer: **Break my hard edges, Lord, and strengthen my center in you. Let me be your friend in all that I am and do. Amen.**

THE UNSHAKABLE LOVE

August 17–23, 1998
Monday, August 17

Soomee Kim ♣
Read Jeremiah 1:4-5a.

"In the beginning..."

Jeremiah was affirmed in his origin: "Before I formed you in the womb I knew you, and before you were born I consecrated you." God knew Jeremiah. God had to know him well because Jeremiah was God's beloved creature. God made him and breathed into him God's own breath, and we might conjecture that God said, "You are good."

Just like Jeremiah, each of us is consecrated even before birth. Have you ever imagined the moment of your creation?

Visualize with me God's creating you in the beginning: Perhaps it is by a creek where cool, clear water flows and sparkling golden clay is abundant. God stoops down on the shore of the creek and scoops up a hearty-sized lump of clay and kneads it very carefully. All God's attention is focused on forming that lump of clay into a figure.

God finishes composing the perfect image of God, then comes back to the face, shaping the eyes, the nose, the mouth perfectly. God looks at the clay figure and says, "It is good!" Then God embraces that figure tenderly and breathes into it the breath of life. The figure becomes a living being.

God whispers in your ear, "You are my child and my beloved. I bless you and the day you are born." What a wonder it is to be reminded that we are made in God's image!

Suggestion for meditation: **Remember God took special efforts to create you. Appreciate all the persons you meet today, for they too are made in God's image.**

♣Ordained minister of Northridge United Methodist Church; Northridge, California.

Tuesday, August 18   Read Jeremiah 1:4-10.

Calling as blessing

God called Jeremiah to be the voice of God while everyone else was facing away from God. The Assyrian Empire had collapsed and was displaced by the power of Babylonia with King Nebuchadnezzar. It was the last days of Judah, just before the deportation of Jehoiakim and other members of the royal family, in 597 B.C. During this unsettling time God called Jeremiah to confront the disoriented people of Judah and tell them what they were not ready to hear.

Like Jeremiah, God calls us to be in ministry. The call often involves doing unpopular things. Frequently God calls us to do the things we've never done before or to do things no one has ever done before. Many times in carrying out the calling we have to take the first step with no previous experience for comparison.

We often fail to recognize divine sanction in God's calling because we are caught up in the enormity of the project or focused on our own insecurity. Calling is a private encounter with God and is a special blessing and a privilege. God calls us not only to give us tasks but also to assure us that we are creatures worthy of God's call. The call also guarantees us that we will receive what is necessary to carry out the calling.

Even in the midst of the opposition, the strong voice of God affirmed Jeremiah, "Do not be afraid of them, for I am with you to deliver you." That same God promises to be with us when God calls us to a task. Even when encountering the seemingly impossible task, our only response to God's calling is, "Here am I, the servant of the Lord; let it be with me according to your word" (Luke 1:38).

Prayer: Give me strength to say "Yes!" to your call, O God. I trust you will lead me all the way. Amen.

Wednesday, August 19   Read Psalm 71:1-6.

The buoyant power of God

Learning how to swim has two stages. You learn the right movements of arms and legs, and you practice turning your head at just the right angle for breathing with the minimum interruption of your speed. Those skills allow you to maneuver in the water with great efficiency. But before you learn the movements, you have to learn to trust the water's buoyancy—to let the water lift you up. This part requires that you relax completely, trusting that you will float. Unless you learn to trust the water, swimming becomes endless kicking and stroking—it depletes your energy and doesn't take you far.

Life is like swimming. We may learn all the right moves and know how to solve problems when we encounter them. But unless we are convinced that God is in control of the whole world, including our lives, life becomes an endless effort. We swim around in circles to the point of exhaustion.

Psalm 71 is a prayer for help that contains petition for lifelong protection. The psalmist's prayer radiates tremendous assurance in God, which results in praises. Even if we live in a world filled with adversity, continuously encountering powerful and persistent challenges, we can remain hopeful when we can affirm and trust that God is in control of our lives. When we have that trust in God, our praise becomes our lifestyle rather than an occasional ritual act.

Like learning to swim, the first thing we need to learn in life is to trust in God. We will surely float above the water of adversity when we have completely surrendered to the buoyant power of God.

Prayer: God of life, you are my hope and my trust. Lift me above life's adversity and strengthen my trust in you. Amen.

Thursday, August 20   Read Luke 13:10-13.

You are set free!

The woman came into the synagogue late—after Jesus had started teaching, hoping to slip into the crowd unnoticed. Maybe she feared the criticism of the crowd or the unforgiving eyes of the synagogue leaders. Being bent over for eighteen years, she was the target of people's judgment: They believed she was possessed by a spirit that had crippled her all these years. Certainly her physical deformity was the consequence of her unforgivable sin. Unable to see straight forward, she probably made her way into the area reserved for women, slaves, and children in the back of the synagogue, trying not to bump into anyone.

But Jesus spotted her. In fact he did more than notice her. He interrupted his teaching and called her to come forward. According to rabbinical law, it was disreputable for a man to speak in public to any woman, let alone a crippled woman. Jesus not only called her, but he invited her to come forward to the place reserved for men. Imagine the shock in the crowd, in the woman herself, and in the synagogue leaders!

She walked slowly forward. People moved aside—not in avoidance but in amazement. Jesus spoke to the woman convincingly, "Woman, you are set free from your ailment." Then he laid hands on her, and she knew she was healed. For the first time in eighteen years, someone recognized her as a valuable human being who deserved attention and dignity.

Like the woman, we have value in God's eyes. God wants to heal us from any restrictions that have caused us to be bent over. Give your ailment to God, receive healing today, and begin praising God with your life.

Prayer: God of wholeness, help me receive your gift of healing. In turn, enable me to extend my hand and touch those who need my attention today. Amen.

Friday, August 21   Read Luke 13:10-17.

Stand up and look straight.

Healing of the bent-over woman causes a stir among the synagogue leaders, but the incident increases Jesus' popularity. The synagogue leaders by comparison come off as uncaring and inefficient. They feel the need to halt the rising acclamation of this itinerant speaker and to restore order in the religious system that has been controlling the lives of people for centuries. So they point out the fact that Jesus has broken the law of Sabbath.

For Jesus, healing could not wait until the end of Sabbath. A person's well-being took precedence over the observance of the law. A religious system that was insensitive to people's suffering could and should be questioned. To restore persons' dignity and to establish the welfare of even the least of humanity, Jesus challenged the tradition and the rules—the tradition and rules that had stabilized society at the price of personal dignity. Jesus demonstrated the importance of love and justice when he healed one woman, a woman who had received no attention for eighteen years. Jesus challenged the system that considered women property, often treating them as equals only with animals.

This passage reminds us of the individual's importance to God. Being made in God's image, we have every right to live fully the life God has intended from the beginning. Jesus' demonstration of love and justice encourages us to stand up and look straight into the present state of our lives. Do you have a sense of hopelessness, doubt in yourself, or an inability to change? Do something about it.

Prayer: O God, give me keen eyes to question the system and challenge it when I am in doubt. May the dignity of individuals be of utmost importance in my decisions. Amen.

Saturday, August 22   Read Hebrews 12:18-24.

An invitation to the new covenant

The author of Hebrews uses the style of comparison to draw a more accurate picture of the nature of the New Covenant. First he draws the picture of the Old Covenant: With thunderous sounds and fearsome atmosphere, God appeared on Mount Sinai and first made covenant with the people. Moses encountered God on the holy mountain with fear and trembling. The sovereign God has power and might, and the people in their fear kept themselves at a distance. No one dared go near the place. Even Moses was ordered to take off his shoes.

In the new covenant, we meet God face to face in the heavenly Jerusalem with no more fear and trembling. Jesus serves as mediator between us and God. Even the heavenly host surround us in their festive spirit and celebrate with us. God is still the judge, but Jesus, with his spilled blood, offers mercy and forgiveness. We stand confidently before the living God because Jesus stands with us, mediating on our behalf.

We have gone far away from God. But the God who labored to shape us in God's own image and tenderly held us to breathe into us the breath of life once more offers us a chance to be with God through the sacrifice of Jesus Christ. The God who consecrated Jeremiah before his birth and who gave assurance to the psalmist offers us grace. As Jesus called the bent-over woman and laid hands on her, God calls us to come and receive God's embrace. Who would not accept that invitation?

Prayer: I hear you calling my name, O God! Give me courage to walk through the crowd and receive your healing embrace. Amen.

Sunday, August 23   Read Hebrews 12:25-29.

Unshakable faith

The earthquake in January of 1994 permanently changed the lifestyles of many residents in Northridge, California, and the surrounding cities. Many have abandoned their community and moved out of the area. But more people have stayed and tried to rebuild their lives, along with their homes. Many lost lifetime collections of porcelain dolls, china, and crystal, along with other invaluable treasures such as precious keepsakes that had been handed down from generation to generation. Despite their value, they were not permanent; nothing could save them from the great shake.

The earthquake gave many a new awareness: Many now know that treasures of a lifetime can disappear in a few minutes. They also know that you cannot buy some things of value. They also know that a certain resilience in them continues to supply hope even after the most devastating disaster.

Today's passage describes the quake that would shake up not only earth but also heaven. It offers us the opportunity to distinguish between what is shakable and what is not. We will discover that many precious things will remain with us: "We are receiving a kingdom that cannot be shaken."

When the unavoidable quake comes your way to shake you from the groundedness of your being, will you remain unshaken? Or even after the shaking, can you find the tranquility that restores your balance?

Prayer: **God of unshakable being, come into me and be the equilibrium that will never lose its balance. Amen.**

Do Remember Me

August 24–30, 1998
Monday, August 24

James W. Kemp♣
Read Jeremiah 2:2, 4-6.

"Do, Lord, O do, Lord. O do remember me." In my childhood that was a favorite chorus at my daddy's childhood church. We made at least an annual pilgrimage to Picket's Chapel. In my first pastoral appointment, that song was again a favorite refrain.

Yet as I reflect on it, the song has the wrong emphasis! Humanity suffers needlessly not from God's failure to remember us but our failure to remember God—and certain people who are easily forgotten. This week the scripture calls us to remember what God has done and to shape our lives in faithful response.

We begin by affirming that God remembers us as those God loves: "Thus says the Lord: I remember the devotion of your youth, your love as a bride." Jeremiah 2:4-6 reflects on the human tendency to forget God's actions. We discover that the things we seek and pursue have the ability to define us. The people of Jeremiah's time [and ours] went after "worthless things and became worthless themselves."

Without a remembrance and center of identity based on the Lord, the God of Israel, we risk becoming worthless. God gives life value and meaning.

In Christ we see God's love in its fullness. We see how much God values us. We are not worthless! God gave Christ for us. God calls us to extend this love to those who are sometimes overlooked—by us, not by God.

Prayer: **Lord, keep your acts always in my memory. Shape my life in faithful response. Amen.**

♣Minister of Encouragement at St. Luke United Methodist Church; Lexington, Kentucky.

Tuesday, August 25   Read Jeremiah 2:7-13.

Persons with short memories forget how far God has brought them: The great miracle of the Exodus and God's provision in the wilderness is ancient history. The people discard the God who gave Israel life and identity, replacing God with other gods who are not gods and who offer no help. Other religious endeavors just don't hold water.

God accuses the people of Jeremiah's day of defiling the land. Without a firm reliance on and sense of gratitude toward God, their ethic becomes whatever is convenient. People and the land appear disposable when they fail to acknowledge God. The crumbling of Jeremiah's world before the exile is attributed to the attempt to replace God with gods who are no gods at all.

The environmental abuse by people today also defiles the land. At times we act as if we can pollute and defile the land with total impunity. We fail to remember our Creator and our place in God's creation. The worthless gods of convenience and profit dictate our actions.

In the arena of entertainment, we face a similar charge of defilement, of selling out to worthless gods of sex or money. It is easy to forget our God and pursue worthless idols of the moment.

Modern idolatry of the perfect body and glowing health leaves little room for those with physical limitations. The gods of speed, convenience, and expense make it expedient to ignore or dismiss the person with a disability who comes to drink from the "living water."

Suggestion for meditation: **What tempts you as a replacement for God?**

Prayer: **Forgive us, Lord God, when we hold anything as your equal. You alone, God of Abraham and Sarah, Moses and Miriam; you alone, God of Jeremiah and Jesus, are the source of living water, the source of strength and life. Amen.**

Wednesday, August 26   Read Psalm 81:1, 10-16.

This call to worship is based on what God has done. The psalmist speaks for God, reminding the people who gather that it was the Lord who provided the strength that enabled the Exodus. It is God's strength that brings forth a "shout for joy." When people fail to remember the Lord's actions on their behalf, both in the past and the present, they are left to the resources of their own "stubborn hearts." Biblical history prescribes this as a recipe for disaster.

Psalm 81 serves as a prophetic exhortation. Beginning in verse 6, God speaks in the first person. In verse 8, God calls, "Hear, O my people, while I admonish you; O Israel if you would but listen to me!" If we consider this a psalm of the Exile, it explains why the people are suffering (vv. 11-12), while offering a word of hope if Israel will just listen and respond (vv. 8-10, 13-16).

The psalm is not only a call to worship on festal occasions but a call to keep listening to and remembering an active God in the midst of God's people. Even when Israel forgets to listen, God still claims them as "my people." Our worship gives us an opportunity to respond by affirming that this is indeed our God.

In Christian worship it is paramount to remember what God has done in Jesus Christ. God identified with us as the one born in Bethlehem. God triumphs over sin and death in the Resurrection. God's actions for us shape our lives. Remembering to listen to God, we can "shout for joy" and face God's future with confident hope.

Prayer: **Lord God, help me remember all you have done in the Exodus and in Jesus Christ. May these memories not bind me to the past but send me confidently into your future. Amen.**

Thursday, August 27   Read Luke 14:1, 8-11.

"Remember your manners!" My mother's admonition still rings in my ears. I called it to mind recently when someone commented on how often I said "please" and "thank-you." "Your mother taught you well," the admirer said. She was right. I thank Mom for my evident manners. Give credit where credit is due.

In this passage from Luke, Jesus gave more than just an etiquette lesson about a wedding banquet. Although his advice was practical in everyday life in his time and place, Jesus taught a great lesson about life in the kingdom of God. He taught, "Go and sit down at the lowest place." Not only does this prevent embarrassment at the wedding party, it acknowledges the host's prerogative to elevate guests to any position. Everyone comes at the gracious invitation of the host. One enters the kingdom by God's invitation.

Jesus warns his disciples about seeking position or prestige in the kingdom of God (Luke 22:24-27). Jesus does not tolerate religious pride. (See Luke 11:37-52 for his chastising words to some of the religious leaders of the day.) God's favor is given, not earned. Religious professionals of all ages can succumb to the temptation to forget who called us into ministry. God calls; we answer. God invites; we respond.

Humility is based on this remembrance. We are invited to the kingdom of God, not because we are great but because God is! Our position doesn't matter. Sit at a place where others are free to come. Anything great or good you accomplish is God's working through you.

Prayer: **Lord, teach me real humility. Remind me that my gifts and graces are not abilities I have earned. Help me use my gifts to the maximum, giving you the credit due. Amen.**

Friday, August 28   Read Luke 14:7-14.

Jesus remembers those persons that many of us choose to forget. It was a lot easier to have a dinner without "the poor, the crippled, the lame, and the blind." Inviting these folks might entail added expense, religious or social ostracism, and great theological debate on the causes of poverty and disease. Besides we don't know these people. We have always avoided their kind. People with disabilities make us uncomfortable. Do we have to invite them?

Jesus had dinner with friends many times without giving blanket invitations. He truly enjoyed meals with friends. But the requirements he imposes for friendship have nothing to do with wealth or physical ability and everything to do with love. Love is remembering that Jesus died for "the poor, the crippled, the lame, and the blind" and everyone else on our social register. It is Jesus' party, God's kingdom. God wants everyone to come.

The measure of faithfulness for a disciple of Jesus and a congregation of Christians may rest in our openness to all. Architecture, attitudes, and invitations to our worship tell whose party and whose kingdom we represent. This may include offering transportation to those unable to see or walk but who are willing to respond to Christ's invitation. If we offer our friendship or association, while holding to our own standards of physical ability, personal hygiene, or financial well-being, is it any wonder that many turn down the invitation?

If it is Jesus' table we surround, if it is God's kingdom we proclaim, we welcome all as Christ's guests—especially those who are often left out. And with the invitation and welcome, "you will be blessed, because they cannot repay you, for you will be repaid at the resurrection of the righteous."

Prayer: **Lord, help me see those who need welcoming love. May those ignored by some find your love in me. Amen.**

Saturday, August 29   Read Hebrews 13:1-8, 16.
(Read both NRSV and NIV, if possible.)

It is not too difficult to love for a moment. It is sometimes very difficult to "keep on loving" (v. 1, NIV). The prisoner who violates parole, the stranger who takes unkind advantage of your hospitality, the one who resists your overtures of friendship can raise second thoughts about "mutual love." It is not humanly possible to be loving all the time!

Chronic illness tests our ability to keep on loving. It is relatively easy to care for someone with the flu or even a broken leg. We can see an end to their limiting condition and can love them throughout. With a chronic illness (I have multiple sclerosis that continues to worsen), it is not as easy. Continued acts of love are required over a lengthy period of time. The person with the chronic condition may not always be appreciative. Time may exhaust our capacity to love, and we may develop what Maxie Dunnam refers to as "compassion fatigue."

That is the point. In and of yourself, it is impossible to muster the strength and love to meet the demands of a disciple of Christ. But remember—you are not alone. You have brothers and sisters in Christ who will help you along. You have God's promise too. The writer of Hebrews quotes from Psalm 118: "So we can say with confidence, 'The Lord is my helper; I will not be afraid. What can anyone do to me?'" (Heb. 13:6).

Keep on! Keep on! Keep on! Remember God is with you and is pleased with your efforts. "Do not neglect to do good and to share what you have, for such sacrifices are pleasing to God."

Prayer: **Dear God, in all my busy activities, help me to remember all you have done. Give me the love, the strength, and the will to "keep on loving" in Jesus' name. Amen.**

Sunday, August 30   Read Hebrews 13:8.

August has no holidays: no expectant joy of Advent-Christmas, no repentant mood of Lent or the celebratory note of Easter or Pentecost. Most liturgical calendars refer to August as "ordinary time." The author of Hebrews is writing to people in ordinary time, people without external reminders.

The readers and hearers of Hebrews faced the difficulties of living in the world after the first advent of Christ, yet before a final consummation of God's kingdom. Was there something they were missing? Was their salvation complete? Was the Christian life supposed to be so hard? How could they best live in ordinary yet difficult times? Their concerns sound much like ours.

In this concluding chapter, the writer of Hebrews warns against loose morality, the love of money, and susceptibility to misleading teachings. Even if things look less than exciting, God is still present with God's people. God's word to Joshua (1:5) as he prepared to cross the Jordan still applies, "I will not fail you or forsake you." (See Heb. 13:5.)

What transpired in the incarnation and resurrection of Christ has significance whether we have special celebrations or not. The good news of Jesus does not fade away, even in our most ordinary times. Remember that "Jesus Christ is the same yesterday and today and forever." This is the good news. No matter what occurs, Jesus is our constant in an ever-changing world.

Prayer: O God, we know about Jesus. We have studied theology. We have heard and preached many sermons. We celebrate Christmas and Easter. But sometimes in the ordinary routine of the everyday, we forget and our lives do not reflect a living Savior. Forgive us. Keep before us all you have done and are yet doing, through Jesus Christ our Lord. Amen.

TO WHOM DO YOU BELONG?

August 31—September 6, 1998   **Rebecca W. Waldrop✤**
Monday, August 31   Read Jeremiah 18:1-11.

God, the original designer, shapes us according to God's own vision, seeing with omniscient clarity the beautiful, sound, unbroken vessels God created us to be. With love and intimacy God's hands touch us, hold us, and place their mark upon us. They work tirelessly in our making.

As we turn on the potter's wheel, however, the feel of God's hands on us certainly does not always bring comfort. Often we feel pressed, pushed, pulled, and stretched. We wish God would work with someone else for a while. At other times God's touch is so subtle that we almost believe we are shaping ourselves. But long before we attend our first silent retreat, begin to pray and study daily, seek spiritual direction or feel the first stirrings of compassion for the poor—God, the potter, has been at work in us, shaping us to God's own divine specifications, and firing us in the pure flame of God's love.

Prayer: **Like the clay vessels described in your word, we come before you: different sizes and shapes, colors and textures, tall and short—some shining and some plain—but all your creations...**
   We come because *we know* you repair the broken pieces.
   Renew the oil of yesteryear—
       fill us with your Holy Spirit
       and empower us to fulfill our calling.
   Through Jesus Christ our savior. Amen.
(Written in 1997 by Sina Kami/Scarritt-Bennett Center; Nashville, Tennessee. Used by permission.)

✤Needlework designer and liturgical artist on staff of Scarritt-Bennett Center in the area of spiritual formation; Nashville, Tennessee.

Tuesday, September 1   Read Psalm 139:1-6.

For all of us who have a prodigal side, these verses offer immense comfort. There is no mad moment of our own defiance that will ever separate us from the God who knows us so intimately (certainly better than we know ourselves). There is no escaping this God whose love floods our lives with grace that cannot be contained.

My granddaughter, Nora Ellen, loves to play hide-and-seek with me. As soon as she could walk, the game began. She runs away from my loving attention and hides. She hides behind chairs, doors, draperies—longing for me to chase her; to find her; to "hem [her] in, behind and before"; and ultimately to gather her up into my arms where she giggles with delight and nestles against me, waiting for the kisses and hugs she knows are coming. Nora does this over and over again, secure in the knowledge that I love her passionately, trusting that I will always search for her and that I will always find her.

This is the God the psalmist knows. It is the God of my experience too. I am God's child. Spiritually, I am just learning to walk in the light. I find myself many times running, hiding, and being found by a pursuing, loving God. Nora is right, of course—there is *nothing* better than being found…over and over again.

Prayer: **O Lord, search me and know me. Hem me in, before and behind. Make me your own. Amen.**

Wednesday, September 2   Read Psalm 139:13-18.

"Remember your baptism and be thankful." The minister placed a small, crystal pebble in my wet hand. Leaving the renewal service, I drove to the after-school tutoring program at an urban church. Mary was waiting for me.

A child of poverty and abuse, Mary was silent and withdrawn at first. When I sketched all the children's faces (so that they could see how beautifully God had made them), Mary watched warily from a safe distance. I sketched Mary too, and one day she crawled into my lap and finished my picture with her bright, red crayon.

Today she led me across the ugly, littered lot next door to a fallen nest of pale blue robin's eggs. She beamed as she held it out to me. In a rush of joy, she dashed off to share it. As she turned, she tripped and fell, crushing the nest and breaking all the eggs. Mary began to cry. Holding her tightly, I began to cry too, filled with grief and rage at all her losses. I reached into my pocket for a tissue to dry her tears, and my hand found the crystal pebble. I placed the iridescent stone in her palm where it gleamed in the sunlight.

"Mary," I heard myself say, "you are God's own child. God loves you very much."

Her face turned up to me, still wet with tears but radiant with joy and wonder. Her small hand closed down hard on the pebble. She raced off to share it. Mary is "fearfully and wonderfully made." All that she has experienced in her life cannot dim the fierce beauty of her spirit. It is the mark of the one who created her.

Prayer: **I praise you, Creator God, for I am fearfully and wonderfully made. Amen.**

Thursday, September 3   Read Philemon 1-21.

In so many areas of our lives, we remain imprisoned although we may spend years fighting to liberate ourselves. Paul knew this very well. Issues of obedience, servanthood, and freedom impact all of us along our spiritual journeys. In God's time and through God's grace, *whatever* paths we take will lead us continually to the same crossroads. And at each crossroads, we must decide whether or not to live in obedience to the one who created us. Onesimus, a runaway slave and Paul's friend, was faced with this choice.

After a time of intense searching, a call invaded my life—my husband's call into full-time ministry. At the time it seemed a hard thing since it was not even *my* call at all. Whoever's call it was, it required an act of obedience on my part. The one thing I *was* sure of in all my confusion and anger was that there was nothing, *nothing* in it for me. I was far more interested in liberation than obedience to God's call. With a great deal of support and love from good friends, I was able to suspend doubt and fear long enough to say "yes." Just as Onesimus's choice to follow God's calling led him home to face the very things he had been trying to escape, I was led home too.

In the ensuing years of struggle and preparation, I discovered to whom *I* belong. Questions of identity that had plagued me all my life were swept away by the God who lovingly claimed me. More remarkable even than the meaning that began to flood my life was the freedom I began to experience. As an artist, I began to open up and stretch creatively. As a woman, I began to heal emotionally. As a child of God, I began to discover, like Onesimus, that the obedience I had fought and feared was the path to the freedom I had longed for all my life.

Suggestion for meditation: **To whom do you belong?**

Friday, September 4   Read Luke 14:25-26.

These verses disturb most of us. We would certainly classify them as "hard sayings." We *know* that the love in our families has helped us understand the love of God. At the same time, many have discovered in their journeys toward greater commitment to Christ a need to undergo some changes in their family relationships. Where relationships among family members are completely healthy, all the members of a family can grow into separate, loving, mature people able to grasp fully their gift of life in Christ.

However, most of us live in less than perfect families. We have to find our way to wholeness out of relationships that are often suffocatingly codependent. We live and work in places where control issues (both ours and other people's) have robbed us of freedom and interfered with spiritual growth. For too long, we have tried to be all things to all people.

Jesus is laying out clearly the cost of real discipleship for those who are literally *following him around*. The question—*to whom do you belong?*—calls into question all the other relationships in our lives. It begins to demand from us a kind of singular loyalty and commitment that is downright shocking. Does this mean that we are not to love our families and our own lives? No. Jesus has too many words to say to us about loving each other. It *does* mean that where the needs and demands of the individuals closest to us interfere with our spiritual growth and our obedience to Christ's claim on us as disciples, we are expected to know without question to whom we belong.

Prayer: **Loving God, make us the kinds of families that will nurture those we love most to embrace your love and become your disciples. Amen.**

259

Saturday, September 5   Read Luke 14:27-30.

Here Jesus is speaking to the large crowds that have followed him all along the road to Jerusalem. They followed him for many reasons. For some Jesus was probably little more than a source of local entertainment. They believed they had joined a parade. For some he was the Messiah come to free them from oppression. They believed they were part of a political movement. For some the need for healing was so desperate that they would have followed him anywhere, hoping for a miracle.

Jesus turns to them all and begins to talk about the cost of discipleship. He asks them to consider up front what the costs will be so that they will be sure they can go the distance.

Commitment to discipleship is a big problem for Christ's church today. Some of us come to church seeking to be uplifted. We need to be fed and filled because we so often feel empty. We are actually too full—full of our own agendas, our own desires, our own ideas. We try to fit the "church thing" into our already frenetic lives. Some of us come looking for rescue. We feel oppressed and put upon. We want someone to take us seriously. We want someone to listen to us. We want power.

All of us come broken, needing healing, longing to be loved. We want to feel better about ourselves.

Do we differ so much from the crowds who followed Jesus? Jesus says to *us*: Do you understand what it *means* to be my disciple? Have you counted the cost? Will you go with me all the way?

***Prayer:* Jesus, teach us what it means to be your disciples. Sustain us with your grace on the journey ahead. Amen.**

Sunday, September 6   Read Luke 14:31-33.

The scriptures tell us repeatedly that, though grace comes to us freely as God's precious gift, the cost of a life of discipleship is high indeed. In these verses, Jesus lays it out for us again: "So therefore, none of you can become my disciple if you do not give up all your possessions." I am sure the crowd on the road to Jerusalem did not want to hear this either, and most of them had less to "give up" than we do.

Discipleship demands more and more from us. Christ wants everything we have and everything we are. I am convinced that somewhere deep inside us we've known this all along.

Following Christ and becoming his companion in the world will take us into dangerous, hurting places. We will have to sacrifice our agendas for his. More and more the things we believed were so important may lose meaning for us. We may not be able to keep the "church thing" under control. Following Christ could become a ministry that will invade every aspect of our lives. We will have to become new people. We will have to learn to love as Christ loves, and we will not come away from that experience unchanged or without suffering.

We will have to let go of some of the feelings and attitudes that have defined us all our lives in order to move out with Christ along the road. Belonging to Christ will change everything. It will change *us* forever. Who will we be? None of us can be sure of that. But we will know, intimately, to whom we belong.

Suggestion for meditation: **Where in your life do you sense Christ's calling you into deeper commitment?**

LOST AND FOUND

September 7–13, 1998   John Indermark ✤
Monday, September 7   Read Luke 15:1-3.

The scene is all too contemporary. Folks whom societal norms deem respectable (*righteous* is the theological expression) are taken aback by the presence in church or among the pastor's acquaintances of "undesirables." The whisper campaign begins in earnest: "Doesn't she know…isn't he aware…what will others think?" Are we talking here of Luke 15:1-3 or last Sunday at church or last Monday at our civic club? Luke depicts a scene that, whether or not it bears repeating, is repeated.

"So [Jesus] told them this parable." Who are "them": the indignant righteous or the welcomed sinners? Sometimes the Gospels are tantalizingly unclear. We aren't exactly sure whom Jesus is addressing, so we listen as if he's addressing us. It's a bit like recess in a crowded schoolyard. A teacher's voice rings out, "You shouldn't be doing that"—and not one but half a dozen or more escapades come to a screeching halt.

"Jesus told them this parable." The parable(s) and other texts will follow this week. But for the moment, take note of this week's theme: "Lost and Found." Most persons will have some personal experience of both. We know what it means to lose and to be lost. We know what it means to find and to be found. But what does God have to say to persons dwelling on each side or to those straddled precariously between them?

Jesus told *them* this parable: the lost, the found, and all sorts in between…which is to say that Jesus tells us.

Prayer: **Teach me to listen, O God, for your word that seeks me out, wherever I am. In Jesus Christ. Amen.**

✤U.C.C. minister, writer; temporary supply pastor to Clatskanie Presbyterian Church; living in Naselle, Washington.

Tuesday, September 8 Read Psalm 14:1-3;
1 Timothy 1:15-17.

Sometimes, the psalmist's fools seem to have the weight of history on their side of the argument. Whether by genocidal conflicts in Third World countries or random violence in First World streets and homes, many events point to the absence of God in human affairs. That absence, however, traces to human choice rather than divine purpose.

God's purpose, if we trust Paul (the ascribed writer of First Timothy), is to seek out sinners (and fools) in order to save. The psalmist minces no words about the widespread folly of the human condition, and Paul just assumes that our folly gives God a bigger pool of prospects (himself included) among whom to exercise grace.

The odd thing comes in discerning what these texts say about being lost and found. The psalm manages to offend our claim of self-secured righteousness in its declaration that "there is no one who does good." However, Paul reveals that not only does God save sinners—but God saves the *foremost* among them (in this case, Paul) in order to give others an "example." In other words, if someone like Paul can be found, then there is hope for the likes of me.

Does this psalm, and does Paul, speak to your life and experience? The psalm offers a pervasive sense of what it means to be lost, even as Paul lifts up God's "finding" activity among those very ones. In a curious way, the theology of Paul depends upon the theology of the psalm. One does not need a God who finds sinners without their confessing the ability of sin to disorient and even "lose" us.

Fools say, "There is no God." Paul says, "Christ Jesus came into the world to save sinners." What do you say?

Suggestion for meditation: **How has Christ "found" you in times of being lost or feeling unworthy?**

Wednesday, September 9   Read Luke 15:4-7.

"Which one of you...," Jesus begins. The gospel is always personal, always seeking an audience from those who might see in it a glimpse of themselves—ourselves.

The story Jesus tells may ring familiar. I recall a painting in a large room of my home church where primary students gathered for worship before dispersing to class: a rocky cliff with thorns and brambles, a lamb either mottled or dirtied on a perilous ledge, a young man reaching down to the lamb to lift it to safety. I wonder how many children pictured themselves as that valiant shepherd—or, perhaps in later years, that grateful lamb. "Which one of you...."

The question Jesus begins with might appear to assume unanimous assent with the shepherd's action. Would you agree with his plan? Would you risk the safety and market value of the ninety-and-nine for only one that is lost? After all, it might wander back on its own, and you wouldn't have to put the others (and yourself) in peril. Besides, the sheep should bear the consequences for drifting from the fold—not an action you'd want to encourage on the part of the others. Now there's a sermon worth preaching!

But that's not the sermon Jesus offered in parable that day nor this day. The issue is not how or why the one became lost. The parable is about the joy of finding. A joy heightened by the risk of leaving the ninety-and-nine behind, just for the sake of the straggler, just for the sake of the wanderer. "Which one of you...," the parable asks. Which one of you celebrates above all else the joy of finding and being found?

***Prayer:* Help me to be a seeker, O God; that having been found, I may help to find. Amen.**

264

Thursday, September 10   Read Jeremiah 4:11-12, 22-28.

One of the corollaries to Murphy's Law ("if something can go wrong, it will") is this: Just when you think things can't get any worse, they probably will.

The prophet Jeremiah offers the ominous forecast of a sirocco (desert wind) blowing in from the east—a likely metaphor for the expanding power of Babylon. Israel thought she merely faced a threat of political and military takeover. Instead, as Jeremiah relates, God's judgment looms in the wind (*ruach*) about to blow: a wind whose result is a reversal of creation—an undoing of Genesis 1, where the *ruach* of God had moved over the waters as creation's prelude. Waste and void, darkness and desolation return to the stage. Just when it seems the Babylonians are as bad as it gets, there is worse. There is God's judgment.

Have we reached, in this midweek of "Lost and Found," the point where all is now lost? Incredibly and graciously, no.

"Yet I will not make a full end." So God slips a hint of redemption into the midst of this overwhelming scenario of judgment. Theologians attribute it to the doctrine of the remnant. People who find themselves caught in desperate circumstances cling to it as light at the end of long and difficult tunnels. Even when creation itself seems to disintegrate around us—by crisis, by illness, by estrangement, even by our own culpability—all is not lost. "I will not make a full end" leaves the door ajar for grace to reenter, for life to renew...for us to be found.

Faith does not insure that things will never worsen. But as long as there is no "full end," fresh beginnings remain.

Suggestion for meditation: **Reflect on how God has brought you and/or loved ones through times that seemed without hope.**

Friday, September 11
Read Psalm 14:4-7;
1 Timothy 1:12-14.

"Have they no knowledge...who eat up my people as they eat bread?" Sometimes folly simply creates amusement. Here however, the psalmist reminds us that ignorance can become cruelty. Ignorance, in its inevitable obsession with self, overlooks the value of others. Those ignorant of the needs of neighbors can feed upon them as surely as ignorance can find ways to confound their aspirations.

And ignorance casts a far wider net than its popular stereotyping among the unschooled and unprivileged sometimes infers. Paul received an exemplary education for a person of his day, if we accept his claims and those of Acts 22:3. Yet in today's reading from First Timothy, Paul admits not only to ignorance but to the excesses—including violence—that ignorance generates.

By the psalm alone, Paul stands judged by the God who brings "great terror" to those whose ignorance harms God's own. So perhaps the closing plea of the psalmist for God's deliverance may remind one of the axiom: "Be careful what you pray for, lest you get it." For in First Timothy, Paul whose ignorance spawned violence is Paul who receives mercy. And not mercy only but grace and faith and love.

Even ignorance does not dig a hole so deep that God's grace may not find us—and not only find but change. God does not leave Paul in his ignorance but transforms Paul in Christ's service. So what of us? Where in our lives, where in our relationships, does ignorance still mar our lives by doing violence to others—if only in overlooking their need? And how may Christ's service lead us, as it led Paul, out of ignorance into love and faith?

Prayer: Holy God, deliver me from knowledge that leads only to self; grant me wisdom that leads to your service. Amen.

Saturday, September 12   Read Luke 15:8-10.

What value do we place on community? Sometimes the answer depends on the quality of support derived from it. At other times, particularly with family, the answer turns on the intimacy of relationships we share with its members.

Consider the value of community depicted in this parable. A woman turns her house upside down in her search for one lost coin. Nowhere does the text mention any involvement of neighbor or friend in this search. Instead, she labors alone until she finds the lost coin. In that finding, though, the text moves from isolation to community. For this woman, joy is contagious. She includes others in its gift. Have you ever been drawn into another's joy, invited to share in the celebration? Or have you ever offered such a gift to another? Joy has the potential to fashion community when shared—*if* it is shared.

Such joy, Jesus concludes, parallels the joy in heaven for one sinner who repents. Why should angels rejoice over one sinner? The answer to that question brings us back to why we value community. The "finding" ministry of Christ initiates Christian community. Those called to be Christ's body share this ministry. Our joy does not come simply in finding persons for our fellowships who look like, think, and socialize as we do. The spark of our joy is in the finding of those who are, in any number of ways, "lost." Such joy has the potential to renew community when shared—*if* it is shared.

The woman calls her neighbors to rejoice in the finding of that which had been lost. What do you hear her saying to you?

Suggestion for meditation: **How does your community share joy; how does joy lead you to seek out others?**

Sunday, September 13   Read Luke 15:1-3; Psalm 14:5*b*;
1 Timothy 1:15*b*.

This week's texts have brought us full circle. We end where we began: "So [Jesus] told *them* this parable" (emphasis added). In Luke 15, Jesus addresses tax collectors and sinners (and all manner of their incarnation today). And in Luke 15, Jesus addresses Pharisees and scribes (and all of their current progeny). Does the parable(s) speak the same word to both groups? Not necessarily. But the point is this: Jesus did not choose one audience to the exclusion of another.

Does the community that bears Christ's name always maintain the ability to reach across such boundaries? I wonder. Surely the criticism of the church as righteous hypocrites has too often been on target, especially where those who do not measure up to *our* standards find no welcome among us. But then again, one could argue that at times the church swings to the opposite extreme, where ridicule of the straight and narrow becomes a fashionable exercise.

The gospel, not to mention the whole biblical witness, forces us to a more inclusive vision for community. Paul's message in First Timothy is unequivocal: Christ came seeking sinners. Yet the message of Psalm 14 is equally unwavering: "God is with the company of the righteous." The church is the meeting place of stuffed-shirts and miscreants alike. And it is so, not because we or they determine it to be, but because Christ so calls and finds us *together.* The one who welcomes sinners and eats with them did the same with Pharisees and scribes—then and now.

This morning at church, look around at the mix of faces and lives gathered in worship; in that mix lies the grace that finds individuals and fashions community.

***Prayer:* Gracious God, help me accept as you accept; help me find as I have been found. In Jesus Christ. Amen.**

September 14–20, 1998   **Herbert Brokering**❖
Monday, September 14   Read Psalm 79:1-9.

Help us.

Forty years ago I saw Hamburg, Germany, laid waste. As I drove through rubble to visit refugee camps on the outskirts, I saw candles in windows where someone found shelter after fierce fire bombings. One night I wrote a poem called "Rubble in the Moonlight"; its subtitle was "Help Us."

The psalmist knew that one part of healing was to cry out, "Have pity, O God. See my sorrow. Help us." Judah had been laid waste; the temple defiled; people taunted, humiliated. The faithful had suffered; the dead did not have a proper burial. Was the Lord's wrath causing the misfortune? The singer prays for punishment on the enemy.

Will the Lord repent? "How long, O Lord?" The song expresses concern: Have pity on Jerusalem. God, why are you beating up on us? The enemy has the upper hand. Your honor is at stake. Defend your glory and authority. Hurry with your vengeance against them. Show us you have not abandoned us.

A child who knows the loving arms of a parent dares to kick and lament because of love. Lamenting is healing. A nation that kneels and laments can receive healing. Only trust will permit a heart to flail against God.

Finally we sink as children into the arms of a parent and sob the words of verse 9, "Our God, you keep us safe. Now help us" (AP). And then the final whimper, "For the glory of your name, …forgive our sins." Let your heart tell it like it is.

Prayer: O God, help me also trust enough to pray, Why have you forsaken me? Amen.

❖Lutheran minister, poet, educator, leader in pilgrimages and global partner projects, and author of several books.

Tuesday, September 15   Read Jeremiah 8:18–9:1.

Cry out.

Jeremiah's message sounds like a newscaster my family listened to during World War II. He reported on the bombing and burning of cities, women, and children; of soldiers' bones left on the ground like trash—much like the slaughter valley in Jeremiah 7.

In my young mind, in night prayers, I prayed for the resurrection of these soldier bones. My father preached about the will of God in the valley of death. As I listened to the radio and to adults, I knew that as in Jeremiah's time, many people had been trapped and put to shame; teachers had turned God's word into lies.

I have walked vacant rubble cities of Europe and guided many through Holocaust prisons of Buchenwald and Auschwitz. "There are no grapes on the vine, nor figs on the fig tree." The prophet is heartsick, grief stricken. As the people are broken, so now the prophet is broken. As the people's suffering is incurable, so is Jeremiah's grief. There is nothing in his voice but lament.

It is important that leaders feel the weight and pain of injured citizens. Expect queens, presidents, elected officers, and judges to weep. Look for mind and for heart when you elect a leader. Listen to the voice and tone of a newscaster. Listen to your heart when you speak.

Where is hope? Where is the balm? Look toward the east, where the sun rises to illuminate Jerusalem, where herbs and trees flower and styrax trees produce resinous gum and ointment as balm. So great is the hurt that all the balm in Gilead will not cure the wound. Cry out for more balm than grows in Gilead.

A good leader, a good prophet feels full pain and mourns with the people. The Jeremiah reading ends, and the prophet's eyes contain a fountain of tears.

Prayer: O God, open our hearts to feel the pain of those who cry out and to be their balm beyond Gilead. Amen.

Wednesday, September 16   Read Luke 16:1-13.

Be smart.

Today's reading is the parable of a dishonest manager, a steward. The rich man dismisses the manager, and he must close the accounts and give up his job. Now what? It's time to think, be smart, plan.

The thought comes to the manager: *Make friends with the network of those indebted to the manager. Help them reduce their debt. Then they will offer me hospitality in time of need. They may hire me if I freelance. I am gifted and trained. I have a family to feed. I will find a way through this crisis. I will be smart.*

The manager was a rascal. We could write him off completely. But Jesus uses the story and redeems one point: The rogue had foresight. I believe Jesus means to say, "I wish you were that smart, determined, and zealous when you respond to God. I wish you didn't run off, whine, complain, and give up. I wish you knew how to do God's business. My parable is about being trusted in a little firm. You are in God's work and that is big business. Being disciples, you are not managing what belongs to someone else; you manage God's riches. Be smart."

The steward did not pity himself, give up, deny what happened. The steward sized up the situation, seized the moment, stayed afloat, acted.

The money in the parable is a foreign currency. The treasure we have is a heavenly treasure, God's riches. When we pray, may we pray for wisdom, thought, and passion so that we can be about God's business and be found energetic, determined, faithful.

Prayer: O God, when I pray, hear the passion behind the words. With all my heart I want to make your work my own. Amen.

Thursday, September 17   Read 1 Timothy 2:1-7.

For everyone

In this letter ascribed to Paul, he writes Timothy, "First of all...I urge that supplications, prayers, intercessions, and thanksgivings be made for everyone." Everyone. Consider praying for everyone, one by one. Begin with someone, add others—a family, nations, everyone. A calming feeling follows.

Praying was precarious in the early church. Authorities looked at Christians with suspicion. In such times it is important to be inclusive and to pray for everyone. Inclusive praying is caring, careful praying. Pray for kings and people in high places, recipients of God's grace and those in need of wisdom and God's grace. Pray for all. Everyone.

News and networking brings the world into our homes. We are not to limit our prayers to family and parish circles. Jesus' prayer begins with *Our,* followed later by "*your* kingdom come, *your* will be done, *on earth* as it is in heaven" (Matt. 6:9-10). Where is this on the globe? Where are these places of the prayer? Everywhere. For everyone.

We can press our prayers to more and more persons, to some we do not know; to a nation, a foe, a ruler. We are to pray for them, stay near them, care and feel for them, understand and give thanks for them. Prayer is toward everyone in all these ways.

What if each week we prayed for one world leader and the people of that nation? Imagine joining millions of others who are knowingly blessing that person and people in the same hour. What if our prayers focused on God's abundant spirit in a particular place? There is space for God's spirit in families, schools, towns, high places, and governments. Prayer gives birth to faith and truth.

Prayer: O God, make room in us for everyone's well-being. Enlarge the circumference of our prayers, in Jesus' name. Amen.

Friday, September 18   Read Jeremiah 8:18–9:1.

Sometimes weep

In my childhood home, a painting of Jesus weeping over Jerusalem hung above our piano. I could feel his tears fall. When we slept Jesus wept; when we woke he wept. This side of Jesus made me feel safe—he never lost compassion.

The time was World War II. Every time we listened to war news we knew about tears. When we saw stars pasted in windows we wanted the feeling of safety. I heard Jesus weeping when polio incapacitated our strong neighbor, when polio swept the countryside like the bubonic plague.

Jesus wept. "O that my head were a spring of water, and my eyes a fountain of tears, so that I might weep day and night for the slain of my poor people!" Jeremiah wailed. Jeremiah scripted a Holocaust symphony and wept while conducting.

We have heard families cry out, seen cities burn, smelled death. I have seen farmers grow silent as hail crushed tall corn, bent down wheat, stripped trees. I have heard gardens shout for drink, felt cities sobbing. When wounded, we weep; we wail.

Tired from weeping, we rest, sleep, heal. Trees drop leaves, sleep, heal. Flowers drop blossoms, sleep, live in their roots in earth. Then come sun, warm spring, soft rain. Gone the crying. Then come green stem, leaves, bud and bloom; no more crying. Done the weeping, done the wailing. God's spirit is alive through us in all seasons.

My doctor says, "Breathe through your pain. Embrace it; acknowledge the hurt; face the thorn; be stronger than the wound. Breathe God's breath, spirit, life through the hurt." When Jeremiah wailed, he cried out through the hurt. Wailing is a form of prayer.

Prayer: O God, free my heart and soul to sometimes wail out loud. When I wail and weep, move your spirit through my hurt. Hold me; and after all my crying, make me still. Amen.

Saturday, September 19   Read 1 Timothy 2:1-7.

Praying space

Prepositions are an interesting part of speech and of living. All prepositions are spatial. They define spaces through which children play as they run in and out, through, over, under, between. Prepositions are important when we play, work, live, and pray.

Look at the prepositions in the Timothy reading. In verse 1 we read that thanksgivings are to be made *for* everyone. We picture ourselves being for everyone—not turned from them—but open to them. See our space in this kind of praying.

In verse 2 we read we are to lead a quiet and peaceable life *in* all godliness and dignity. Imagine being in godliness, not beside it or over it, not beneath but *in* godliness—surrounded by godliness and God's dignity. See our space in this kind of praying.

In verse 5 we read, "For there is one God; there is also one mediator *between* God and humankind, Christ Jesus, himself human." How do you imagine this picture in prayer? Christ *between* God and all humankind, *between* each of us and God. See such space in prayer and tell another what you see.

In verse 7 find the space of Paul in prayer: "*For* this I was appointed a herald." Christ Jesus is Paul's whole speech, the topic for his heralding. This space is about commitment.

Among all prepositions, *of* may best describe closeness, nearness, connectedness. In verse 7, Paul claims to be "a teacher *of* the Gentiles *in* faith and truth." Where was Paul in relation to this truth and faith? He was *in* faith, *in* truth. Prayer space surrounds us.

Prayer: Glory be *to* the Father, *through* the Son, *by* the Holy Spirit. Amen.

Sunday, September 20   Read Psalm 79:1-9.

Prayer pool

We are part of a prayer pool. Some of us have descended from people of great prayer. People around us pray. Prayers, songs of praise, great music, glory seem to be in our genes.

We also inherit fear: "Do not remember against us the iniquities of our ancestors." Early in life I reviewed my ancestors. I thought of four grandparents I never knew, of distant relatives talked about in family stories, of the inheritance in my mind and body. I looked at family albums and saw resemblances between ancestors and myself. I knew about those who went before. Sometimes I traced myself back to disciples locked in fear behind closed doors. I did not know about genes. But I knew there were emotions and gifts, both good and bad, passed on to me from those who lived before. We all inherit inequities.

After major surgery I felt like a city—burned, bombed, laid waste. I cried. A doctor asked me about my wasteland, my ancestors, my inheritance. Six months he asked me questions: I cried out like the psalmist. Then the light became brighter; I found a bright and joyful inheritance.

Verse 8 still is true: "Let your compassion come speedily to meet us." How do we in prayer embrace our inheritance? How do we through prayer leave good offerings for those who will follow us? How do we embrace the light, the glory of God's name?

I like my name. When I was very little I had a stuffed dog with my name embroidered on it. I hugged my name at night to go to sleep. I had to learn to do that again fifty years later. Drawing on my inheritance, I learned.

Prayer: O God, you have given us your own name, a glorious name, to deliver us. Our ancestors are from you, O God. Amen.

DYNAMIC FAITH FOR OUR TIME

September 21–27, 1998
Monday, September 21

Afrie Songco Joye✤
Read Psalm 91:1-6.

Throughout history, the Lord has disclosed countless manifestations of faithfulness. This week's meditations reflect on the dimensions of a dynamic faith in a world characterized by pervasive mistrust, hostility, despair, as well as consumerism and materialism. The texts bring timely messages on living a life of faith and hope at different stages and periods of struggles, suffering, and pain.

Our text today gives a brief sermon, rich with images and metaphors, on God's care and protection even in the face of crises and suffering. The psalmist addresses the assuring words to a "someone" but writes the psalm to all who live and abide in God's presence and peace.

A dynamic faith genuinely trusts in the providential care and secure power of the Almighty, believing that one may depend on God to keep promises. A dynamic faith acknowledges God's faithfulness and goodness. Tragedy, loss, pain, and hurt can cause us to question God's faithfulness. Yet God's cooperation with the laws of nature does not replace God's fulfillment of promise to be with us always.

Those who abide in God's hope accept the reality of danger, destruction, and death; yet they believe that God protects and saves them from hopelessness. May we be people whose dynamic faith lies in God's abiding hope.

Prayer: **God, our refuge, fortress, and deliverer, thank you for your ever-present care and protection. Help me trust that whatever happens today and each day of my life, you are always with me; giving me hope, strength, courage, and faith. Amen.**

✤Pastor of St. Paul's United Methodist Church; Tarzana-Encino, California; author and educator.

Tuesday, September 22   Read Psalm 91:14-16.

Faith without knowing is passive and weak; faith without love is hypocrisy, for faith is human response to divine love. Some assume that faith is a blind acceptance of anything, including the unprovable and unreasonable. Others think it is surrender to the inevitable. However, true faith is genuine trust and commitment; it is courageous confidence and confident courage, using our best informed judgment and working from the perspective of the gospel.

Dynamic faith involves knowing and loving God. The psalmist declares that God provides safety, protection, honor, long life, and salvation to all who truly know and love God. Here is the immanent and transcendent God we can trust even in times of trouble, danger, toil.

The knowledge of God in Jewish thinking includes both mind and heart—one's whole being. To know God, therefore, is to take God's image, embrace it, live it. This image of love embodies a life of faith. The core of Christian discipleship is our love for God.

The dynamic movement of God's power; the strength of a faithful community; and our creative, healing responsiveness can transform our faltering faith into a dynamic faith. Remember these four Cs as you reflect on a dynamic faith for our time: certainty of God's promises; commitment to believe in God's promises; constancy in clinging to God's promises, even when they become dim or far-fetched; and conviction of unseen reality.

Prayer: **Ever-faithful God, thank you for having faith in us. Give us grace and power to live in faith and in love. May we know you and love you with our whole heart, mind, soul, and strength. Amen.**

Wednesday, September 23   Read Luke 16:19-26.

Seeing and hearing the cries of the hungry of the world can so overwhelm us that we become numb and unresponsive. A German theologian at the Vancouver World Council of Churches Assembly made a statement to the effect that in the third world, stomachs are empty; in the first world, hearts are empty. Our faith calls us first to accept the reality of suffering; second, to feel with the sufferers; third, to discern and discover the more direct, tangible ways we can help the hungry, the homeless, the poor, the marginalized; and fourth, to act on our discovery.

Dynamic faith involves action. Jewish law (see Deut. 15:4-11) and Christ's teaching demand that we care for the poor and hungry. In our story the rich man refuses to hear and act on the cries of poor Lazarus. Denial of the reality of suffering and refusal to respond worsen the problem. Who can help but you and I?

A few years ago, I joined the telephone hotline of the local chapter of Bread for the World, a national group that lobbies for petitions and bills to support the poor and the hungry around the world. I felt that in a small, specific way, I could actively show my solidarity with some of the oppressed people. I was amazed at how the phone calls I and others made to our senators and congresspeople affected their voting on those petitions and bills; a small voice can be heard across the nation by powerful, decision-making leaders. Your voice and vote do make a difference.

Our Christian identity and vocation require that we manifest God's image of love and that we follow the way of Christ, which is the way of liberating people from the oppressive bondage of poverty, hunger, injustice.

Prayer: **Compassionate God, forgive me for my insensitivity and selfishness, for caring only for myself and being unwilling to give a small part of my time, my resources, my gifts, myself in helping alleviate the suffering of your children. Speak to me; let me listen. Put me to work; let me do your will. Amen.**

Thursday, September 24   Read Luke 16:27-31.

Today's text emphasizes the importance of scripture, specifically the words of Moses and the prophets, for faith formation and transformation. Abraham's reply to the rich man that the latter's brothers should listen to the teachings of the people of faith from the Hebrew Scriptures attests to the essential place of scripture in a life of faith.

Dynamic faith involves taking the message of the scripture seriously and finding manifestation of its meaning in our personal and public life. The fundamental teachings of the gospel need to undergird our intrinsic and external values.

We might be tempted to conclude that the rich man is not saved because of his stinginess and lack of compassion. A corresponding assumption would be that if the rich give to the poor, they will receive a secure, safe position in the heavenly abode. Our faith, however, affirms that salvation is not by good works but by the free gift of God's grace through faith in Christ. Faith and good works, individual piety and social action rooted in love and justice go hand in hand.

A forty-five-year-old man living with AIDS met with me to plan his memorial service and to designate the estate gift he intended to leave to various church ministries. He wanted to make sure that I included in my homily the significance of prayer, scripture, and the church in one's growth of faith.

Bringing the scripture message into life requires attentiveness to God's voice and vision and our own voices and hopes, God's infiniteness and our own finiteness. Only then may we respond to God in awe, wonder, praise, thanksgiving, and service.

Prayer: **Everlasting and ever-loving God, help me set my priorities straight. In the midst of my busy, hurried, and harried life, enable me to take time with you. Help me dig deeply into scripture, for in knowing the truth, I shall be free. May I live with compassion and passion for the truth. Amen.**

Friday, September 25   Read 1 Timothy 6:11-19.

Paul, a faithful follower of Christ, summons us to leave behind the anxious, all-consuming primary pursuit of material wealth; and in its place, to strive to do the right, to be holy. Paul calls us to embrace the spirit of Christ; that is, the spirit of love, gentleness, acts of faith, endurance, righteousness, and godliness. Here we find what it takes to live a dynamic faith.

The text calls us to strengthen our connectedness with the creating, redeeming, healing, reconciling God. Divine-human relationship grows as we grasp every moment—giving meaning, beauty, and love in and to those moments.

A life of faith does not eliminate hardship, crisis, conflict, persecution. Dynamic faith gives us strength to endure the suffering and pain that we—as individuals, as a community, and as a global village—continually encounter both firsthand and vicariously. As we confront difficult issues and situations of injustice and oppression and try to find concrete manifestations of an alive faith, may we turn to the ever-present, ever-faithful God for love, wisdom, and strength.

Our firm foundation is in God, ruler of all, King of kings, Lord of lords. To God be all glory and honor. God alone—not money—meets our deepest needs and hopes. God's providence and provision last; possession of money does not. Let us trust and hope in God.

Prayer: **All-knowing, all-powerful, and ever-present God, fill me with your power and love so I can love in an unloving world, be just in an oppressive world, be generous in a selfish world. Give me strength to endure, not allowing anyone or anything to weaken or destroy my faith in you. Amen.**

Saturday, September 26   Read 1 Timothy 6:6-10.

Paul points out that a life of faith and godliness is more satisfying and fulfilling than a life motivated primarily by getting rich. Paul gives convincing reasons for setting low priority on acquiring wealth and high priority on holy living. He says that (a) material possessions stay on earth and cannot be part of life beyond earthly existence; (b) temptations, traps, and self-serving motives come heavily for money-driven people; (c) the love of money can weaken people's faith. People obsessed with the ultimate goal of material possession can lose sight of their identity and vocation as children of God and as members of the community of faith. They can become insensitive to the deep longings of their heart and to the cries of their hungry neighbors.

We might find it ironic to affirm the belief written on our coin and paper money: "In God we trust." Humanity's belief in the power of money, particularly the love of it, has caused the breakdown of relational foundation and has sapped the spirit of many people drawn by a consuming, materialistic society.

Many individuals, churches, and synagogues put making money as their top priority and fulfilling their mission and vision as last on their agenda. Christ's disciples worship God not because of what they will get from God but for the intrinsic value and experience of peace and joy in communing with God. The "be-religious-and-you-will-be-prosperous" propaganda does not have a place in a life of dynamic faith. Saints of the past and the present confess the restlessness of their souls until they find rest in God. When we sow the act, the habit, and the character that manifest the lordship of Christ, we reap a lasting communion and redeeming partnership with Christ.

Prayer: **Source of life and giver of all good gifts, take from me the nagging intense desire to have more material possessions. Fill my thirst with your soothing presence, your comforting peace, and your fulfilling love. Amen.**

283

Sunday, September 27   Read Jeremiah 32:1-3*a*, 6-15.

Here is a story of faith in action—a story of hope, an act of obedience. While in exile, the prophet Jeremiah hears the Lord's command to buy a piece of land from his cousin Hanamel. Jeremiah answers the call: He purchases the field at a time when his people have lost their homes and land during the Babylonian siege and fall of Jerusalem. Jeremiah's detailed account of the public record of land ownership means that Babylonian captivity is not the end of life.

Jeremiah believes that God's providence has guided him in the public act of land purchase, authenticated by the specific record of payment in cash, the signing of titles and deeds, verification of witnesses, and public filing of the copies of transaction. What a potent sign of faith and hope at a time when life is in disarray.

A church lost the lives of several members and its building in a devastating tornado. The pastor, whose child was killed in the disaster, and the members who lost their loved ones kept their faith and hope alive. They rebuilt their sanctuary. Most importantly, they renewed their faith. They confessed and affirmed that nothing—not even destruction and death—can separate us from the love of God through Christ Jesus our Lord.

Saleem Al-Anati, a Palestinian physician, serves as the only medical doctor for the 15,000 Palestinians living in Shoafat camp in Jerusalem. Despite the harsh realities of poverty, disease, displacement, and oppression, Dr. Al-Anati continues to trust and hope in God. He believes peace and justice will reign someday.

A dynamic faith hears and follows the call of God both in good and bad times, in small and big decisions of life.

Prayer: **Ever-trusting God, increase our trust and hope in you. We know that nothing and no one can separate us from you and your love. When crises, disasters, or suffering come, hold us tightly so that we look to you, our Redeemer and Sustainer. Amen.**

ACCOUNTABILITY

September 28—October 4, 1998   **Woodie White**✤
Monday, September 28   Read Luke 17:5-10.

"The apostles said to the Lord, 'Increase our faith!'" This is a plea of all Christians. New converts and seasoned disciples alike are met with the reality that spirit and deed do not always dwell together. The head is not always at the same place as the heart.

The disciples watched the Lord close up. They not only had the benefit of his teaching but of his daily living. It must have been difficult at times to watch one whose will and deed were one. Their own failings were the more glaring in his presence.

"Increase our faith!" they implored. They wanted earnestly to believe more totally and to act more consistently. Yet, they were aware of their own reluctance. They knew their moments of doubt, even times of utter disbelief.

The Lord's response must have been startling to the disciples. They needed faith only the size of a mustard seed, he told them.

The mustard seed, while tiny, grows rapidly into a large and lively plant. Thus, the message in part to the disciples is that faith does not come full-blown, mature, in an instance. Faith often begins in small portion and, when grounded in the living Lord, grows deeper in each experience of one's journey.

Prayer: **Dear Lord, we pray this day only for enough to get us through the day. That is enough for now. Amen.**

✤Resident bishop, Indiana Area, The United Methodist Church.

Tuesday, September 29   Read Lamentations 1:1-6.

I was born in what was then the largest city in the United States. I especially remember my "inner city" neighborhood as vibrant and alive, with apartment buildings filled to capacity.

Small neighborhood businesses were plentiful, and neighbors knew one another, even watched and corrected one another's children. The city held such promise; it was the place to be.

I went back to my neighborhood after some years. Now apartment buildings, once full with growing active families, are boarded up, burned out, torn down, or abandoned. I walked the streets of my city and wept.

So many cities—large important metropolitan areas, once crown jewels of their region—are today abandoned, even by the church. These places of promise in another era seem today to be a burden to government and others. They are places undesirable for living or rearing a family and are to be avoided.

The lament over Jerusalem, devastated by the Babylonians in 587 B.C. is a painful reflection over this once vibrant holy place. It is a sad reminder of what happened to this city of promise and hope. I cannot read these words from Lamentations over Jerusalem without my own lament for so many cities in the world today. They experience their own special devastation, and they are in need of my prayerful action.

Suggestion for meditation: **Focus on those who must struggle to survive living in large cities. Think of ways you can be an advocate for them.**

Prayer: **Dear Lord, we pray this day for cities. May they again be places of hope and promise. Amen.**

Wednesday, September 30   Read Psalm 137:1-3.

*By the rivers of Babylon—there we sat down and there
we wept when we remembered Zion.*

Sometimes all we can do is weep. While I grew up in an era
that socialized males for the most part to avoid tears, I did
observe men who unashamedly wept.

There is a time in the course of difficult and painful circumstances to determine how to move on from the place of hurt or
disappointment. One cannot forever remain in a posture of
defeatism or sorrow. People of faith are also people of hope.

But there are times when one must first weep. The pain is
great, the loss so unbearable, the destruction so total, that all the
stuff of human emotions collapses. There are no words adequate
for the moment, and reason fails. Even when you know in your
heart some tomorrow will be better, today you must weep.

One weeps over a child or spouse, a nation or a city, a friend
or a colleague; some even weep over the church. Sometimes we
weep from homesickness—we long to be in another place. Good
times and people are remembered—loved ones, happy events,
holy moments.

Soldiers in a far-off land, a college student only miles from
home, or a relocated or resettled group who may never return to
the place called "home," remember and weep.

Who cannot identify with the psalmist weeping for Zion?

Sometimes all you can do is weep!

Suggestion for meditation: **Remember the last time you wept.
What made you cry? Were they tears of joy or of sadness?**

Prayer: **Thank you, Lord, for the healing of tears. Amen.**

Thursday, October 1   Read Psalm 137:4-9.

How could we sing the Lord's song in a foreign land?

In the wake of Jerusalem's defeat by Babylon, the psalmist seems to voice the dismay of exiles who are haunted by another day and another time. It is a Jerusalem alive with the sounds, aromas, and the songs of a determined people.

Now in a foreign land, humiliated and defeated, how does a faithful people remain faithful? It would almost seem a desecration to observe rituals of holiness and to sing hymns of joy and praise in a place thought to be the antithesis of the sacred.

How does one sing in an unfamiliar, even a hostile, environment? Indeed, a greater temptation is to become accommodated to a foreign place, seduced by it, forgetting one's native place—even its songs. It remains a challenge to stay alert and faithful when all around us speaks doom, failure, and defeat.

There are exiles today. Sadly, wars and civil conflict have forced people to be exiled sometimes in their own land. Others are blessed to be welcomed to lands of safe haven.

There is yet another exile: when changing values, mores, and conditions in one's own land turn a once-familiar and beloved place into something quite unfamiliar. It is when home no longer looks or feels like home. Some are strangers—exiles—in their own homes.

How does the Christian sing in the midst of suffering and pain, hostility and oppression? With confidence! With confidence!

Suggestion for meditation: **Try to imagine what it would be like to be taken from your home. In what ways would you stay close to God in such an exiled condition?**

Prayer: **O Lord, in the midst of suffering and pain, give us your song. Amen.**

Friday, October 2   Read 2 Timothy 1:1-7.

Today's scripture recalls one of the more moving and meaningful relationships in the New Testament—that of the apostle Paul and his young "beloved child" in the faith, Timothy.

The opening verses inform the reader of Timothy's deep Christian roots. He is a third-generation Christian. Paul reminds Timothy of the faithful witness evidenced in his (Timothy's) grandmother Lois, and his mother, Eunice.

There is talk in many circles about roots—genealogy—and the importance of racial-ethnic identity. While important, they may describe more physical identity than character or spiritual formation.

When Paul reminds young Timothy of his roots, he is pointing to a faith identity. It is important because Paul is attempting to prepare Timothy for the struggles and challenges of ministry. The counsel to Timothy is that he should remember how he has been nurtured in the household of faith.

One is blessed indeed, to be a part of a nurturing, faithful household, one that seeks to build emotional and spiritual fortitude for life's journey. Not all households are such nurturing places.

To learn of God so early in life that one cannot recall a time when there was no knowledge of God is a gift. To witness faithful living by parents and family is a blessing.

Suggestion for meditation: **Remember those in your family who have nurtured you in your faith. Have you passed their nurturing on to the "beloved" children of your life?**

Prayer: **Thank you, Lord, for loving, faithful Christian households, where the young learn of you by word and example. Amen.**

Saturday, October 3   Read 2 Timothy 1:8-14.

Today we come to the heart of Paul's message to Timothy. Having reminded Timothy of his godly heritage, as well as the challenges to be faced as a Christian in the midst of hostile circumstances, Paul's counsel is clear: Do not be ashamed of the Lord and the good news, even when to speak out could mean ridicule, persecution, imprisonment, even death.

In the face of competing philosophies and religious teachings, Timothy is to maintain the "standard of sound teaching" learned from Paul and his mother and grandmother. What Timothy has learned, observed, and experienced is the gospel of Jesus Christ. It is a "good treasure" entrusted to him to handle with care and to share generously.

This word is still a relevant one. Amid many competing ideologies, each claiming to be the truth or a truth, the Christian is still challenged to remember the Word, to test all other claims against the teaching of Christ Jesus. Yet it is in a spirit of love that faith is affirmed and other claims rejected.

To be faithful Christians today may still be difficult in the face of competing values and changing mores. In some places, living out one's faith is a choice of life and death. Paul's counsel to Timothy is also a word for us!

Suggestion for meditation: **What changing values and mores have given you difficulty in maintaining the Christian life? How do you help others deal with such changes?**

Prayer: **O Lord, may we guard the good treasure entrusted to us with the help of the Holy Spirit living in us. Amen.**

Sunday, October 4   Read Lamentations 1:1-6.

Not all suffering and pain is undeserved. What a hard reality! Not all catastrophes are inexplicable.

The writer of Lamentations believes the transgression of Jerusalem is the cause for its predicament: "Jerusalem sinned grievously" (v. 8).

There is a time of sowing and reaping. Actions have consequences. Not even a good God shields forever against poor choices, especially those made in the light of day when consequences are clear.

When we read this lament, we hear a penitent heart. Here is no "victim" mentality; there is an owning of failure, misdeeds, unfaithfulness.

Today we seem to be living in a victimization culture, where failure to accept responsibility for poor choices, riotous living, and irresponsible actions is in vogue. Somehow we found it convenient to blame society, our circumstances, sometimes even our parents.

Lamentations teaches us a lesson here: There are consequences. Ours is not a morally neutral universe. And God is both gracious and just.

There is integrity in holding one's self accountable. With freedom of choice comes responsibility. With confession comes forgiveness.

God is gracious, just, and merciful when we acknowledge our own failings and shortcomings.

Suggestion for meditation: **In what ways have you accepted responsibility for your shortcomings? Think of consequences you have experienced from irresponsible actions.**

Prayer: **O Lord, our God, thank you for your gracious mercy. Give us courage to acknowledge our sin so that we may grow into a people of spiritual integrity. Amen.**

AT HOME WITH GOD

October 5–11, 1998   **Aida Luz Beltrán-Gaetán✤**
Monday, October 5   Read Jeremiah 29:1, 4-7.

The prophet Jeremiah received a message from God for the people of Israel who were exiled in Babylon. The message is a series of directions: to build houses, to plant gardens, to marry with the Babylonians and grow. It adds, "But seek the welfare of the city where I have sent you into exile, and pray to the Lord on its behalf, for in its welfare you will find your welfare." To be an exile is painful, even when a person chooses to leave her or his country voluntarily. A person may leave behind family, friends, community, culture, career, and language. Such uprootedness may cause identity and values crises—much more if it is forced exile due to captivity by an overpowering force.

Yet God's message offers a word of encouragement: In the worst of conditions for life, choose to live. Do not give up on life. Furthermore, intercede for those who wield power over you; contribute to their future, for both your futures are entwined.

Today in cases involving citizens and aliens, we sometimes ignore the one side or the other of Jeremiah's message. The message implied for the Babylonians is this: Those in exile are God's people, sent there within God's design for their future. But the oppressors' future depends upon the aliens' intercession and contribution. Jeremiah's two-faceted message is in character with the living God: It is a two-edged sword that cuts both ways.

Prayer: **Most gracious God, protect us from forced exile. May the aliens among us intercede for us. Enable us to receive the contribution of their gifts among us to embrace life for mutual benefit. We are all yours. In your mercy, hear our prayer. Amen.**

✤Clergy member of the North Georgia Conference of The United Methodist Church; conference missionary to implement the National Plan for Hispanic Ministry.

Tuesday, October 6   Read Luke 17:11-19.

If the lepers stood before Jesus today, Jesus would probably say, "Go to church." Would the lepers follow Jesus' direction? What if we were the lepers? The lepers in Luke's story went in obedience and trust that the one directing them was worthy. Jesus is still worthy, and he invites us to follow his directions in a spirit of obedience, out of love for him.

Why does Jesus make an issue about the forgetfulness of the lepers who did not return? They followed his directions and went on their way to the priests. Why take issue with it?

The Samaritan leper, the foreigner, takes more to heart the relationship with Jesus who has restored to him the gift of life in community. The Samaritan, a foreigner and outcast within the Jewish community, recognizes who Jesus is and presents his offering of gratitude. The Samaritan's first priority is to God; his restoration to community and family is in second place.

In our journey we must remember religious rituals simply guide our desire to deepen our relationship with God, to recognize whose hand or word heals us, and to express our gratitude from our heart. Without this desire, our rituals and our restoration to community become shallow and shaky, an empty ritual void of the vital sign of glorification of God.

Suggestion for meditation: **Pray that the hearts of the ones who go through ritual motions may be grateful. Meditate on the implications of this passage for us as the church in our relationship to those among us who are from other countries.**

Prayer: **Most gracious God, how wonderful you are that you heal us even when we may be outcasts and foreigners. Thank you for restoring us to community and family life through your healing power. We choose to obey you. Assist us. Amen.**

Wednesday, October 7   Read Psalm 66:1-12.

The psalmist calls upon all the earth to praise God. The call comes out of a recognition of God's awesomeness. The psalmist recognizes that everything worships and praises God, that God's doings are extraordinary—changing even the constitution of things: the sea into dry land, for example.

In the midst of the praise, the psalmist includes a relevant remark: "[God's] eyes keep watch on the nations—let the rebellious not exalt themselves." Keeping an eye on someone does not necessarily imply curtailment or censorship. It may simply imply care. But the last phrase puts a different tone on the watching: on rebelliousness and arrogance.

Indeed God loves us and, as the psalmist declares, has brought us out to a spacious place where we may enjoy abundant life. But God will not take our national rebelliousness and arrogance lightly. God will not ignore how we ignore God—the God who created all that is created, even the alien among us. The one so different from us was created by God and may praise God in ways unknown to us. All God's creation, all the earth, gives God glorious praise. All the earth, including its inhabitants, worship and praise God.

After the acknowledgment and the exhortation to praise God, the psalmist declares that God tries us all like silver. Is silver tested to determine if it is silver or not? Could it be that God tests us to discover whether we are truly God's children, born of God, born anew? God comes to us as a stranger, the alien among us. What would Jesus say about our response to the alien? Jesus said, "I was a stranger and you welcomed me" (Matt. 25:35). Fascinating!

Prayer: **Most gracious God, watch over us, all your nations. Let us not be rebellious nor exalt ourselves. May we recognize how awesome all your deeds are. May we enjoy the privilege of passing the silver test and praising you. Amen.**

Thursday, October 8 Read 2 Timothy 2:8-15.

Paul was in prison, but even though he seemed to be defeated and forgotten, he had found something solid, permanent: the word of truth. He had determined not to give that up no matter what his circumstances were. In spite of his situation, he was not going to give up his memory of Jesus Christ, who had risen from the dead to give salvation to all humanity. Jesus the faithful one was with him and within him. Paul was not ashamed.

We well know how Paul (then Saul) persecuted the ones of the Way, which was more than enough reason for him to be ashamed. But once he had an encounter with Jesus, Paul did his best to present himself to God as one approved by Jesus Christ, giving faithful testimony of who Jesus is and of his gospel, rightly explaining the word of truth.

What is the truth? Pontius Pilate asked Jesus as he attempted to judge him. Many are seeking the truth. Some are heartsick because everything seems fake. Nothing is solid, permanent, true. Or so it seems.

What is the truth? Jesus is the truth—the Word of truth. That "word of God is not chained." Neither are those who proclaim it, even if the bars are thick.

Prayer: **Most gracious God, we remember Jesus Christ who is free and who has set us free. Sometimes it seems and feels like nothing is true. Remind us that Jesus is the Word of truth and dwells in us. Amen.**

Friday, October 9   Read Luke 17:11-19.

In an age when medical science has developed in extraordinary ways, and hospitals experience miracles daily, we still have communities invaded with uncontrollable disease. Imagine when leprosy had created outcast communities in society. These persons were deprived of medical help, of family association and care, of social participation, and of hope for the future.

Some lepers had heard about Jesus, who was healing people in the cities. They needed what he had, and when they saw him they asked for what they needed: mercy. They received it on their way to see the priests.

Why would Jesus direct the lepers to the priests? The priest was at the Temple, the place where community was declared. Their priest had the power to declare them restored to the community, to their faith community, to their family, to their rights in society. A healed body and soul without restoration to the community is incongruent.

Jesus Christ, our high priest, has visited us and healed us of our spiritual leprosy through the power of God. We have received mercy, and he has restored us to the community of God's people.

Restoration to community is the miracle that medical science cannot provide, and it is available to us by God's grace. Like the lepers, we have heard the news. We too can call out to him today: "Jesus, Master, have mercy on us!" Everywhere we worship God and become community, we receive the miracle of true wholeness. Though many believe things will not get better, the news that Jesus is in the city healing gives us hope for the future.

Suggestion for meditation: **Pray that the church may become a healing place for the outcasts of society throughout the world.**

Prayer: **Most merciful God, thank you for Jesus' visitation to our diseased communities. Give us compassionate hearts and heal us on our way. Amen.**

Saturday, October 10   Read Jeremiah 29:1, 4-7.

Today's passage begins by saying that Nebuchadnezzar had taken the elders, the priests, the prophets, and others into exile from Jerusalem to Babylon. Yet in verse 4, the Lord claims responsibility for their current situation: "Thus says the Lord of hosts, the God of Israel, to all the exiles whom I have sent into exile...." This claim seems to contradict historical fact, but in Jeremiah's perspective, God controls history. Though people may seem to be in control, God is still the Sovereign One.

Jesus might say it this way: "No one takes [my life] from me, but I lay it down of my own accord" (John 10:18). Historically, humanity makes decisions. Theologically, God works out God's purposes for humanity through history. God has a plan for us in whatever situation we find ourselves and is always working with us for our good. (See Jeremiah 29:11.) No place or circumstance is so hopeless that God cannot redeem it for us. As we view current events, we must remember that God is at work; God has not abdicated God's throne. God's will shall be fulfilled for us and for humanity. With or without us, God's will shall be fulfilled. Hope says we should surely join in!

Suggestion for meditation: **Reflect upon the significance of the present-day exiles among us. What is God up to? What does God expect from us? What would God have us do? How would Jesus expect us to relate to the ones that "Nebuchadnezzar" has brought among us, knowing that it is the Lord who has sent them?**

Prayer: **Help us, God, to see you revealed to us among the exiles. Give us wisdom and courage to respond according to your will. In Jesus' name. Amen.**

Sunday, October 11   Read 2 Timothy 2:8-15.

This passage in Second Timothy brings us to the heart of Paul's gospel: "Remember Jesus Christ." Someone has referred to these words as "the memory that redeems." And certainly upon reflection, these three words bear witness to the gospel we have come to know and affirm: They bring us back to the center from which all Christian faith and life take direction; they remind us that Jesus was God made flesh, not mere abstract thought but revealed in a person in our history. It is this gospel that we affirm and acknowledge when we state, with the author of Second Timothy, that "the word of God is not chained."

God's word is not chained to us or anything. When we remember Jesus Christ, God's word flows freely, bringing freedom to all who will hear it and live by it. We join the early church in their affirmation: "The saying is sure: If we have died with him, we will also live with him; if we endure, we will also reign with him; if we deny him, he will also deny us; if we are faithless, he remains faithful—for he cannot deny himself."

Let us rejoice in God's unchained word that comes to us freely. In the midst of all that life brings, let us remember that by God's word we were created and by God's word in the power of the Holy Spirit all things are recreated. On this day of rest and renewal, let us remember Jesus Christ.

Prayer: **Gracious God, revive within us a desire to know your word, to know the truth, and to follow it. Let us never be ashamed of your word revealed to us through Jesus Christ. Help us recover the power of your word for us today. Amen.**

RESTORING SPIRITUAL PASSION

October 12–18, 1998   **Kathleen Stephens**✤
Monday, October 12   Read Jeremiah 31:33-34.

Tucked in among the seven deadly sins is the unappealing-sounding word *sloth*. More insidious than a tendency to watch a lot of television, sloth is spiritual listlessness, despair, inertia, a lack of desire for God or the good. The current of life constantly pulls us toward that kind of spiritual lethargy, but God never intended that we live like that.

As evidenced in scripture, challenge and risk mark God's activity in a life. Abraham left everything familiar and set out in search of a city "whose architect and builder is God" (Heb. 11:10). Esther put her life on the line to intervene on behalf of her people. Paul exchanged a life of privilege for an insecure, peripatetic existence. Rather than settling for status quo mediocrity, God is always prodding us to live with a from-the-heart kind of passion.

When spiritual passion wanes, we ought first to look at our relationship with God. Spiritual passion doesn't spring from a terrific sermon or a book or a small group. Rather, the source of our passion is in the deep places of our heart where we know God intimately. In this deep place the problem arises; in this deep place we find restoration. Those of us who sense a growing coldness toward the God who created us and sustains us may relish this week's meditations. We will look at ways to recover a spiritual passion that makes our lives not only fruitful but joyful.

Prayer: **God, examine me and illumine any lethargy or boredom that has crept into my work and worship. In your mercy, open my eyes to the truth of the life to which you have called me, so that I can worship and serve you with all my heart. Amen.**

✤Associate editor, *Weavings: A Journal of the Christian Spiritual Life*; Nashville, Tennessee; seminar leader on the Christian spiritual life.

Tuesday, October 13   Read Jeremiah 31:27-34.

Receive the new covenant.

A lover spurned, a covenant broken..."though I was their husband, says the Lord." The people of Israel had made a shambles of God's covenant relationship with them. This same God "took them by the hand to bring them out of the land of Egypt." How could they have known a God so personal and loving as this and then broken the covenant between them? While this may seem inconceivable to us, we make the same choice by opting for shallow pleasures rather than walking with God.

God had every right to reject the people of Israel. God had made a way for them, and they had rebelled against it. Why bother with these rebellious people any more? But God did not destroy the people. What God chose to do takes our breath away—God gave them a second chance.

In response to rebellion, God gave the people of Israel—and us, their spiritual descendants—a new covenant. Rather than giving us what we deserve, God said, "I will be their God, and they shall be my people." This action reveals a God who is always reaching out, reconciling, forgiving, restoring.

Jeremiah indicates that the new covenant provides inward motivation for obeying God and the law. God's breathtaking, restorative love motivates our passion for service. A love that goes to such great lengths to give us another chance creates in us a passionate desire to love and serve God in return.

Prayer: Loving God, you astound me by the lengths to which you go to restore and forgive me. What amazing grace you have heaped upon me! Yet in light of the new covenant, I stand before you and ask with all confidence, "More." Amen.

Wednesday, October 14　　　　Read Psalm 119:97-104.

Fall in love with God's law.

Words have an undeniable power to capture life. A treasured letter read and reread, folded and unfolded until it threatens to come apart bears testimony to that power. The words on that worn page are precious because they somehow unite us with our loved one. In them we vicariously experience that person's character and emotions—the essence of his or her being.

We find God in scripture in much the same way. Mysteriously, through one-dimensional words on a page, we experience God's character, power, and love for us; and we respond to the Person revealed there. Through the word we find relationship. We love God's law because it unites us with our beloved Creator.

In today's reading, the psalmist loves God's law for the richness it brings to his life. He has discovered that meditation on the law brings wisdom, understanding, right living, and pleasure. In it he finds everything needed to understand life and to thrive. But more than these obvious benefits of meditation on God's law, the words evidence a passionate relationship between the psalmist and the living God who can be found between the lines and among the words on the page.

God's law elicits a passionate response in us too because it reveals a God who loves us passionately. "Oh, how I love your law!" we cry with the psalmist, because there we meet our Divine Love.

Prayer: **Open my eyes, loving God, to the riches of your law. Help me see that contained there is everything I need for abundant life. As I meditate on your law, breathe your life into the words on the page and into my life as well. Amen.**

Thursday, October 15   Read Luke 18:1-8.

Keep praying.

A judge ignores the pleas of a poor widow, presumably because he sees no gain in helping her. The widow keeps bothering him until he relents and gives her what she wants. His reason for the change of heart? "So that she may not wear me out by continually coming." Hardly an outpouring of love and concern for the woman.

But beneath this strange little story lies a great lesson on prayer. What is important here is the contrast between the unjust judge and the character of God. If after repeated requests the widow finally gets her audience with the unjust judge, how much more will God hear the requests of God's chosen ones who continually pray to God?

This passage of scripture reminds us that what is important about prayer is to keep at it. Endurance and persistence count when it comes to answered prayer. We need to hear this, because we tend to give up too easily on God. We may pray but when immediate answers are not forthcoming, we assume God is not interested; we lose heart. By expecting too little from God, we miss all that God has in mind for us. As C. S. Lewis points out in *The Weight of Glory*, "Our Lord finds our desires, not too strong, but too weak" in light of the incredible promises of scripture.

Spiritual passion, which gives vitality to our faith, can be ours if we keep praying, never losing heart, never giving up.

Prayer: God of overwhelming generosity, when I'm tempted to believe that you do not care about what concerns me, remind me of the widow who never gave up until her need was met. How much more will you meet my needs. Amen.

Friday, October 16   Read Psalm 119:101-104.

Do the right thing.

I once read a newspaper account of a man who had managed to live to a ripe old age. His longevity was his claim to fame and the reason for the article. He gave the usual advice for those younger than he—don't drink, don't smoke, don't ever try to tell a woman what to do.

But one piece of advice captured my attention. He said, "To the best of my ability, I have lived my life so that I would have no regrets at the end." When I read this article as a young person, that thought profoundly affected me. I purposed to live a life that would cause me no regrets in the end.

The psalmist also determined to live a life of no regrets. He decided to take the narrow path despite its hardships because it led to a greater reward in the end. "I hold back my feet from every evil way," he says, indicating deliberate choice.

Holding to the right paths—doing the right thing—in little ways each day is how we arrive at the end of life with no regrets. Granted, making those kinds of choices over a lifetime is no walk in the park, but it produces a crown of righteousness for those who endure.

Doing what is right—preaching the word, visiting the sick, encouraging the weak, calling to account those who are in sin— even when the emotions are not there will lead to an eternal weight of glory as well as a passionate life here on earth.

Prayer: Lord, when I am faced with choices today, remind me that doing what is right and good always builds upon an eternal foundation. Amen.

Saturday, October 17   Read 2 Timothy 3:14-17.

Recognize what we have.

Paul, the ascribed writer of Second Timothy, is a reliable guide for us as we explore how to restore spiritual passion. His love for God and for the gospel never seemed to flag, even in the most trying situations. Paul writes to encourage believers. He reminds them of the role scripture has played in their faith and then he makes a bold statement: "All scripture is inspired by God and is useful for teaching, for reproof, for correction, and for training in righteousness, so that everyone who belongs to God may be proficient, equipped for every good work." We require nothing else to fulfill the divine call in our lives.

The many learning opportunities available to Christians can easily overwhelm us. New books arrive daily in my office. I shelve them, and they proceed to haunt me. I don't doubt that each contains great ideas, but I'll never have time to read them all.

Most of us want to keep up with new ideas and new resources that can enhance our ministry. But at times that means running at breakneck speed as we read more books, attend more seminars, and study for another degree. However, in our souls remains the gnawing realization that we can never keep pace no matter how fast we run. In the midst of our anxiety, Paul stills us with this reminder that God-breathed scripture is enough to equip us "for every good work."

Spiritual passion doesn't come from some new thought or resource but from holding fast to God's holy word. It equips us for ministry—intellectually, spiritually, practically.

Prayer: God of all, when the desire to stay atop the flood of available information overwhelms me, remind me of this basic truth: Your word is adequate. Amen.

Sunday, October 18   Read 2 Timothy 4:1-5.

Remember that God is with us.

A superficial view of life and ministry creeps into our minds sometimes. We hear it in the little voice that tells us that we are alone and therefore accountable only to ourselves for the way we live out our call. *Why not do whatever seems right in our eyes, what will benefit us? What does it matter? No one will know.*

The writer of Second Timothy probes deeper. No, he says, we are not alone—we live in the presence of God, who observes all and judges and rewards. All of our life is lived under the gaze of God.

What a difference it makes in the way I work, play, worship, and care for others when I am aware of God's eyes upon me. I am more apt to choose right ways when I consciously acknowledge that God sees the good and says, "Well done, good and faithful servant." Conversely, I tend to avoid doing wrong when I am aware that God sees the unkind or selfish things I do, knowing that it brings God sorrow.

The psalmist raises the question, "Where can I flee from your presence?"(Ps. 139:7). The answer is, of course, nowhere. But God's gaze is not intrusive. Rather, it is proof of a divine relationship, an invitation to know and be known by our Creator. And in the knowing, we receive an invitation to change—from glory to glory.

Paul encourages us to live every day *coram Deo*—"before the face of God." Doing so restores in us a spiritual passion that fuels our work, our worship, and our love of one another.

Prayer: O God, your gaze is not an intrusion but a source of rock-ribbed security for me. Let me never forget that wherever I am, you are with me. What comfort that brings me as I live out your call in my life. Amen.

ENCOUNTER WITH GOD

October 19–25, 1998
Monday, October 19

Timothy Jones✤
Read Psalm 65.

A fellow church member once shared a remarkable experience with me. In her apartment living room one Sunday afternoon a sudden awareness overtook her—God simply showed up. She found herself immersed in a cleansing Presence, wrapped in divine power. The God of Christianity she had espoused for years became vivid reality. It was life-shaking, even unsettling, but not terribly surprising.

Our encounters with God happen in different ways; we use varied expressions and we reflect on our experience through the filters of disparate backgrounds. But if we open ourselves to God's presence, we, like the psalmist, find ourselves praying, "Happy are those whom you choose and bring near to live in your courts." The object of theological speculation becomes a personal presence. In our praying and worshiping, something "clicks"; we find ourselves in an encounter charged with grace.

In spiritually hungry and curious times such as we live in now, it is good to know that, as verse 4 tells us, "We shall be satisfied with the goodness of [God's] house." Our times of personal prayer and corporate worship can be rich with a God who becomes wonderfully real.

Today reflect on how your faith can be a matter of heart as well as head, earnest desire as well as careful deliberation. God will eagerly take you to a new place of happiness and profound satisfaction.

Prayer: Lord, let not my faith remain a static or unfeeling thing. Warm my heart and remind me how willingly you draw me to your loving presence. In Jesus' name. Amen.

✤Editor of Special Projects, Upper Room Books; author, retreat leader.

Tuesday, October 20   Read Joel 2:23-27.

Out jogging in undeveloped woodland near my home, I came upon a Caterpillar tractor. It was rolling down a dirt road that led to a construction site. A backhoe shovel jutted from the front like a crab's leg, and the tractor had the metal tread and cogged wheels of a tank. And while the driver pushed the engine at top speed, the tractor only crawled along. Nevertheless, I had a sense of unstoppable momentum. For all the tractor's slowness, nothing, it seemed, would halt its progress.

I was to see just how true that was while out jogging again. This time the tractor perched on the edge of a cavern built for a drainage duct. Beside the tractor was a mountain of dirt. The tractor had done its slow, powerful work.

The people in Joel's time worried about God's slowness: Was God about to help them in their distress? Could they trust God's power? Whatever the historical setting (and we know little about Joel or when he prophesied), the people needed reassurance. "O children of Zion, be glad and rejoice in the Lord your God....The threshing floors shall be full of grain....I will repay you for the years that the swarming locust has eaten." The people needed a reminder, as do we sometimes, that in every circumstance we can trust what someone has called "the slow work of God."

Yes, God's deliverance may take time. But the mighty force of a Cat tractor gives the merest glimpse of the momentum and power that God has set in motion in the world. We can rejoice and be glad in God.

Prayer: **Lord, sometimes I get impatient. Sometimes I forget how surely you work out your purposes in our world, in my life. Please restore my trust. Amen.**

Wednesday, October 21   Read Joel 2:28-32.

A few years ago a friend and I were discussing our experiences in the Christian faith. Despite lifelong involvement, my friend confessed that church sometimes left him bored and empty. "I have been attending and teaching Sunday school classes for years," he admitted, "but I never seem to get anywhere."

A woman I know once shared similar longings in a small group. "During all those years I was growing up in the church," she said, "we talked about God's power. We sang about God's power. But I never experienced God or God's power in a dramatic way."

Joel the prophet deeply believed there could be more to religion than mere form and habit. "I will pour out my Spirit on all flesh," Joel said, speaking for God. "Your sons and daughters shall prophesy, your old men shall dream dreams, and your young men shall see visions." It was to be a grand and glorious time, one the earliest Christians would later believe was vividly fulfilled in their midst. (See Acts 2.)

God is still fulfilling Joel's prophecy. God does not stand back, nor does God confine God's workings to a narrow strip of first-century Palestinian geography. God can make a glorious difference when our Christian life grows stale.

The great Methodist missionary E. Stanley Jones once wrote about a minister who passed a church with an intriguing slogan on its notice board: "Jesus Christ is in this place. Anything can happen here." The minister went in, knelt at the altar, and surrendered his frustration and emptiness. "Jesus Christ was in that place and met him," Jones wrote. "He went out of there a new [person]."

So can we.

Prayer: **Lord, help me to experience the glorious, life-giving power of your Spirit. Amen.**

Thursday, October 22   Read Luke 18:9-14.

A junk mail offer crossed my desk; I found it amusing. It touted a book entitled *How to Do Everything Right.* The promotional included sample tips from the book to whet your appetite—tips like "How to get off the phone fast without offending the long-winded party on the other end." Especially amusing was the caption about the book: "421 inside ways to live better, smarter, longer, safer—and richer—in uncertain times when you need to be an expert on everything."

Sometimes, in matters of faith, we feel the pressure to be experts. Sometimes the church conveys a subtle message that everything must be done "just so." Our standing with God becomes our goal, our achievement, our "project."

But Jesus offers another view in his story about the Pharisee and the tax collector. Here the point is not rightness but humble dependence. One had done everything "right"; the other had failed miserably. But strange news! All the display, all the veneer of religiosity, all the right-sounding eloquence of the Pharisee's prayer was prattle. And the downcast mumbling of the tax collector was music in the ears of God.

God cherished the tax collector not because of any spiritual expertise but because of his honesty. The man looked at himself with a stark realism that drove him into the merciful arms of God.

We in the church, Pharisee and marginal member alike, need to rely on grace. We need God's gift of grace, perhaps most of all when we feel good about ourselves or feel that we manage to do everything right.

***Prayer:* Lord, help me, like the tax collector, to turn to you saying, "God, be merciful to me, a sinner." Help me rely on your goodness and grace, knowing that I need only your forgiving touch. Amen.**

Friday, October 23   Read Luke 18:9-14.

"When I finally got past my pride at being a good church member and upstanding citizen," confessed one middle-aged woman, "I could finally experience grace for the first time."

The Pharisee in Jesus' parable needed a similar breakthrough, which is not to say you might not have liked him had you gone to synagogue with him. To many contemporary people's surprise, the Pharisees were not joyless legalists. They resembled respected church members like you and I perhaps more than we would like to acknowledge. But under the veneer of immaculate attention to detail, something was profoundly wrong.

What most condemned the Pharisee in this parable was not his religion but his pride. What made him turn his nose up at Jesus was less his theology than the condition of his heart. His confidence in his goodness made him impervious to grace. His reliance on an impeccable spiritual pedigree and prodigious achievement allowed him to impress others and himself—but not God.

On the other hand, all the tax collector had to commend him was what the psalmist called "a broken and contrite heart" (Ps. 51:17). But that was enough—indeed, far better.

Think about your own attitude toward your faith and church participation. Is it a source of pride? Does it insulate you from confronting your radical need for grace? Does it make you think Christ did not really need to live and die for the likes of you?

Try today to think of God's loving mercy, not your goodness or accomplishments.

Suggestion for meditation: **Reflect on places in your life that need God's mercy. Thank God for God's forgiveness.**

Saturday, October 24   Read 2 Timothy 4:6-8, 16-18.

I found the story almost unbelievable, but a newspaper reported that for eight years a woman tended the dead corpse of her husband as though he were still alive. While it was obvious that the man had been dead for years, the sheriff of the town explained, "The family sincerely thought he was fine, the way he was being treated." They even changed his bedding and clothing, and while the body's skin had dried leathery and tough, the woman managed to convince her teenage children that their father was alive.

Part of us would like to cling to the past too, instead of seizing the present and turning toward tomorrow. But in today's reading we see another way. Paul, the apostle and ascribed writer of Second Timothy, knew that he could not hold on forever to what had been. Despite his rich ministry, Paul saw no point in hanging on to yesterday's glories. Even while sensing his imminent death, he wrote, "I have finished the race....From now on there is reserved for me the crown of righteousness."

Paul celebrated what had happened to him and through him. But that did not stop him from embracing what God still had in store with joyous and wild anticipation. He knew God's future was too wonderful not to greet it gladly.

Prayer: Lord, remind me that no matter how good things have been—in my life, my family's, or my church's—the best is yet to come, because you are constantly at work. Amen.

Sunday, October 25   Read 2 Timothy 4:6-8, 16-18.

As Minister of Christian Education at our church, my wife writes a monthly newsletter for teachers. In one issue she inadvertently subtitled an article, "Never estimate what God is willing to do through you." Of course, she meant to say *underestimate*. But the more she thought about it, the more she realized it wasn't such a big mistake. Whenever we try to predict how God will use us, we are likely to miss the big picture. "This week," she wrote in the next newsletter, "don't even bother to estimate. Tell God you're available for use whenever, however, whatever."

Paul seemed to share the same philosophy. While in 4:16-18 Paul feels compelled to defend his ministry in a specific controversy, he offers us a striking glimpse of how God used and guided him. The Lord stood by Paul and strengthened him, we read. God enabled Paul to preach to the Gentiles with power and conviction. God even rescued Paul from the "lion's mouth."

Paul learned the futility of putting boundaries on how God would work. And ultimately, Paul concluded, "From now on there is reserved for me the crown of righteousness, which the Lord, the righteous judge, will give me on that day, and not only to me but also to all who have longed for his appearing."

So live boldly! Serve without reservation. And know that God will guide and protect you. In the end, the reward will surpass anything you or I could imagine.

Prayer: **Lord, keep me from forgetting how great you are and how willing you are to enlist me in your great purposes. Amen.**

THE ETERNAL WHY

October 26—November 1, 1998
Monday, October 26

Martin E. Marty✤
Read Habbakuk 1:1-4; 2:1-4.

Habbakuk is one of those tiny overlookable books tucked in toward the end of the Hebrew Scriptures. But this minor prophet speaks to moderns in an especially clear voice. His cry matches our own when we are in agony or bewildered. One commentary on Habbakuk was called *The Eternal Why*, for good reason. Through the ages people have asked and they will continue to ask "Why?"

Why must the righteous suffer? Why does a good God not come immediately to help those who believe—and help them unmistakably? One glance at this morning's paper will lead readers to identify with the prophet: Why, he asks and we ask, must we see so many accounts of injustice and wrongdoing and see them go unpunished?

Shouting about injustice or whining about our culture are ineffective strategies for dealing with evil. The prophet has a better idea, an idea full of resolve: "I shall stand at my post" (2:1, REB) and be alert to the signals from God. One comes. It consists of the promise of a vision "for the appointed time" (2:3, REB). This vision inspires the righteous to "live by being faithful" (2:4, REB). Picture this day as one in which we, at our posts, live faithfully—and begin to get a vision of God's answers to our "Why?" question.

Prayer: **Faithful God, stand by us at our posts today. Amen.**

✤Teacher at The University of Chicago, senior editor at *The Christian Century*, and author of numerous books on Christian themes.

Tuesday, October 27   Read Psalm 119:137-144.

Three pages into the psalm that is so long that readers begin to let their minds wander, comes a wake-up call, a set of verses that help refocus the mind. The words startle; they can provide a framework for the day's dealings.

Believers like it because so much of it could work for their own autobiographies. "Though I am overtaken by trouble and anxiety. . . ." (v. 143, REB) That speaks to us. Even on good days, there are enough perplexities and disappointments to cause us to cry out. On bad days we are left with nothing but a cry—but, says this psalm, also with a God to whom we can direct that cry with the promise of a hearing.

Not immediately, however. There is more autobiography: "I am speechless with indignation" when enemies neglect God. "I may be despised and of little account" might read like a diary page of most of us ordinary people. The psalmist gets all the anxieties and complaints laid out on the table—and then finds more important things on that table.

More important? Yes, they come when believers get lifted out of themselves and learn to see God as central in life. This God is pictured as "just" and as the author of a law and an exemplar of a love that is "steadfast."

Days like today and tomorrow can take different shapes. They can be threatening or deadening if the believer, in half-belief, concentrates only on the injustice around and the anxieties within. They can be life-giving if the same believer, in a more vivid expression of faith, concentrates on the character of God who—this psalm reminds us—makes justice and "delight" available now and on all days.

Prayer: **Let your promises, O God, give the shape of delight to our days. Amen.**

Wednesday, October 28   Read 2 Thessalonians 1:1-4, 11-12.

The computers and chroniclers tell us that more Christians are being persecuted and martyred these years than they ever were before—even when, as the old stories have it, they were being tossed to the lions. But most of us are remote from what an ancient church letter calls "the persecutions and troubles you endure" (v. 4, REB).

Fortunately for most of us, however, the writer of the letter talks about "troubles" that have been endured and, we must surmise, are to be coped with even now. Troubles can come in the form of confusion or setback. They may have to do with separation and alienation, with loss and mourning. Hearts break. Where then is God?

For biblical writers, the address to trouble is faith. Paul, the ascribed writer of the letter, knows that some growth in faith has begun in those who will receive this letter. But one does not leave weak faith alone. Left alone, weak faith does not prosper. Paul bursts out with a "thanks" to God because "your faith keeps on increasing and the love you all have...grows ever greater" (v. 3, REB). And the believers are steadfast, as we get to be, where faith rules.

How did Paul know this about everyone in the community to which he wrote? A Thessalonica phone book might have spelled out their names, but what did he know about each? What could a proclaimer of faith know about each of us? One thing: that if we in faith are part of the company of those who respond in thanks, "the name of our Lord Jesus" will be glorified in us, and grace will spill into all corners of our lives.

Prayer: **O God, grace us with the faith that helps us move beyond troubles into a life of love. Amen.**

Thursday, October 29   Read Luke 19:1-10.

In today's world, a forklift or a cherry picker would have solved matters for a short man named Zacchaeus. He wanted to see Jesus, but the crowd was too massive and towering. So he did what all other agile parade-goers might do: He climbed a tree. Voila!

The encounter is only half over. Zacchaeus is still only a voyeur, a gazer at celebrities. There would be no point in zooming in on his portrait and setting it before busy moderns. Odds are good that the story was told and preserved for people of all heights and all ages, in all ages, so they would themselves draw closer to Jesus and recognize the presence of God.

Zacchaeus wants "to see what Jesus [looks] like" (v. 3, REB). But Jesus sees him and invites himself to the home of the most hated man in town. Jesus says he must come to the house of the sinner, and does. Let the other townsfolk grumble at the favor Jesus shows their despised neighbor. Only one thing matters now: the status of Zacchaeus's soul.

In the course of things, Zacchaeus does what many of us do. Drawn to Jesus, he gets drawn to others and offers to give goods to them. Jesus acts as if he does not notice that repentant response. His mind is on what is really happening: He sees Zacchaeus being adopted into the company of the people of God.

Where we perk up today is at the end, where Jesus says that as Son of Man he has come to "seek and to save what is lost." Lost often enough to care, we usually concentrate on God's *saving*. Today we will not overlook the other verb: God's *seeking*. Seeking us is what God is about today.

Prayer: **May your seeking go well today, O God; here am I, looking up from my troubles and down from my tree, to welcome you. Amen.**

Friday, October 30   Read Ephesians 1:11-23.

Our outward eyes look out. Fair enough. We are gifted with vision to see what surrounds us. But the writer of a letter to the Ephesians does a twist on the concept of seeing and speaks of our inward eye: "I pray that your inward eye may be enlightened, so that you may know what is the hope to which [God] calls you" (v. 18, REB).

Once the inward eye gets enlightened, it sees what ordinarily gets overlooked. The author can hardly contain himself as he spells out what comes along with the "wisdom and vision" that the Holy Spirit brings with that enlightened eye. Let him pile it on, and let us realize all this and put the benefits to work on a day that might be cloudy and gray—either outwardly in the weather around us or inwardly, in the soul, where the climate really matters.

Here goes: We henceforth get to know "how rich and glorious is the share [God] offers...among his people" (v. 18, REB). Try this for an elaboration, and see what it can do for us: "How vast are the resources of [God's] power open to us who have faith" (v. 19, REB). By the end of the chapter we read about how the glory of the risen Jesus is "filling the universe in all its parts." No place is left where he will not be.

And all these resources get backed up for us when we look at the record of what God has done in Christ. Christ "raised from the dead" is pictured as now being above and beyond all the earthly powers that would dominate us. Call that liberation theology: It certainly announces our freedom-in-faith. If only we turn the inward, liberated eye on it.

Prayer: **God of liberating love, help me overcome the astigmatism and myopia that cloud my vision of you and your promises. Amen.**

Saturday, October 31   Read Daniel 7:1-3, 15-18.

Each day these pages begin with a command. Today, simply: "Read Daniel 7." If it said "Read Cicero," or Shakespeare or Tom Clancy, we might do so for education or amusement. But this command or counsel is designed to help draw us closer to God.

Some days the appeal to read is followed by a text that speaks directly. Today is not one of those days. The world of the Bible and the world of everyday life are far apart when we crack obscure dream-filled books like Daniel. Daniel in the lion's den? Fine. Daniel the dreamer? Those who use puzzling biblical books to spin out their theories about the end of history ponder it. Most of us skip it.

Today Daniel gets another chance, this time to spell out a feature of his vision. He is "troubled" and "dismayed." The details of what he heard when he dreamed his question do not concern us here. Let the line-for-line scholars ponder it. For the busy, there is a bottom line: God is in control of history. Let the kingdoms of the earth gain power and think they can hold it. "The holy ones of the Most High," the people then being persecuted, and all the "holy ones" ever after among whom God dwells will be the ones who will receive the power and get to retain possession of it "for ever and ever."

Perhaps the holy ones can fulfill some of God's purposes if they grasp just enough power for each day, any day, such as this day: a power to love.

Prayer: **Empower me, O God, to take courage and face what troubles might stand in my path—and yours—today. Amen.**

All Saints Day

Sunday, November 1   Read Luke 6:20-31.

You won't find the word in ordinary dictionaries, but the big antique ones like the Oxford say that *macarism* is rare. It means simply "beatitude" and comes from the Greek word *makarios*, which means "blessed." Read on and you will see that you can macarize someone, which is what the Jesus of this Gospel is here doing for the reader who believes: "to call [someone] happy or blessed."

In Catholicism, to be named "blessed" or to be beatified is halfway to being named a "saint." But this All Saints Day we can take a shortcut and see that in the eyes of Jesus, all who hear in faith are the saints. Being blessed by God through Jesus is enough.

The fact that most of us know some beatitudes or macarisms from memory might lead us to mishear them, to fail to note their staggering claims and powers. So rich are the blessings to those "in need"—we like that; or who "go hungry"—it's spiritual mealtime!; or "who weep"—which too often is ourselves; that we overlook what goes with the blessings. Read on: There is also a command to love, including to love and bless the enemies. Some of them will be on our figurative mounts and plains, waiting for our acts of love.

Many scholars have pondered the idea of being commanded to love. Must not love be free, uncoerced, and spontaneous? The more we read the scripture the clearer it gets: For people of faith the word is not so much "you've got to love" as "you get to love," thanks to a power given us.

Prayer: **God of love, I ask you to "macarize" me, to bless me, thereby empowering me to get to love those I consider saints and those who are enemies. Amen.**

319

WHAT DOES THE FUTURE HOLD?

November 2–8, 1998
Monday, November 2

John O. Gooch ✤
Read Haggai 1:15*b*–2:9.

Upon their return to Jerusalem and their homeland, the exiles did not rebuild the Temple first. First came homes, then shops and workshops. Those are all important, says the prophet, but they aren't the full story of the future. The first chapter of Haggai warns that drought, crop failure, inflation, and low wages are more than leading economic indicators: They are signs of God's displeasure. The people live in houses, but the Lord does not. Disobedience and neglect of worship have consequences in the real world of economic time and space. The primary problem is not just trying to get an economy back on its feet; the primary problem is that the people have neglected the worship of Yahweh.

In today's text we hear, even as the rebuilding of the Temple has begun, the word that the future is in God's hands. Perhaps the most comforting word any of God's people could ever hear is, "Take courage...for I am with you, says the Lord." Keep on working, because I am with you. God has kept the covenant God made with the people when he brought them out of Egypt.

That's the key to the future—the faithfulness of God in past and present. We have trusted God in the past. We trust God in the present. We can trust God with the future. And knowing that we can trust God with our ultimate future means we can trust God with the future that lies just beyond the edge of this page, when we put the book down and begin our daily tasks.

Prayer: **O God of past, present, and future, help me trust in you and not be afraid. Amen.**

✤United Methodist minister, writer, consultant/trainer, and youth minister; Nashville, Tennessee.

Tuesday, November 3   Read Haggai 1:15*b*-2:9.

The Lord instructs Haggai to find some people who had seen Solomon's Temple and invite them to compare it to the Temple being rebuilt now before them. The response: It looked like nothing to them. It had none of the richness and splendor of Solomon's Temple.

Then the prophet says, "Take courage." You're grieving over the way the Temple looks? Take courage! Remember, I am the Lord, who brought you out of Egypt. My spirit is among you—don't be afraid.

At the crucial point of decision making in any building campaign, some fear the future. They are unsure that what they want to do can be done. And at the same crucial point, we find those who say, "We need to have faith, now more than ever. Let's not be afraid of the future." Those same two spirits do battle at every crucial decision-making point in the life of the church—and in our personal lives. What does the future hold? Should we be afraid? Should we go forward?

God promises that the future will be better. In just a little while, God will shake the heavens and the earth and all the nations, so that the treasure of all the nations will come to Jerusalem and the splendor of the new Temple will be even greater than the first Temple. What a powerful image—God's shaking the nations, turning them upside down, so their treasures fall out of their pockets and rain down on Jerusalem!

Is it too much to say that when we trust God for the future, God gives us an even brighter future than we had imagined?

Prayer: **Lord, I don't want to be cocky about the future, but I do believe that you are in the future, calling us to come to you. I believe that you will bless my future if I trust you with it. Help me to live what I say. Amen.**

Wednesday, November 4   Read Psalm 145:1-5, 17-21.

One of the all-time greatest scenes in American musicals is that magical dance of Gene Kelly in *Singin' in the Rain*. Gene is out on the street in a downpour, dancing in deep puddles, getting soaked to the skin—and totally oblivious to the whole thing. He has just discovered he's in love, and that is more important than anything else in the world.

The psalmist says that's what life is like for those who live in God's kingdom. We live in this world—in the midst of downpours—focused on the overwhelming love of God for us. And we dance for joy.

Christians affirm that the fundamental reality in the world is the caring and compassionate love of God. And God's love looks on the world with different eyes from the world's. In God's kingdom, the poor, the people who are beaten down by society, who don't "fit in," are lifted up. The hungry are fed, because God is a God who satisfies the desires of all. God is just; that is, God treats persons fairly according to God's standards.

Our experience of life in the world reflects the unfairness of people with power and wealth who take advantage of people without power and wealth. Life in God's kingdom carries its own sense of inequity because God treats the poor and powerless and outcast the same way God treats the rich and powerful.

Praise is often about what the future holds. We join all creation in giving thanks that God's power shows itself in grace, compassion, love, and faithfulness in the midst of life's inequities and pouring rain. Remembering God's overwhelming love, we dance!

Prayer: **Lord of the future, help me live in hope and openness toward the future. Amen.**

Thursday, November 5   Read 2 Thessalonians 2:1-5.

The year 2000 offers several very different visions of the future. One vision that haunts us takes place in the computer world: Our apocalyptic nightmare is that computers will go berserk and charge us for ninety-nine years of back taxes. The religious world generates another vision: People begin to think about Jesus' return and the end of the world. With those two visions in mind, we can begin to appreciate Paul's problem with one of his churches.

People in the church at Thessalonica were upset. They were afraid the day of the Lord had come (that Jesus had returned), and they had missed it. This was not a light matter. The words "shaken in mind and alarmed" imply a state of great agitation, so much so that the people are actually mentally unstable. Paul has to deal with this agitation, while helping the church understand the real truth about the coming of the Lord. It's apparently unclear, even to Paul, how the problem started. He mentions several possible ways the word could have come. But he is clear about the solution: The day will not come without the "lawless one" (v. 8) preceding it.

Paul says that at this point the future looks bleak. The "lawless one" is yet to come, and his coming can only mean bad things. But all that is still in the future; it's foolish to panic in the present. Trust God for both the future and the present.

How often we worry about things over which we have no control—indeed, that have not even happened yet. Some of them are apocalyptic, computer-breakdown, worries. Some are more ordinary, everyday kinds of worries. Paul reminds us, in the midst of our worries, that the future is in God's hands.

Prayer: **Help me give over my worries to your faithful control, O God. Help me leave the future in your hands, where it and I will be safe. Amen.**

Friday, November 6   Read 2 Thessalonians 2:13-17.

The future holds glory and sanctification! You are the "first fruits for salvation," Paul says. "First fruits" is a reminder of the Jewish festival where the Israelites offered the first of the harvest in the Temple as a sign that all the harvest belonged to God and was a gift from God.

What does it mean to be "first fruits for salvation"? It's like saying, God has saved you through Jesus Christ and will save others through you. It's like all the glorious promises of the service of the Baptismal Covenant, where we affirm that a person being baptized is "initiated into Christ's holy church ....incorporated into God's mighty acts of salvation and given new birth through water and the Spirit" (*The United Methodist Hymnal*, 33). We can't see it or touch it, but the promise is from God, so we believe it and trust that it will come to fullness in the future. That is God's gift!

We are "first fruits for salvation through sanctification by the Spirit and through belief in the truth." We have been saved by God's act in Jesus Christ. We are being saved as we believe the truth about Christ and live it out every day. We are being saved and will be saved as the Spirit works in us to sanctify us. In the New Testament and the early church, sanctification did not mean moral perfection. It meant completion, wholeness, fulfillment of God's intentions for us. So the saying, "Be patient. God isn't finished with me yet" is a true one. The Spirit is still working in us to bring us to the fullness of who we are as children of God. No wonder the future holds glory!

Prayer: **God, I know you aren't finished with me yet. Grant that your Spirit might continue to work in me to bring me to the fullness of your love and plan for me. In and through Jesus Christ, who lives and reigns with you and the Holy Spirit, world without end. Amen.**

Saturday, November 7   Read Luke 20:27-38.

The ultimate question about the future, of course, is "If mortals die, will they live again?" (Job 14:14). Many of us agonize over that ultimate question, both for ourselves and for our loved ones.

There was a time when Israel did not believe in resurrection. Our text states that the Sadducees supported that conviction. They believed that one lived on in one's descendants. Therefore, if a man died without children, Torah said that his brother was obligated to marry the widow and have children by her to perpetuate the dead man's name. The Sadducees' question assumes this ancient practice. To point up the moral muddle of resurrection with its untenable quality, they don't ask, "What happens to the family name?" but "Whose wife will the woman be?"

Much as we'd like to, we can hardly scoff at the Sadducees. After all, church history is full of long, passionate, debates on issues just about that important and filled with arguments that make just about as much sense. So it might pay us to look carefully at Jesus' answer to the question.

First, Jesus says in effect, "You've asked the wrong question. The life of the age to come radically differs from this life." Then he responds in this fashion, "Here's the right question: Are the dead raised?" And the answer to that question is, "Yes."

Now that does not answer a lot of our questions about heaven, but it deals with the most important ones: Is there life after death? What is the ultimate future like? The ultimate future is about a living relationship with a living God.

Prayer: **Hope of the world, thank you for the promise of resurrection and life with you. Help me live this day in the presence of your eternal Spirit. Amen.**

Sunday, November 8   Read Luke 20:27-38.

The future so far transcends anything we can imagine that speculation about the life of the world to come cannot begin to touch its reality. That seems to be the point Jesus is making with the Sadducees.

It is still legitimate to ask about the nature of the resurrection, however. I remember as a boy of twelve, finding great comfort in the thought that, in heaven, I would be reunited with my grandmothers, who had died when I was nine and ten. I still believe that. A similar hope sustains each of us. We don't often breathe the rarified air of abstract thought—we cling to hopes that we can understand.

As a husband of some thirty-eight years, I hope that relationship will continue beyond death; Jesus' statement that we will neither marry nor be given in marriage in heaven makes me uncomfortable. On the other hand, I can imagine that persons who have lived in abusive marriages would breathe a sigh of relief at the statement. So how do we handle this scripture? What about relationships in heaven?

The most comforting word is that the resurrection—and the reality of relationships in the resurrection—is in God's hands, and we can trust God with them. Given that, I still find it hard to imagine that meaningful, loving, and nurturing relationships in this life will somehow cease to exist in the life of the world to come. I've given up the idea of quizzing Paul on some of the obscure passages in his letters (that now seems a bit presumptuous), but I still anticipate renewing relationships with my grandmothers—and my parents and friends and all those other relationships that have enriched my life.

Prayer: **God of the living and of the resurrection, we live in hope that relationships with you and with our loved ones will continue. Sustain us in that hope, we pray. Amen.**

November 9–15, 1998
Monday, November 9

Ben Campbell Johnson❖
Read Isaiah 65:17-25.

A new earth vision

"I am about to create new heavens and a new earth; the former things shall not be remembered or come to mind."

There are moments in history when we need a new vision, a new earth vision. The old vision has failed or run its course or been corrupted, and the people of God need a new vision for themselves and their world.

Imagine the mixture of pain and distress that gave birth to this prophecy of new heavens and a new earth. Exiled in a strange land, persecuted and alienated from neighbors, an oppressed minority lived in a state of fear and hopelessness—not too unlike many oppressed persons today.

Yet out of this mixture of dread and powerlessness, a prophet arises with a vision, a vision of a new way of being on the earth. The prophet sees a world in which babies do not die, old men and women are not robbed of health, houses are not confiscated, and fruit orchards provide for the planters and tillers. The new earth vision promotes life as we imagine it ought to be.

Do we not need such a vision today? I believe God stands ready to inspire another prophet with the vision of an alternative world, if she or he will but listen! What power resides in a vision. Like a star, it draws us into the future; it guides us on our way; and it pictures the goal worth living and dying for.

Prayer: Dear God, slow me down so that the wind of activity does not blow away the seed of vision. Amen.

❖Professor of Christian Spirituality at Columbia Theological Seminary; Decatur, Georgia; Presbyterian Church (USA).

Tuesday, November 10   Read Isaiah 12.

Dealing with distress

"You will say in that day: 'I will give thanks to you, O
Lord, for though you were angry with me, your anger
turned away, and you comforted me.'"

What does a disciple do when the face of God has turned
away? How does the servant of God deal with the sense of
aloneness, lostness, and thick darkness?

I believe the prophet Isaiah was dealing with this issue in his
own life when he recognized God's anger and a feeling of
abandonment. In that moment he experienced the pain we feel
when we are left on our own to do a ministry beyond our ability
unaided by God.

What is going on, we wonder? *Is God angry with me? Am I
experiencing the chastening rod of the Father? Is this my cross to
bear? Why should this come at this time in my life?* These and a
thousand other questions plague us when we grope around in
darkness searching for a glimpse of the face of God.

What are we to do? The prophet says he will give thanks to
the Lord. How can we be thankful for pain? for darkness? for
distance between us and God? Did you ever notice how much
more often you think about God when you hurt? After being
asked to do a life-review, one minister in the seminar asked,
"When am I ever going to finish wading around in the muck of
my life?" "When you can be thankful!" came the reply.

Strange but true, the muck of our lives provides the fertile
ground from which ministry grows! In the muck we trace the
image of grace. Give thanks for the pain, for the darkness, and
for the confusion of life. God is there with you.

**Prayer: O God, when I am tempted to ask "Why," give me the
courage to say, "Thanks!" Amen.**

Wednesday, November 11   Read 2 Thessalonians 3:6-9.

Imitating the saint

> "For you yourselves know how you ought to imitate us; we were not idle when we were with you....This was not because we do not have that right, but in order to give you an example to imitate."

Learning to be Christian requires seeing, looking, watching and imitating. How bold of this writer to invite young believers to "imitate" him. This gesture reveals either a runaway egotism or the self-conscious confession that Christ motivates his behavior.

If the spirit of Christ drives his behavior, the writer can risk inviting other disciples to imitate him. Perhaps he knew long before our day that "Christianity is better caught than taught." Yet it is a lesson each of us could relearn. To draw closer to Christ, find someone who is closer and spend time with him or her.

When I was a young minister, I copied every great preacher I heard. I thought, *If I can say the words he said, with his tone of voice, with the accents and gestures he uses, then I can be as mature and effective as he.* (In that day the minister was always a "he.")

While we may begin the journey of faith as imitators, there comes a day when we must dare to become our own persons, create our own examples, become models for others. In that shift we become leaders not followers, creators not copiers. Each becomes his or her own version of Christ. In maturity, beyond copying and creating, I believe we come to the place where we simply focus on being the person God created us to be. Our search for authenticity and integrity saves us from both phoniness and vanity.

Prayer: **Christ, the Pattern, help me to be a new example of you without paying too much attention to it! Amen.**

Thursday, November 12   Read 2 Thessalonians 3:10-13.

Overcoming weariness

"Brothers and sisters, do not be weary in doing what is right."

"Serving God is a joy, such a delight!" I have heard people say that. I have said those words and meant them. But sometimes I get weary in the service of the Lord.

When we are serving God in a church that fights over most every issue on the table, or when we are living with a person who never sees any good in us, or when there is hardly enough money to pay the bills at the beginning of the month—we do get weary.

Our weariness may come not from tough situations but from poor health, lack of rest, slack discipline, a work-driven ego, or a false messiahism (that is, we are God's special representative in all things).

On the other hand, sometimes weariness comes from doing what we must: taking a mother with Alzheimer's into our home, adopting interracial children, or caring about homeless persons. Hard tasks can be thrust upon us, leaving us no choice but to obey at a great price.

In our weariness may we listen to the voice of God. Perhaps our weariness speaks moderation or the need to make personal changes to live more effectively in our circumstances. Perhaps our weariness is a catalyst for us to examine our motives to see what is driving us into the ground.

If we listen to God, I wonder what we will hear. Might the Voice say, "There is only one God, and it's not you"?

Prayer: **Dear God, please accept my resignation as general manager of the universe. Amen.**

Friday, November 13   Read Luke 21:5-19.

Enduring to the end

"By your endurance you will gain your souls."

How do you keep on keeping on? For those engaged in ministry, this question has never been more urgent. Whatever the full meaning of Jesus' teaching about the temple, one message is clear to us, "Hold steady; endure to the end!"

I don't know if the birth of a new millennium marks the end of the world, but it does mark the end of an age—an age disrupted by enormous change. In this era of pervasive anxiety, pastors often become the scapegoat for the fears of the congregation. Many ministers are tempted to "cut and run."

In nearly a half century of ministry, I have never seen so many pastors in pain. Many are being bitten, chewed up, and spit out by angry congregations. The ministry of Christ is heavy enough by itself without the added weight of blame from the baptized.

I recently visited a church in which the minister was under heavy attack. During his ten years as pastor, the church has grown each year; the budget is larger than ever; mission giving stands at a record high; old and young are experiencing the transforming power of Christ. About ten percent of the membership is determined to rid themselves of this minister with smear tactics, whispering campaigns, and character assassination. When ministers like this one are persecuted, what does the future hold for the rest of us?

As ministers, let us care for one another; as members of congregations, let us support and encourage our ministers.

Prayer: Dear Christ, help us consider your endurance of the attacks against you so that we can gain new strength for the work that is ours. Amen.

Saturday, November 14   Read Psalm 118.

Living in the present

"This is the day that the Lord has made; let us rejoice and be glad in it."

Dealing with conflict and distress is the "stuff" of ministry; it is the daily bread of service. The two greatest distractions to the life of faith arise from the past and the future: worry about the past, anxiety about the future.

Sometime this past year, this suggestion came to me: "Come to the present! Come out of your past to the present; come back from your imagined future to the present. Be present now to your world, to your life, and to me!" Because this suggestion seemed to be from God, I began trying to live in the reality of the present moment.

One weekend I found myself serving in an unwelcoming situation. The chair of the worship committee had questioned my suggestions about change. I went to lunch with my wife. While waiting to order, I found myself rehearsing what this person was thinking, what he was saying about me and my new ideas—I felt anxious and mildly depressed.

Then, I "came to the present." The person on my mind was not in the room, nor was his criticism. In the present was a loving woman, a waiter, a menu, music, and the choice of food. I came to the present, and all the wild negative imaginations died. Worry evaporated. I learned that God indwells "the present moment" but does not bother to inhabit our excursions into an unreal future.

Join me in this adventure. "Come to the present" and find yourself in the Presence.

Prayer: O God, give me the power to capture my thoughts and imaginations that I may become present to the Presence in the present moment. Amen.

Sunday, November 15   Read Psalm 118.

A thankful life

"O give thanks to the Lord, for he is good; his steadfast love endures forever!"

Some persons seem to sleep through life. These are the Rip Van Winkles who snooze as life goes by; they suddenly awaken to discover that amazing changes have occurred. Others seem to live their whole lives in unawareness, never awakening.

Maxie Dunnam once posed the question from the child's prayer, "If I should wake before I die" (rather than "If I should die before I wake"). What would it mean if we should wake before we die?

If we should wake before we die, we would discover that the old Enlightenment world has died. A new day has dawned for faith. Old certitudes born in the Age of Reason seem shaky today. Believers don't seem so crazy anymore.

Abba Anthony, the first of the desert fathers, predicted the world of the Enlightenment, suggesting that a time was coming when people would go mad and when they saw someone who was not mad, they would attack him or her saying that they were mad; they were not like we. That age has come and is now dying. Wake up to the age of God!

If we should awake, we would begin to see the world as it is— permeated with the presence of God! This awareness would so shock our existential imagination that it would fill our breasts with wonder—the wonder that we are, the wonder that anything is, and the wonder of a beautiful world. And we would wonder at a love so great as to share itself with us.

Wonder like this gives birth to gratitude, and gratitude is the only proper response to the God of all grace.

Prayer: Thanks be to God for all that is—for me, for you, for all things! Amen.

333

CHRIST THE KING

November 16–22, 1998   **Reginald Johnson**✤
Monday, November 16   Read Luke 1:68-79.

What it would be like to spend over nine months unable to communicate through speech to others? Zechariah experienced a God-imposed silence from the moment he asked the angel Gabriel, "How will I know that this is so?" until the day of his new son's circumcision. More than three hundred days of silence would be almost more than some of us could bear. During the time a son was developing in Elizabeth's womb, disbelief was turning into wonder in Zechariah's soul.

What would be the first word out of Zechariah's mouth after three hundred days of silence? *Blessed!* The words tumble out, image upon image, one on top of the other. Each is an evocative picture of what Zechariah realizes God is about to do in human history. We who have been enslaved, God is redeeming. We who have cowered before our enemies, God is delivering. We who are held in the iron grip of hostility, God is setting on the way of peace. We who have lost our way in the darkness, on us the tender mercy of our God, the dawn from on high, is breaking!

Perhaps we need some extra space for silence in God's presence today so we can hold the mystery in our own hearts a little longer and so we can imagine more vividly just what it is that God has done and is doing for us through Jesus Christ.

Suggestion for meditation: **Think about a place in your own life where you are experiencing a healing from hostility or bitterness, a passage out of some fearful darkness or deliverance from an enslaving bondage. Let meditation lead into prayerful gratitude.**

✤Dean of the Chapel and Professor of Spiritual Formation at Asbury Theological Seminary; ordained member of The North Carolina Conference of The United Methodist Church.

Tuesday, November 17   Read Luke 1:68-79.

"By the *tender mercy* of our God, the dawn from on high will break upon us" (italics added). Stay with those words. Trace them with your fingers. Highlight them in your Bible! Zechariah is taking us into the very heart of God. How does God feel toward us? God is full of "tender mercy" (yearning compassion, merciful kindness).

In the original language, the words are striking. The Greek words translated as "tender mercy," actually referred to what the Greeks understood as the "noble viscera": heart, liver, intestines. It is metaphorical language for the inner springs from which our deepest emotions rise. The verb form of the word is the same as that used in the Gospels to characterize Jesus' feelings for the widow whose son was being buried, the people who were like sheep without a shepherd, or his feelings for the crowd which came out in the country to hear him teach—but came without food. Jesus has tenderness for us in our grief, our suffering, and our lostness. Jesus' feelings and actions toward people reveal the way God feels toward you and me.

It is possible for us to be able to explain God's grace to others and yet be filled with disdain for ourselves. We may feel that we don't measure up, or that we are inferior to others whose gifts are so much greater.

Has it yet soaked into the layers of your psyche that God's feeling toward you really is one of tender mercy, merciful kindness, and yearning compassion?

Suggestion for meditation: **Read Luke 1:78 over again and again, personalizing it as you do by inserting your name in place of the word "us" at the end of the sentence. Let the significance of the words sink in as you imagine what they mean.**

Wednesday , November 18   Read Colossians 1:11-14.

Far too often we live as if we were waiting for a "savior" to appear; a savior who will finally liberate us from destructive patterns or habits of addiction or will release us from seemingly hopeless situations in which we feel trapped. The writer of Colossians shakes us awake by showing us the reality in which we now live.

Notice the ringing finality in the words: *rescued, transferred, redeemed.* Imagine the experiences they describe. We are persons whose lives were dominated by a terrible darkness, but a rescue operation has brought us out. We had lived in the grip of a suffocating fear, but we have been ushered into a new realm where we now breathe the fresh air of God's love. We had been enslaved by guilt and shame, but our freedom has been purchased by one whose blood was spilled as payment for our sins and whose death demonstrates our tremendous worth to God. A new reality characterizes our lives now: an intimate relationship with the living, loving God!

"May you be made strong with all the strength that comes from his glorious power." The trials we face do not change the truth about our lives but give fresh opportunity for us to demonstrate how God's living presence in us can enable us to transcend difficult circumstances by being "prepared to endure everything with patience, while joyfully giving thanks to the Father." However bleak things may appear on the outside, we realize that our lives are truly in God's hands so we can now rest, assured that ultimately, all shall be well. Conscious of God, we will find strength for our trials, as have the saints before us.

Suggestion for meditation: **Dwell on the new situation that characterizes your life—a personal relationship with God, opened by Jesus Christ. In the light of this, talk to God in your own words about whatever trials or difficulties you are facing.**

Thursday, November 19   Read Jeremiah 23:1-6.

Leadership is about using our powers to influence outcomes in a certain direction. Each person has such capacities and moves in circles where he or she can exercise leadership. So the question then is not "Am I a leader?" but rather, "What kind of leader am I?"

This passage in Jeremiah has to do with leadership. The prophet lived at a historical juncture when his beloved nation was falling apart, spiritually, morally and politically. His people had suffered at the hands of leaders who destroyed rather than built, who scattered rather than unified, who exploited rather than showed care, and who drove people rather than led them. In the opening verse, Jeremiah sadly announces the leaders' certain doom.

But even when the situation seems most hopeless, Jeremiah realizes that God is not yet finished. The divine plan is threefold: (1) God will act on behalf of the exiles who are broken, fearful, and dismayed. God will gather the scattered home, making their lives fruitful and their land productive once again. (2) Like a sprig of new life appearing from a felled, dead tree, God will raise up a "righteous Branch." This Messiah will "reign as king and deal wisely, and shall execute justice and righteousness in the land." (3) God will raise up good shepherds who will lead with the same goodness and justice that characterize the messiah-king to whom they belong and whose name describes him well: "The Lord is our righteousness."

Reflecting on this passage, perhaps we need to consider the way we use our influence and exert our leadership.

Prayer: **Good Shepherd, who cares so intimately for each of us, fill me with your love so that I might use my opportunities in my circles of influence in harmony with your yearnings, embodying your Spirit. Amen.**

Friday, November 20   Read Luke 23:33-38.

Rubens filled his great painting *The Crucifixion* with activity. A woman stands at the foot of the cross, extending her hands in a futile attempt to restrain a horseman whose spear is gouging into Jesus' side. A comrade of his has drawn his horse nearer, leering at the gory spectacle. But what always strikes me with pathos are the horses. The soldiers' horses are straining, pulling their heads away, refusing to look in the direction of the cross. It is as if they—along with the tiny circle of those closest to the cross who love Jesus most—cannot bear to witness what is happening to their beloved.

Notice the verbs Luke uses to depict the attitudes of those in the scene: The people *stood* by, *watching*; the leaders *scoffed* at him; the soldiers *mocked* him. All have had a hand in the dark turn of events that have led to this tragic moment.

Jesus speaks his first words from the cross: "Father, forgive them; for they do not know what they are doing." In one sense, of course, they knew full well what they were doing. What Jesus means is that since they don't recognize his true identity, they have no idea what is actually taking place—the sinister nature of this moment and the magnitude of their actions.

Here is the scene: There are those who understand but can't bear to look; there are others who don't have a clue but who are determined that they won't miss a moment of this sordid hour. But there is also a third (and invisible) group—we who sit on this side of the event but who are no longer moved by the scene because we fail to perceive either the repulsiveness of our sins that necessitated a savior or the depth of Christ's love, which led him to give his life for us.

Suggestion for meditation: **Choose a hymn with the theme of Jesus' death on the cross. Singing or reading softly, let the words of the hymn become your prayer.**

Saturday, November 21   Read Luke 23:39-43.

What a contrast! From the crosses on either side of Jesus: One man mocks; the other prays. A person's exercise of faith when life comes crashing down and all of life seems to contradict any notion of a caring God at the center of the universe is noteworthy. But it is even more extraordinary for one to look upon a helpless, crushed, and dying "savior" and believe that—against all evidence to the contrary—this victim is about to reign; this weak and powerless man is actually about to receive authority to grant favor and show mercy. Can you imagine praying to such a helpless-looking savior as this!

What could have brought the second man to penitence and trust? What had he seen or heard on the way up to the place of The Skull or from that adjacent cross that led him to express faith—despite such contradictory surroundings? Perhaps seeing an innocent treated with such injustice but refusing to defend himself caused him to realize that he was in the presence of a moral purity and integrity greater than he had ever known. Perhaps the unfathomable grace of those words, "Father, forgive them; for they do not know what they are doing," awakened faith.

"Remember me," prays the dying criminal. "Remember me when you come into your kingdom." Notice Jesus' response: "Truly I tell you," are emphatic words, as if to say, "Now, listen to what I am about to say"—"Today you will be with me in Paradise." The criminal had asked only for remembrance, but Jesus promises to take him along—to make him a special guest! The answer far exceeds his prayer.

Suggestion for prayer: **Talk to Jesus conversationally about how he seems to you in this passage. Talk to him about his response to the criminal's request. Realize that this is exactly how he responds to you. Imagine the implications. End your prayer in praise and gratitude.**

Sunday, November 22   Read Colossians 1:15-18.

I praise you, O Christ! When I grasped the tremendous love you demonstrated when you went to the cross, I realized that I was seeing right into the mysterious being of God. You showed me that at the center of the universe is not blind fate but a heart of love.

I know now that your loving presence did not originate in a manger but existed before time began. In fact, I know that the love I see in you was the inspiration and intention behind all creation; it is your love that holds everything together.

As creation's "firstborn" you have always been its pattern and prototype, revealing the way life is meant to work. From atoms to galaxies, everything contributes to the whole; nothing need be lost. We were all made to fit, for we were all created to give. Your caring heart and self-giving love are written into and shine through all that exists.

Christ, you gave everything its start, whether visible or invisible, everything in heaven and everyone on earth. Grade upon grade of angels and rank upon rank of heavenly agents all owe their existence and find their purpose through you. They exist to do your bidding.

Help me to see everything in the light of your presence and to make you central in all that I do. Help me never to allow anyone or anything to usurp the place of preeminence that you deserve in my life. Enable me to refer to you my every concern and to offer to you my every action so that loving you will be my deepest motive and serving you the ultimate objective in all that I do. Amen.

Suggestion for meditation: **Spend a few minutes in quiet, realizing Christ's presence within you, sensing his love irradiating all that exists.**

Learning War No More

November 23–29, 1998
Monday, November 23

Robert Reddig♣
Read Isaiah 2:1-3.

With the coming of Advent we enter into a season of hope and preparation. Isaiah, whose words are like fanfare for great ceremony, signals to the believer that great and glorious things are about to take place in the days to come. Isaiah speaks to the people of his time with language of the land. He urges them to be drawn from the hills of their lives to the mountains, and among the mountains to the highest pinnacle, visible to all nations, where none but God resides and teaches. The poetic image of a pilgrimage undertaken by all peoples to the mountain of God urges us to envision peaceful assembly above our differences, petty strivings, and prideful certainty.

Peace requires two things: We must leave what we are doing and the place where we are doing it; and we must be teachable, open to something new. Peace in heart and relationship is not simply a lull following our triumph over someone or something. Peace is something that breaks above us, something new, something larger than the small hills of our rights and prejudices.

First see the mountain of God and then make your pilgrimage to it. In the process you will merge with others who have come from different spiritual and emotional territories but who are nevertheless on the same journey.

Peace starts with a vision of what is possible, and it requires our departure from the landmarks of our conflict. Isaiah proclaims that the mountain of God has something new, and it is near.

Prayer: **Gracious God, draw us from the lowlands to the mountain of your grace and power. Amen.**

♣A psychotherapist in private practice; Nashville, Tennessee.

Tuesday, November 24   Read Isaiah 2:4-5.

Isaiah proclaims that in a time, certain and coming, the Lord will judge among nations, and nations will learn war no more. His proclamation tempts us to feel exempt if we are not carrying obvious weaponry. Who among us carries spears? Who among us brandishes a sword? We do not conspicuously prepare for war. Come to think of it, we rarely if ever plow or prune. We may garden on our own property, simply removing weeds and pests. How civilized!

However, old images fit our old natures perfectly. Isaiah is talking about the transformation of one of our most significant enterprises: killing off our foes. Who among us does not wish to spear a competitor at work or slice the heart of a rival for recognition or affection? It is fascinating to take stock of how much we prepare for war each day. Often we brace ourselves, arming for conflict rather than for understanding, forgiveness, compassion. Our cars and computers, more sophisticated than plows and pruning hooks, would seem ideally suited for bridging distances and differences among us. And while many of us are blessed with convenience, we are also cursed by competition. We continue to learn war. We have more enemies than we can count.

Isaiah proclaims that God has a plan to transform us. God not only wants to take our instruments of war and bend them to useful purpose; but more importantly, God chooses to transform our hateful hearts. Without this last transformation, you and I are capable of using virtually anything—charm, gender, race, money, status, even scripture itself—as a blunt or pointed instrument against those we dare not love. God's plan is not merely to make our wars more polite but to declare a lasting peace.

Prayer: **Help us to know and believe that we are the objects of your abiding love, Lord. May we extend that same love to our enemies. Grant us peaceful hearts. Amen.**

Wednesday, November 25   Read Psalm 122.

The small country church in North Dakota where I first learned the lessons of faith heavily emphasized the memorization of scripture. I remember Psalm 122, and with it some uneasiness as I recited the opening verse.

I was expected to go to church, and while it was often fun to see cousins and friends from other farm families, I cannot recall feeling glad when someone announced that it was time to go to church. Saying the verse from memory I felt vaguely dishonest, because even then, in a time with little competing entertainment, going to church was more an obligation than a joy.

Nor, I'm afraid, did I think it was important that there be peace within Jerusalem for the sake of relatives or friends. The greeting "Peace be with you" seemed feeble and passive. I recall some light comedy when we spoke of "peas" being with one another, for few of us liked them.

That was then. As a child in a spartan and sparse environment, I could easily imagine more exciting places to visit and more exciting greetings than those described in Psalm 122. Perhaps there were then, and there are now. But the psalmist is proclaiming wisdom that he has discovered. He is bearing witness. We can imagine that he too has been places other than the house of the Lord and spoken words that were not peaceful.

Psalm 122 is an invitation to release our attachments, to enter into the place of the Lord's full safety and security. And the psalm expresses a wish that others too will find relief from striving within the sanctuary of Jerusalem. It comes as no surprise to most of us that God and God's sanctuary are usually not our first choice. We can imagine other places and circumstances being more exciting. Grace leads us to the dwelling place of the Lord, and there we find lasting peace.

Prayer: **Mighty and enduring God, we are grateful for the place you have kept for us. Lead us home. Amen.**

343

Thursday, November 26   Read Romans 13:11-12.

"Wake up and smell the coffee!" Depending upon voice inflection, these words can be either a delightful invitation to a new day or a harsh judgment about being ignorant of what is going on and about to happen. As the season of Advent approaches, most of us are anticipating the turmoil of preparation. All of us have our own urgencies about holiday events, gift giving, correspondence with friends, strained family relations, and the overlay of responsibility upon lives that are probably too hectic already. For some, the Christmas season is a nightmare from which they hope to recover in January. Well, wake up and smell the coffee!

Today's scripture taken from Paul's letter to the Romans is both an invitation and a judgment. It is an invitation to be lifted from the law by the new and transforming commandment to love. It is a judgment upon the frenzy of trying to calculate to whom we owe what, of trying to decide who is worthy of our concern and who is not. Paul declares that to love is to obey the whole law. (Wouldn't we all like to satisfy our gift-giving "obligations" with one simple and profound gesture?)

The most troubling dreams and nightmares of our sleep present themselves to us as truth. We do thrash about with urgency; we fear falling; we try to run and cannot escape; we try to speak and the words will not come. We are asleep but in the throes of pointless purpose. Well, wake up and see the love of God, the babe in the manger, the gift of love. And have a second cup of coffee as it all sinks in.

Prayer: **Loving God, awaken and stir in us the urge to offer simple acts of love. Amen.**

Friday, November 27   Read Romans 13:13-14.

Few of us feel that the good things we do are adequately illuminated. We would like to put them in the spotlight to showcase our talents, to highlight our resumes, and to photograph our shining moments. Advertisers have created ingenious ways to put their products before our eyes with billboards, special effects, and commercials that often overshadow the programming they sponsor. And in what seems like a headlong dash for our moment of celebrity, we feature our own web pages and design vanity license plates or congratulatory bumper stickers.

We have, in short, fallen in love with the light and have assumed that it is the light that matters most. As more and more of us climb up on stage and bathe in the light, we are not apt to notice that audiences are dwindling, that they are coming up onstage to get some illumination and recognition as well.

I doubt that Paul, in writing to the Romans, had this image in mind when he urged them to conduct themselves as people who live in the light of day. He had in mind conduct that was so exemplary that it need not be disguised or hidden. He had in mind conduct that was the polar opposite of our darker natures, driven by impulse and desire.

It is a measure of our cultural ingenuity that we have highlighted and featured some of the darkest parts of our natures, as if light itself would transform our actions and turn them into the stuff of virtue. It has been said that character is what we do when no one is looking, what would be applauded if it were known and seen. It is the love of God through Christ that lifts us from the darkest parts of our natures to the light of loving obedience. It is a process unrelated to our entertainments and our fame.

Prayer: **Turn us, Lord, to the light of your love, that we may see things more enduring than our own deeds. Amen.**

Saturday, November 28   Read Matthew 24:36-41.

The human record of knowing the important turns in history before they come to pass is not really very inspiring. As we read biblical accounts of the foolishness and waywardness of both faithful and unfaithful servants of God, we are tempted to think that we could do better, that we could predict God's intent and plan for our lives, and that we could follow instructions much better than the patriarchs and matriarchs. We are tempted to believe this because we have such elaborate structures with which to pattern our lives and pattern our strivings.

We act as if we know the future, our own and that of the world. We enter into contracts, commit to mortgages, develop five-year plans, establish our financial portfolios, set career goals, save for college, calculate our circumstances at the point of retirement. We act as if we know much more than is ever given us to know. Perhaps part of the human condition is to act as if our plans determine and control the future.

A central requirement for the Christian life, perhaps common to all deep spirituality, is our surrender to that which we cannot control or know. We are given the central truth that God is love. We affirm as well that God is all-knowing. But like children at their father's study door, we often presume to possess the wisdom within because we are so lovable.

In my personal life and in my spiritual life I have belatedly but fervently accepted two truths that guide everything I do. The first is that God is love and constantly reveals that love to me. The second truth, related to the first, is that God will surprise and amaze me. My plans, set in this context, are an amusement like my multifeatured digital watch. And so they should be.

Prayer: **We lift our praise to you, O Lord, who loves us before and after all our plans. Amen.**

First Sunday of Advent
Sunday, November 29   Read Matthew 24:42-44.

For the past ten years or so, it has been a family tradition for my wife, son, and me to drive from Nashville, Tennessee, to Venice, Florida, and spend the Christmas holiday with my wife's parents. As traditions go, it is quite ordinary. But we three have come to love the journey and the brief transformation it brings to our otherwise busy lives. We cruise down Interstate 75 from Chattanooga to Tampa, listening to Christmas music and chatting in the cozy capsule of the car. We make no plans along the way and schedule nothing unusual once we reach our destination.

We enjoy this time because we are fully available to one another. With nothing that must be done, we are available for surprise and the unexpected—a nice circumstance for Advent to come upon us. It is a delightful way to wait.

We live in a culture that is in love with Christmas, a culture that tells us that Christmas is much more fun and advantageous for us than Advent. And as Christians we sometimes feel we have done our part when we revere the nativity story or listen to some magnificent portion of Handel.

The deepest truth of Advent is that God is coming to us—not to the shepherds and wisemen of history but to the hearts that are now beating within us. Scripture tells us that we humans are not so good at being ready for what is coming, for what is really important. Advent is our most important waiting, for that which is most important is coming.

Prayer: **Dearest Lord, prepare our hearts and minds for the surprising gift of your deepest love. Amen.**

GOD'S COVENANT PEOPLE

November 30—December 6, 1998　　　　**David M. Griebner✤**
Monday, November 30　　　　Read Psalm 72:1-7, 18-19.

One of the primary themes in Advent is how God keeps God's promises and fulfills the covenant. This week we will explore seven things covenant people dare to believe about themselves and their world. We begin a with a simple affirmation.

First, *covenant people dare to believe that God created this world and is still involved in it.* Covenant people believe that the universe is the result of an intentional decision and that the One who made the decision to create is still involved with creation and available to us.

"Give the king your justice, O God," begins the psalmist. "May he judge your people with righteousness." The king models for God's people the way of living God desires, and he defends this way of life. Furthermore, the hope is that one day obedience to God's way will fill the whole earth. All the earth will know the creator, know itself as God's creation, and live accordingly.

All this points us toward a greater truth: In Advent we await the moment when eternity and time will join in the Incarnation. Advent includes the ancient longings of God's covenant people, but it concludes with an event that exceeds all expectations. This event creates a new covenant people who know and affirm that the psalmist's prayer for a just king finds its embodiment in Jesus Christ.

Suggestion for meditation: **How does my life express the belief that God created this world and is still involved in it?**

✤Pastor of Riverside United Methodist Church in Columbus, Ohio; husband of Sande and father of Claire, Hannah, and Jordan; author of many stories.

Tuesday, December 1   Read Romans 15:4-13.

This week we are exploring seven ways covenant people see themselves and their world. Today we affirm that *covenant people dare to believe that God is for us.*

This does not mean God is at our beck and call to gratify every want or desire that pops into our heads. It means that God stands with us in covenant intimacy to help us make the kind of choices that are best for us. Paul writes in Romans 15:4 that "whatever was written in former days was written" for our instruction, encouragement, and hope.

The purpose of the biblical record is to reveal God to us in such a way that instructs us in the right way of life, encourages us to live as God desires, and gives hope that we are becoming the people God wants us to be.

Covenant people know that great personal desire lies behind everything that happens. This desire is not neutral. Behind everything is God's desire for everything to be better for everybody.

In the Hebrew Scriptures, the Hebrews believed that God was on their side and against the Egyptians, the Philistines, the Canaanites, and so on. God had chosen them, and their election served a deeper purpose than simply becoming king of the hill.

In the New Testament, Jesus proclaims the kingdom of God and invites everyone into God's dream to make everything better for everybody. This powerful conviction drives Paul to preach to the Gentiles. God is on the side of what is best for me and for all creation, in order to make everything better for everybody.

Suggestion for meditation: **In what way do I believe that God is for me? What changes is God asking me to make?**

Wednesday, December 2   Read Isaiah 11:1-10.

God's covenant is not just a declaration of general intent but of a specific plan: *Covenant people dare to believe that God has a plan for this world and for us.*

Isaiah proclaims that as the result of an inbreaking into history that is yet to be revealed, "The wolf shall live with the lamb, the leopard shall lie down with the kid,...and a little child shall lead them....They will not hurt or destroy on all my holy mountain; for the earth will be full of the knowledge of the Lord as the waters cover the sea." God's plan for this world includes all relationships, even the ancient predatory rules of the natural order. Everything will one day honor the eternal purposes of God.

Furthermore, this obedience will not come from ignorance, instinct, or luck but from knowledge. We will know what we are doing, for whom we are doing it, and why. Today we participate in this plan by faith, as Paul says, "dimly" (1 Cor. 13:12); but one day God's plan and purpose will become self-evident, clear, and truly inclusive of everything and everybody.

I believe that if we accept this truth we can begin to listen for it and look for it. If we listen for it and look for it, God will give us ears to hear and eyes to see what is still largely a dream. Daily God invites us to wait, secure in the knowledge that the plan is still in place, and to watch for signs. Isaiah can dream of God's plan. Isaiah can imagine it. Can we? Do we?

Suggestion for meditation: **Do I truly believe that God has a plan for this world?**

Thursday, December 3   Read Matthew 3:1-12.

Continuing to move deeper into our experience of covenant intimacy, today we affirm that *covenant people dare to believe we have a purpose in God's plan.*

We are all important. We are all chosen. We all have a purpose. When John the Baptist appears in the Bible, the idea of purpose is always nearby. God sends John for a reason. John has a purpose, and his purpose is twofold. First his purpose is to fulfill ancient prophecy. God's plan is not a new thing. Pieces have been falling into place for centuries even when no one was paying attention. Now it is time to sit up and take notice.

Second, John's purpose is to prepare the people of his time to receive the ministry of the messiah. The key concept of repentance yokes John's ministry and Jesus' ministry together. Long ago Isaiah declared, "In repentance and rest is your salvation" (Isa. 30:15, NIV). John anticipates the Lord, greeting the seekers who come to hear him preach with the stark words, "Repent, for the kingdom of heaven has come near."

Sometime ago while pondering the meaning of repentance, I decided that repentance is the *acceptance of responsibility.* In the act of repentance, I acknowledge that I have done something wrong. I have turned against the truth. I have harmed myself and others.

All too often we compromise the health and intimacy God offers us by refusing to accept responsibility. I have sinned; I am responsible. This acknowledgment is the first step toward healing. It is the first step to becoming useful to God and finding our place in God's plan.

Suggestion for meditation: **Where do I need to repent?**

Friday, December 4   Read Isaiah 11:1-5.

We revisit a portion of Isaiah for our fifth truth about covenant intimacy with God: *Covenant people dare to believe that God can reveal our purpose to us.*

Isaiah declares that one day someone unique and connected to the royal house of David will enter history. The spirit of the Lord will rest upon this person as a "spirit of wisdom and understanding." It feels like Isaiah is describing some form of spiritual discernment.

Discernment is the gift of seeing clearly what is going on around us, what God is doing, and what response to make based on that knowledge. Isaiah goes on to tell us that other gifts this person will possess include being able to accomplish what he perceives God is asking him to do ("might") and the discipline to stay focused on God alone ("His delight shall be in the fear of the Lord").

I often feel as if my own attempts to obey God leave much to be desired. I have experienced discernment as a very inexact practice. Even when I think I'm on to something, I still have to muster enough courage, discipline, and will to get it done—to say nothing of explaining it to those affected by my decision.

Nonetheless I believe that as covenant people God invites us to live according to the will and purpose of God and that this living is truly possible. I believe we can make this way of life our intent in all we do, which will greatly affect how we make our decisions. With Thomas Merton, I believe that while we may not know if we are doing God's will, our desire to please God does in fact please.

Suggestion for meditation: **Do I really want to know God's purpose for me?**

Saturday, December 5   Read Matthew 3:1-12.

Several themes begin to converge now. We revisit Matthew to affirm a sixth expression of covenant intimacy: *Covenant people dare to believe that God will equip us to take our place in God's purpose.*

John addresses the Pharisees and Sadducees who have come to be baptized and says, "Do not presume to say to yourselves, 'We have Abraham as our ancestor'; for I tell you, God is able from these stones to raise up children to Abraham." As covenant people we stand within a larger plan and purpose that was in place before us and will be in place after us; but we cannot rest in this fact.

What counts is finding our purpose in this larger purpose. John has come to prepare the way for Jesus whose baptism is fire to John's water. He comes to announce that a process of sifting is about to commence. The context suggests that people will be separated by their response to the Messiah.

Something that has always troubled me is the difference between style and substance. When I played soccer in high school, I remember being almost as concerned about wearing the right socks as I was about my skills with the ball. Something in me whispered, *If you look good, you are good.*

The good players in every sport are not always the ones who look good but the ones who get the job done. John looks at those who have come to hear him preach and declares that neither he nor God will be persuaded by appearance. Appearance consistent with a substantive response to God is what counts.

Suggestion for meditation: **If you were to do one thing today that you believed was truly in keeping with God's will for you, what would it be?**

Second Sunday of Advent
Sunday, December 6   Read Romans 15:13.

Covenant people dare to place their hope in God's covenant no matter what.

Paul commends no glib or untried hope to believers in this verse. Elsewhere he remembers what he has suffered for his perseverance in the gospel (2 Cor. 11:23-32): imprisonment, floggings, beatings, stoning, bandits, and the like. How can a person experience life in this way and still have hope?

Margaret Wheatley discusses "chaos theory" in her book *Leadership and the New Science.* Scientists have long observed that the universe evidences both order and disorder. We can observe things that act in a completely predictable and orderly way. Gravity, for example, obeys laws we can understand and predict. However, other observable systems and events produce a completely random result. For such we see no discernible order; chaos reigns.

At least this is what we thought was true. With the advent of computers, scientists have been able to study chaos and disorder more deeply. They have discovered that if we observe chaos long enough, order emerges. The most chaotic system stays within certain boundaries. Every chaotic system seems to have a strange attractor, an often elegant center that holds.

In my best moments I know this is true for my life and all life. There is always a center that holds. There is always a reason to hope even when events happen that defy explanation. Today's scientists are discovering the experimental evidence for what simple people of faith have always known: Our God reigns.

Suggestion for meditation: **How have I experienced God's order in my life? How is God sustaining hope in me right now?**

THE DESERT SHALL BLOSSOM

December 7–13, 1998
Monday, December 7

Ray Buckley✤
Read Isaiah 35:1-4.

Famine does not create an appreciative eater. It creates a desperate one. It means long periods where there is some food but never enough; when there is only a handful of seeds and sometimes none at all. In those moments, each seed is savored, each drop of water truly tasted. Nothing from that time on will ever be capriciously consumed again. A drop of rain will never be carelessly wiped from the face. It is the desert experience.

To those who have learned not to expect more than the desert, one does not yell, "Look, flowers!" One looks into the eyes of those who have seen the destruction of Zion and their lives and have resigned themselves to dryness: There is almost a pleading, "Don't tease me."

The voice of the prophet calls to those who know the wilderness with a painful familiarity: Strengthen the hands that cannot hold on any longer. Lift those who cannot stand. Something is happening. In the desert, with no expectation of change, God is here. We cannot believe it until we see it. We think it is a mirage until a crocus begins to bloom, and we hear the drop of water.

Prayer: **Water of Life,
flood over me.
Saturate my life,
until I bloom,
Precisely because you are here. Amen.**

✤Samples and Curriculum Promotions Coordinator, United Methodist Publishing House; Native-American United Methodist layman, residing in Nashville, Tennessee.

Tuesday, December 8   Read Isaiah 35:5-7.

They wait. People of the "desert." The ones beyond the right words to say. Beyond our ability to grow green again. People, places, and situations become dry. It is easier to abandon them to the desert. It seems a less embarrassing thing to do.

These are not waiting for the "annual rain." They are used to the quick fixes that have come and gone with the first hot wind. They endure the promises of those who do not know the desert. It has become easier to expect burning sand instead of water, and know the company of jackals. Stoicism hurts less. Hope has become brown and dry.

Then God comes. Nothing God touches can remain the same. It is not a flash greening. It is a deep-down watering, which permeates the core of being. It is the restoration of ground-water, not seeping but flowing in a current, so that all of life is changed. Roots begin to grow deeper. Stoicism turns to hope. Once hope has rooted, joy appears.

Gradually, the wilderness is greening. Pools of water appear where sand burned weary feet. Water rushes over stones that knew only the wind. Jackals seek out other deserts.

The eyes of the blind are opened. Some receive their sight, but all see. The ears of the deaf are unstopped. Some catch the rush of water, but all hear. Spirits long dry begin to feel, for whatever God touches is changed.

We have waited for God, not really expecting an appearance. And God has come.

Prayer: **Master of the desert,**
        God of the impossible and improbable,
        Lord of time,
        wet me,
        according to your will. Amen.

Wednesday, December 9   Read Isaiah 35:8-10.

In the desert, the bones of the brave lie next to those of the prepared. It is the place of the unexpected and the predictable, of cold nights and days of despairing heat. Was there a road in this place? To what destination did it lead? Some have followed it and left in confusion. The desperate find easy prey. Scavengers, both human and animal, search for the lost; the place that once flowed with milk and honey has become a place of fear.

Into the desert God has come. In this place of hope bleached white, God has come. And in the wake of God, salvation has become a road, a highway for those freed from bondage. It is for those who have traded dryness for Living Water. Those who have stepped beyond the desert to a new green.

God has made a way. It is not just a road that leads away from the desert. It is a way that leads through the desert, reclaiming it, and forever changing the hold of fear the desert brings. It is a way from which one cannot be lost—a way secured by God so that those who would impede the journey have no power here.

There is a sound that has not been here before. It is not the sound of the forlorn. It is the sound of the human voice. Through the desert air it is lifted on the wind. Joy has invaded the place of desolation. Those who have been set free are singing!

God has stepped into the place of the lost and reclaimed it. Moss grows on sheltered rocks. The sound of water is heard. Grass grows beside quiet pools as the ransomed sing. God has come! Nothing will be the same.

Prayer: **O God who makes a way,**
             green me.
          There is no desert
             that you cannot change.
          Touch this dryness
             with your presence,
          and I will sing. Amen.

357

Thursday, December 10   Read Matthew 11:2-6.

He was an oddity. People had come out of the city to hear him speak. They might have thought him overzealous. But he had been born for this. Born to be the one who stood in stark contrast to the norm; to be the stone over which the spiritually complacent stumbled. He had been born to be the one who would interrupt the smoothness of religious routinism.

The spiritually hungry and curious had stayed to listen. He spoke of one who would follow after. He spoke of repentance. He had stood in water and offered them symbolic cleansing. They called him the Baptist.

The *he* came. The Baptist, standing in the water, put his arms around the body of the Son of God. Together they stood, wet, as the voice of God spoke from heaven.

As he lay in Herod's prison, far removed from the water and the dove, John the Baptist felt the stone and darkness. Separated from the ministry and surroundings that defined him, John felt alone. Could he have been wrong? Was Jesus the one?

The answer of Jesus was not, "Yes, John." It was, "Tell John what you hear and see." That Isaiah's prophecy is coming to fulfillment. A statement of fact. The impossible has become reality. The disenfranchised have been adopted.

Removed from the things that we think define us, we feel our own stones and darkness. Seed-sowing is for the hopeful. To have hope one must know despair. "Are you the one, or shall I look for another?" our heart asks. The answer comes with more certainty than the question. Lives are being changed—the broken, mended. The wounded are being healed. And we ourselves, awaiting the One, are already recipients of the promise.

Prayer: **Lord,**
> **When I can't see you in my today,**
>> **let me see you in another's today,**
>> **and give me peace until tomorrow. Amen.**

Friday, December 11   Read Matthew 11:7-11.

To the crowd it is not always important *what* is happening. It is simply that *something* is happening. And they come. Some come to criticize and thereby reestablish their own position of importance. Some come for entertainment. Some come to gawk. Many come because not coming would mean being left out. One can be lost in the crowd without definition or commitment. Such is the legacy of jesters and prophets.

Jesus steps in front of the crowd and knows them. Really *knows* them. Jesus both confronts and defines the crowd, using the ministry of John as a tool. His first question assaults the pretenders—the pseudo-intelligencia. What had they gone to the wilderness to see? He leads them with an absurd thought. Had they gone to see a reed being shaken by the wind? Jesus plunges deeper, forcing them to define their purpose. What then did they go to see? Someone dressed in nice clothes? No, the beautifully dressed live in palaces. What then? A prophet? The absurdity of his questions hits home, exposing the crowd's spiritual hunger. They had come looking for spiritual truth.

Jesus uses familiar words of scripture to define John, and in so doing, to define himself. The crowd is confronted. They are confronted with the Messenger, the Messiah, and their own search.

"Give me God, anything of God," the crowd of all ages exclaims. And we run to the wilderness to hear the voice of one prophet and then another. The search becomes an end in itself, and we exult in being part of the crowd. Then we are confronted, not with the voice of God but the body of God. In that moment we are defined. Professional searchers or disciples.

Prayer: **God become flesh,**
　　　　　confront me.
　　　　　Invade my "social correctness."
　　　　　I wish not to search
　　　　　but to follow. Amen.

Saturday, December 12   Read James 5:7-10.

Seed-sowing is for the hopeful and sometimes the arrogant. The arrogant do not always stay until germination. They are captivated by the novelty of beginning something new and intimidated by the loss of status that failure might bring. They are quick to interpret the success or failure of other seed-sowers and are masters of the "you should have...." Still, it is in the plan of God that even the arrogant sow.

It is the hopeful who plant their lives with the seed—living not for the breaking of new ground but for the emergence and maturity of the fruit. Having carefully selected the seed, they pull the weeds, give all the water their arms can carry, and wait. At times, the wait is long. The certainty of the moment in which they held the seed is obscured. They wait and work. They work and pray.

Deep within the faith-seed is the promise of God, pregnant with life. Whether sown by the hopeful or the arrogant, it lives. Its germination is both guaranteed and determined by God's plan. There is no risk, and therefore no need to argue.

In the face of utmost certainty there is no speculation. We time the planting, expecting the fruit at harvest time. But the seed is God's. It often grows what we did not choose. Its germination is longer than we thought. But it grows. It is not often what we thought we had planted. It is always what we need.

Prayer: **Seedmaker,**
        teach me that all which comes from you
            is certain.
        Remind me
        that I am the product of someone else's sowing,
            and how long I have taken to grow. Amen.

Third Sunday of Advent

Sunday, December 13   Read Psalm 146:5-10.

The rain was hitting the ground hard enough to beat down the grass. "What is God's name?" I asked.

He was quiet for a moment. "To the people, God is called Wakan Tanka, 'The Great Mysterious,'" he said softly.

"Doesn't God have another name?"

"Yes."

"What's that?"

"When you have walked with God for a while, then you will know what name to use."

Yahweh. Jehovah. The Creator, Maker of heaven and earth. God, who caused the planets to form and breathed life into all living things. God, whose will and purpose pulled the tides and gave rain to return water to the earth. God, who hid stars in cottonwood branches and laughed color into flowers and feathers. With incredible contrast and incredible consistency, the nature of God creates worlds and helps the fatherless.

The Lord will provide. The faithful one. The righteous one. Almighty God grieves over the condition of humankind. The Creator, having destroyed creation once, chooses to redeem it.

"Happy are those whose help is the God of Jacob." There is no fear in going out on a limb, if the limb is strong. There is no uncertainty in certainty. In the greatest creative act of all—to redeem humankind—the One who sent galaxies reeling lies softly breathing, the small form cradled in grass, created by the hands of God.

Prayer: **O God, who lets me call you mine,
My God, you have written my name on your hand.
Write your name on my heart,
   my mind, my entire being,
until I am covered. Not with self,
   but you. Amen.**

A SAVIOR FOR YOU

December 14–20, 1998   **Andy Langford✤**
Monday, December 14   Read Matthew 1:18-25.

Where is God? When will God do something good? Spiritual persons throughout the ages, in the midst of strife and turmoil, have always asked this question.

Joseph's life is falling apart. Joseph just wants a quiet life as a carpenter, with a faithful wife and children of his own. He has became engaged to a lovely young woman. But now his fiancee is pregnant, and the child is not his. Divorce is the just alternative. Joseph questions, Where is God? Why must I suffer like this?

As the sun sets earlier each day, our world seems engulfed in darkness. Millions of children wake and go to bed hungry. Races and religions war against one another. In our own lives and communities, marriages and relationships crumble. Human bodies fall ill. People die. We all question, Where is God? When will God do something good?

In the night, an angel asked Joseph to let God be in charge. Marry the woman. Assume the responsibility of fatherhood. The child, Jesus, will be a sign that God is with you. May we also hear this message: God is with us.

Prayer: **Light of the nations, break into our darkness. When all else fails, remind us that you are near. Amen.**

✤United Methodist pastor in the Western North Carolina Annual Conference; author of ten books and editor of *The United Methodist Book of Worship.*

Tuesday, December 15   Read Isaiah 7:10-16.

Where is God? When will God do something good? The enemies from Damascus and Samaria surrounded Jerusalem. The land and people of God were doomed. No rescue appeared imminent.

Then, through the prophet Isaiah, the Lord asked King Ahaz to seek a sign, to ask for a blessing, to pray for deliverance. If Ahaz would simply ask, the Lord would respond. God would grant Ahaz anything under heaven or earth. Not wanting to put God to the test, however, Ahaz refused. In self-righteous humility, Ahaz turned God down.

Often we also refuse to put God to the test. We make God too small. We are self-reliant, self-sufficient, and independent individuals who need no one. Persons who need other people and persons who need God are weak, undisciplined, and lazy. We holy ones save up our prayers and requests for significant crises, not everyday life. We act like Ahaz and turn down God's offer of help.

God grew tired of Ahaz's unbelief. The land was destroyed; the temple torn down; the people sent into captivity. Ahaz's self-reliance doomed him and his people. God was there, but Ahaz chose not to seek help from his Lord.

Our unbelief can destroy us also. We cannot fix all our own problems. In each of our life's crises, however, God is not absent. Let us learn anew to call upon the Lord. We will not be disappointed.

Prayer: **Lord, help my unbelief. Help me to trust that nothing can separate me from your love. Amen.**

Wednesday, December 16   Read Isaiah 7:10-16.

God was there. God is here. Although God grew weary of Ahaz's unfaith and the land was destroyed, God still loved the chosen ones. Although the temple was dismantled and the people banished into exile, God did not disappear.

The prophet Isaiah had eyes to see God. Isaiah was less a predictor of the future and more a keen observer of how God operates. God's love for Israel was as passionate as a mother's strong arms and as steadfast as a father's hugs. In the midst of destruction, God would act.

Isaiah foretold the birth of a special child, whose name would be Immanuel. His mother would be young, his diet and lifestyle simple. His birth would signal God's destruction of every enemy.

The signs of God's presence still surround us, if we too have eyes to see. The birth of a child continues to be a miracle of life. The joy in young children's faces as they sing the Christmas carols with conviction reminds us that the story is true. Teenagers carrying food to the home of a shut-in proclaim the presence of God. The smiles of older adults as they come to worship on Christmas Eve announce that the Christ child has come. Those who have eyes, let them see.

Prayer: **Immanuel, you are with us. Angels sang of your glory; shepherds crowded your room; star gazers fell down before you. Help us to see you also. O come, O come, Immanuel. Amen.**

Thursday, December 17   Read Psalm 80:1-7, 17-19.

Seven hundred years before the birth of Jesus, the northern kingdom of Israel was ready to fall. Where was God? Although God had been faithful in the past and had watched over Joseph like a shepherd, the people saw God nowhere. This collective song of lament, sung by worship leaders and people, acknowledged the turmoil and distress among God's chosen ones. God's anger caused tears among the people, invited the scorn of other nations, and evoked laughter among Israel's enemies.

This song could have been written at many times in the life of Israel: during captivity in slavery in Egypt, after defeat at the hands of outsiders, in the midst of famine or drought, or as the northern tribes vanished from the face of the earth. Still, the people of God sang.

We too sing songs of lament. When children go to bed hungry, when teenagers lose their lives to violence, when older adults spend days without speaking to another human being, we sing of our pain. In our personal lives, relationships are never perfect. Children, spouses, parents, and friends fail us. Troubled thoughts cruise our minds. Sickness often overwhelms us. Death stalks. As we sing of our pain, however, God's ears are open to our cries.

Prayer: **Lord, you have been faithful in the past. Be present today. Listen to our pleas. Come down out of heaven to set us free. Restore our relationships, our minds, and our bodies. Shine your light on our darkness. Amen.**

Friday, December 18   Read Romans 1:1-7.

Paul knows the answers to the questions. Where is God? God is present in Jesus Christ. When will God do something good? God already has done good. Paul knows the answers. How? Because the persecutor had become an apostle.

On the road to Damascus to persecute the followers of the Way, a bright light struck Saul blind. In that brilliant moment, through Saul's blindness, Jesus spoke to Saul, and Saul became a new man. After this encounter with the Lord, Paul never doubted the presence or goodness of God. As Jesus Christ had revealed himself to Saul, Paul would spend the rest of his life revealing Jesus Christ to others.

Romans is Paul's greatest epistle. In this salutation, he begins the longest, most complex, and richest of all his letters. The first seven verses are just one long and convoluted sentence. Too often we jump over Paul's first words to concentrate on weightier issues. But at the beginning of the Christian year, at the birth of the Child, Paul's first words ground us in the reality of God's love.

Our knowledge of and about God ultimately are not abstract but personal. Where is God? God is intimately engaged at every moment of our lives. What is God's purpose? God's purpose is to touch us, to care for us, to help us become all that God created us to be. We recognize the gift of the Christ child only when we first recognize the gift of God's love in each of our own lives.

Prayer: **Son of God, child of Mary, help me remember the gift of your grace and peace to me. Amen.**

Saturday, December 19   Read Romans 1:1-7.

Paul had evidence of God's presence and goodness. Promised by the prophets, spoken of through the scriptures, this revelation of God became flesh in the family of David. Even more importantly, Paul knew the reality of Christ because Jesus personally spoke to Paul, calling him to be an apostle. Paul never met Jesus in the flesh. Paul never spoke about Jesus' birth. He seemed not to have cared about Mary and Joseph, the shepherds, magi, or angels. The resurrected Jesus Christ, however, had personally transformed Paul's life. Paul, therefore, was an apostle of the living and loving Jesus Christ.

Jesus also called the Romans who, like Paul, had never seen Jesus Christ or knelt at his manger or seen the angels. Yet these Romans had become saints because each one of them had also experienced the living Jesus. They too were a visible sign that God is Immanuel.

And so it is for us. Many people say: "Oh, I wish I had been there that night of Jesus' birth." "Oh, I wish I had been at Calvary the day Jesus' died or at the tomb on Easter morning." Paul, however, reminds us that all who have experienced the resurrected Christ are still saints. How do we know? Because through bright lights or in songs of pain or in a quiet angelic voice, the living God who loves us has transformed our lives.

Prayer: **Loving Lord Jesus, you called Paul and the Romans to be your saints. Call me anew to be one of your saints as well. Amen.**

Fourth Sunday of Advent

Sunday, December 20   Read Matthew 1:18-25.

Over two hundred years ago, Charles Wesley reflected upon Matthew's good news and wrote this poetry:

Hark! the herald angels sing, "Glory to the new-born King; peace on earth, and mercy mild, God and sinners reconciled!" Joyful, all ye nations rise, join the triumph of the skies; with th' angelic host proclaim, "Christ is born in Bethlehem."

Christ, by highest heaven adored; Christ, the everlasting Lord; late in time behold him come, off-spring of a virgin's womb. Veiled in flesh the God-head see; hail th' incarnate Deity, pleased with us in flesh to dwell, Jesus, our Emmanuel.

Hail the heaven-born Prince of Peace! Hail the Sun of Righteousness! Light and life to all he brings, risen with healing in his wings. Mild he lays his glory by, born that we no more may die, born to raise us from the earth, born to give us second birth. Hark! the herald angels sing, "Glory to the new-born King!"

Where is God? God is here with us, in a child named Jesus. When will God do something good? God already has, through offering God's own self to us in human flesh.

Prayer: **Ever-present God, open our ears that we may hear your song; open our eyes that we may see you near; open our lips that we may tell others; open our hearts that we may be drawn closer to you. Amen.**

DO NOT BE AFRAID!

December 21–27, 1998   **J. Philip Wogaman**✤
Monday, December 21   Read Isaiah 63:7-9.

Some years ago a good friend of mine lay dying of cancer. While racked with physical pain, he told me of a deeper spiritual pain. He said he had come to see that a physical crisis is also a spiritual crisis. He said, "I look across that dark void, and there is no answer."

In the end, some weeks later, he found the answer. Several friends gathered in his room for a last Communion and a kind of blessing from him for each of us. It is the answer we anticipate in Advent and celebrate with Christmas. God is with us; God is really with us; we do not have to be afraid.

The passage from Isaiah 63 is about that. The Lord "became their savior in all their distress." This verse underscores the point that God does not send the message—across that dark void—by messenger. God does not fax it or send it by e-mail! God delivers it in person, by God's *presence*. "In his love and in his pity he redeemed . . ." That is the point of Advent and Christmas: God present in love. We will continue to have troubles, but with God at our side we need not fear.

Suggestion for meditation: **Reflect on your deepest fears, some of which may gnaw at you subconsciously. What does it mean to you that God really has reached out to us in Christ? It is not easy to banish fear; but if God is with us, what really is there to fear?**

✤Senior minister, Foundry United Methodist Church; Washington, D.C.; Professor of Christian Ethics, Wesley Theological Seminary.

Tuesday, December 22   Read Psalm 148.

We know more about the vastness of the universe than the psalmist did. According to astronomers, there are billions of galaxies of stars with 100 million to 100 billion stars per galaxy (more or less). The human mind cannot conceive such immensity. At least this mind cannot! It is also frightening, particularly when we think of the billions of years since the universe began and the billions of years the physical universe has yet to go. Who are we, puny little human beings, in face of the immensities of space and time?

The psalmist may not have had the factual knowledge of modern science, but Psalm 148 helps us overcome our fear. We should not be afraid of all this grandeur; we should praise God who created it. "Praise him, sun and moon; praise him, all you shining stars! Praise him, you highest heavens....for he commanded and they were created." The one whose coming we anticipate in Advent, whose presence we celebrate at Christmas, reveals the true nature of the Creator.

One of John Greenleaf Whittier's hymns speaks of how "Jesus knelt to share with thee the silence of eternity, interpreted by love!" In other words, the love of God expressed directly in Christ is the true meaning of all of that immensity of time and space. Our fears can give way to grateful wonder.

The night sky, even when most brilliant, displays but the smallest fraction of God's actual creation. We can gaze upon it as a work of creative love—not a threat to our vulnerability but as an invitation to a life of gratitude and praise.

Prayer: **We praise you, O God, for the wonders of creation and for the precious gift of life we are privileged to share. Amen.**

Wednesday, December 23   Read Psalm 148:11-13.

In the midst of this psalm of praise, the psalmist surprises us. It is a psalm of Israel, but we suddenly find that it is not limited to Israel. The psalmist calls upon "all peoples" to "praise the name of the Lord." One reads no word of hostility here directed against the peoples of other lands, no hint of fear of those who are not of the psalmist's own community. They too belong to the same God—the God of everything and everyone. It is not unusual for people to fear those whom they consider to be enemies, and it is easy to regard strangers as enemies. But it helps to know that God is God of all.

This point is emphasized by the psalmist's inclusion of "all rulers of the earth." Most of us fear power somewhat, particularly when exercised by rulers who are not accountable to us. That fear sometimes can be healthy! But this psalm views political power as a part of God's greater providence. The rulers of this world are responsible to God also. They too should join in praise of the one who has created us all.

When we overcome our fear of strangers and rulers, we also see our responsibilities more clearly. To praise God is to serve God. To serve God is to work at transforming the world. None of us can have the whole picture. But as we work to transform the part of the world to which we have access, we are helping God transform it all.

Prayer: **Creator God, let all share our hymn of gratitude, that all may rise above earthly hatreds and fears and seek your realm of righteousness and love. Amen.**

Thursday, December 24   Read Luke 2:1-20.

It is Christmas Eve, and the story of the shepherds captivates us again. Do not be surprised that their first reaction to the "glory of the Lord" was one of fear. Our first awareness of God's reality overpowers us, being brought up short by our creatureliness and by the blinding power bearing in upon us. So it was with the simple shepherds who had never had anything much happen to them before.

But then the word of kindness: "Do not be afraid." There is nothing to fear. The angel had come to bring them good news, not bad news—and great joy. We are given to believe that they had been singled out because in their humility they could receive the good news—not because they were religious leaders and certainly not because they had done anything wrong and had any reason to fear.

The message was to them, but it was also through them. They "made known" what had happened to them, and all who heard it marveled. The heart of the message was, I believe, contained in the angelic word: "Do not be afraid." Humanity, all tied up in its anxieties, now has a deep basis for trust.

We recall the words from a beloved Christmas carol about the dark streets of Bethlehem: "The hopes and fears of all the years are met in thee tonight." Yes! But not just "met." The fears exist there in the dark streets of human life, but now the good news overtakes them. Our deepest hope will not let us down.

Prayer: Gracious God, give me the openness of humble shepherds to receive the good news of Jesus in a fresh way this year. Amen.

Christmas Day

Friday, December 25   Read John 1:1-14.

The Gospel of John says nothing about the actual birth of Jesus, but the magnificent prologue to the Gospel says a lot about why it mattered. There we read that "the light shines in the darkness, and the darkness did not overcome it." Without the light of Christ, we struggle in the world's darkness. Without that light we either give up in despair or endlessly and uselessly plot ways to ward off the ultimate futility of life. We fear the darkness, but we are powerless to overcome it. Now comes the light, and we can see our way.

John proclaims the essential point: "The Word became flesh and lived among us, and we have seen his glory...full of grace and truth." Christ is God's grace to us. Christ freely offers God's love, which we could never merit on our own and which draws us out of our despair. Christ can be God's grace to us because Christ is also the truth about God. Christ is who and what God really is. Now we know. Now the darkness of our ignorance and fear has been broken.

The essential truth about life has to appear in human form in order to touch us. God cannot be remote and speculative to penetrate our deeper self. The heart of the meaning of God, the Logos, the "Word," somehow must be present in the flesh or we shall never get it. On Christmas we celebrate God's true presence to us in Christ.

Suggestion for meditation: **The secular holiday atmosphere often seems to eclipse the deeper spiritual meaning of Christmas. Most of that is innocent enough. But this is a good time to reflect on how our frantic efforts to conform to holiday expectations express deeper fears that can be overcome only by the one who is grace and truth.**

Saturday, December 26   Read Hebrews 2:10-18.

This passage from Hebrews is complicated. You do not have to get it all to grasp the main point: "I will put my trust in him." He who shared our humanity with us and who treats us "like his brothers and sisters in every respect," helps us overcome our fear. For the writer of Hebrews, the ultimate fear is the fear of death. In fact, we are slaves of that fear until Christ destroys in us the power of fear.

As a pastor, I am often called upon to be with people as they approach death and then to minister to their surviving loved ones. It seems to me that only in a real community of faith is it possible to face the reality of death and to grieve honestly. When death is feared as the final extinction of life, people search for ways to camouflage the reality: soft music, a vast display of flowers, soothing words ("She seems so peaceful"; "He has entered into rest").

I do not criticize. But fear is not so easily dissipated. It takes more than rose-scented air and sweet music. Among a people of trust, it is possible to face grief, to comfort one another, to celebrate a life in the confidence that the life is safe with God.

We must not overlook the realism and humor of the line "he did not come to help angels." No indeed, people are not angels! Still, our very human hearts do not have to be so fearful now. We know that God has reached into our humanity.

Prayer: **Still our restless hearts, O God. Renew our confidence in the one whose coming overcomes our bondage to fear, even the fear of death. Amen.**

Sunday, December 27 Read Matthew 2:13-23.

Today's reading from Matthew is about healthy fear and real tragedy. The Lord warns Joseph in a dream that the wicked King Herod wishes to kill Jesus. The little family had better flee to Egypt to avoid something awful that really could happen.

Then comes the atrocity: Babies are massacred. Such things really do happen. How many infants, too young to know left hand from right, have been slaughtered in recent memory? Who can number the precious lives lost in "ethnic cleansing," genocide, indiscriminate shelling, terrorist bombing? Who can measure the grief of parents for children, of children for parents?

And yet, real as these outrages have been, they do not have the final word. In due course, Herod was gone. In the end, Herod is always gone. Hitler is gone; Stalin is gone; Idi Amin is gone—at least from power. Such figures, obsessed with power, do not consider Christ much of a factor in the real world. But they come and go, and in the end humanity instinctively turns toward home.

In one sense we do well to fear the real damage that evil can inflict upon the world. In another sense Christ liberates us from the crippling power of that fear. Those who care passionately about peace and justice are always tempted to despair. Yet the truth of Christmas lingers on. Just when we are ready to give up, the sheer power of God's love breaks through again. God is with us! Do not be afraid!

Prayer: **God, grant us the grace to believe where we hope, to act where we believe, and to be wise where we act. Amen.**

375

ALL THAT GLITTERS MAY NOT BE GOLD

December 28–31, 1998   **George Hovaness Donigian**✤
Monday, December 28   Read Psalm 72:1-7.

Current conventional wisdom offers an updated Golden Rule: "The one with the gold makes the rules." This week's readings offer physical and spiritual gold.

Psalm 72 brings to mind power and discretion and the difficulty of thinking that life has ever been simple. Scholars identify this text as a coronation psalm, beseeching God's blessing on royalty. It offers the conventional images of any national psalm: "May there be abundance of grain in the land" (v. 16). Yet the beginning of the psalm makes us aware that it moves beyond conventional thinking.

"Give the king your justice, O God" can intend only a radical upsetting of the balance of power. To think about the justice of God draws us into a new understanding of the world and all that is within it. To follow the commercial assault of Christmas with an appeal for God's justice shows the heart of biblical spirituality, which includes a concern for the least of our brothers and sisters. Such spirituality celebrates the love of God for all people. The psalmist asks God to grant that the king may "defend the cause of the poor of the people, give deliverance to the needy, and crush the oppressor." These words hardly mirror the opulence of a royal court but point the royalty to see with new eyes and to hear with new ears the plight of those who are poor and needy and to establish a proactive stance against those who would oppress. In that message is genuine gold.

Suggestion for prayer: **Seek silence to reflect upon those around you who are oppressed and those who oppress them.**

✤Writer, editor, and children's teacher; ordained in The United Methodist Church; living in Nashville, Tennessee.

Tuesday, December 29   Read Ephesians 3:1-12.

Most scholars label Ephesians 3 as a prayer for wisdom. Though Paul, the ascribed writer, may begin prayerfully, he moves into a rambling discourse concerning his mission before returning to the prayerful portion of the chapter. In the parenthetical comment (vv. 2-13), the writer offers insight into his own personality and his understanding of the gospel.

The phrase "although I am the least" brings to mind Jesus' statement in Matthew 25 about the least of the brothers and sisters. We know little of Paul's life, though we piece together details from the epistles and the Acts of the Apostles. We know that once upon a time he was a rabbinical student who became an itinerant, and on a road trip this angry person became open to God's loving acceptance in Jesus. He was not oppressed but the oppressor and persecutor of Christians. Yet God's grace comes to the oppressor. His conversion goads him to become one who defends the cause of the poor and to speak loudly against those who oppress.

"This grace was given to me to bring to the Gentiles the news of the boundless riches of Christ." This phrase, *the riches of Christ*, stirs up a smorgasbord of imagery related to God's love. Foremost among those riches is God's loving acceptance of all persons, those who are wealthy and those who do not have the riches of the world. Connected to that portion of riches is the knowledge that God does not show favor to individuals because of their merit or their status. Related to these riches is that sense of God's mercy, which extends to all. Another quality on that table is God's justice, which exalts the meek and the lowly and levels the mighty.

Mining for spiritual gold helps us unfold the mystery of God's love.

Prayer: **Plunge us, O God, into the depths of your mystery that we might claim the fortune of your love. Amen.**

Wednesday, December 30 Read Isaiah 60:1-3.

Hear these words in your own time of exile:

"Arise, shine; for your light has come.
    …Nations shall come to your light,
        and kings to the brightness of your dawn."

The promise of restoration is a rich word for the parched spiritual condition of Israel in exile. Imagine the effects of being carted away from all that is familiar to a land that feels alien. Imagine having lived with a sense of God's special blessing and then experiencing the exile. If that becomes your experience, what happens to your understanding of blessing and of God?

My family also was scattered and exiled involuntarily because of religious conflict. Some landed in Brazil, some in the United States, some in Lebanon. Others remained in the old country. During this exile, the church continued to bear witness to the light. A people who seemed no people continued to tell the stories and to remember the sustaining power of God's rich love.

These words of Isaiah 60 almost seems a sham when heard from the perspective of cultural wealth or security. We may accept the promise too easily. We may feel persuaded by a cultural perspective that confuses national identity with a godly promise. And we may feel spiritually parched, wondering where the glory of the Lord may arise and whether we may really witness such a glory.

During the exile, a word of hope came from God to a parched people. The promise is so luxurious that we might miss it. Were we homeless persons today sleeping or resting on a heating grate in the center of a large city, would we understand the extravagance of this promise? Maybe the heart of God appears in such extravagance.

Prayer: **Lead us boldly, divine Light, that we might burn with the intensity of your spirit. Amen.**

Thursday, December 31   Read Matthew 2:1-6.

To scare a Middle Eastern despot requires an audacity not normally associated with the benign magi from the East. The notation in my New Oxford Annotated Bible (NRSV) states that Herod's "fears were aroused that his own children might be excluded from the throne." Without arguing with those commentators, my reading into the history of the family of Herod shows little concern for any offspring and a concern only to preserve the personal power of the incumbent thronesitter. Indeed, the family Herod tended to treat its slaves better than its children. Whether the Gospel writer knew the reality of the Herodian set of family values, other reasons suggest the inclusion of this curious sentence concerning Herod's fear.

Perhaps that fear stemmed from the intensity of the magi. Perhaps that fear in Herod stemmed from an awareness that these magi had crossed many difficult miles in search of a baby. Perhaps that fear grew from the implications of what might have inspired these men to assume such a journey.

Or perhaps Herod's fear stemmed from his own spiritual antenna, which sensed that the God of his ancestors was about to do something new. Perhaps Herod recognized that God was calling forth a new creation in which the coronation psalm (Psalm 72) would no longer be a set of words in meter but words set in the reality of God's justice. Perhaps Herod sensed that the baby would turn all that Herod cherished upside down. Perhaps Luke thought of all this as he envisioned a small scene incorporated in this Gospel.

Perhaps we, as we sing carols of joy, can also tune our spiritual antenna to see the wealth of newness that God is doing this very day.

Prayer: **God of the atom and of the ever-expanding universe, for the sake of Jesus, keep us open to that which you are doing new. Amen.**

The Revised Common Lectionary*
1998
(*Disciplines* Edition)

December 29—January 4
SECOND SUNDAY
AFTER CHRISTMAS
Jeremiah 31:7-14
Psalm 147:12-20
Ephesians 1:3-14
John 1:(1-9), 10-18

NEW YEAR'S DAY
Ecclesiastes 3:1-13
Psalm 8
Revelation 21:1-6a
Matthew 25:31-46

January 5–11
Isaiah 43:1-7
Psalm 29
Acts 8:14-17
Luke 3:15-17, 21-22

EPIPHANY
Isaiah 60:1-6
Psalm 72:1-7, 10-14
Ephesians 3:1-12
Matthew 2:1-12

---

*Year C—Advent/
Christmas, Year A.
The Revised Common
Lectionary copyright ©
1992 by the Consultation
on Common Texts (CCT).
Used by permission.

January 12–18
Isaiah 62:1-5
Psalm 36:5-10
1 Corinthians 12:1-11
John 2:1-11

January 19–25
Nehemiah 8:1-3, 5-6, 8-10
Psalm 19
1 Corinthians 12:12-31a
Luke 4:14-21

January 26—February 1
Jeremiah 1:4-10
Psalm 71:1-6
1 Corinthians 13:1-13
Luke 4:21-30

February 2–8
Isaiah 6:1-8, (9-13)
Psalm 138
1 Corinthians 15:1-11
Luke 5:1-11

February 9–15
Jeremiah 17:5-10
Psalm 1
1 Corinthians 15:12-20
Luke 6:17-26

February 16–22
TRANSFIGURATION
Exodus 34:29-35
Psalm 99
2 Corinthians 3:12–4:2
Luke 9:28-36, (37-43)

ASH WEDNESDAY
LECTIONS:
Joel 2:1-2, 12-17 (*or*
Isaiah 58:1-12)
Psalm 51:1-17
2 Corinthians 5:20b–6:10
Matthew 6:1-6, 16-21

February 23—March 1
FIRST SUNDAY IN LENT
Deuteronomy 26:1-11
Psalm 91:1-2, 9-16
Romans 10:8b-13
Luke 4:1-13

March 2–8
SECOND SUNDAY IN LENT
Genesis 15:1-12, 17-18
Psalm 27
Philippians 3:17–4:1
Luke 13:31-35 (*or* Luke
9:28-36)

March 9–15
THIRD SUNDAY IN LENT
Isaiah 55:1-9
Psalm 63:1-8
1 Corinthians 10:1-13
Luke 13:1-9

March 16–22
FOURTH SUNDAY IN LENT
Joshua 5:9-12
Psalm 32
2 Corinthians 5:16-21
Luke 15:1-3, 11b-32

Lectionary Readings

March 23–29
FIFTH SUNDAY IN LENT
Isaiah 43:16-21
Psalm 126
Philippians 3:4b-14
John 12:1-8

March 30—April 5
PASSION/PALM SUNDAY

Liturgy of the Palms
Luke 19:28-40
Psalm 118:1-2, 19-29

Liturgy of the Passion
Isaiah 50:4-9a
Psalm 31:9-16
Philippians 2:5-11
Luke 22:14–23:56
   (or Luke 23:1-49)

April 6–12
HOLY WEEK
(selected lections)

   Monday: Isaiah 42:1-9;
   John 12:1-11

   Tuesday: Isaiah 49:1-7;
   John 12:20-36

   Wednesday: Isaiah
   50:4-9a; John 13:21-32

   Maundy Thursday:
   Exodus 12:1-4, (5-10),
   11-14; Psalm 116:1-2,
   12-19; John 13:1-17,
   31b-35

   Good Friday: Isaiah
   52:13–53:12; Psalm 22;
   Hebrews 10:16-25;
   John 18:1–19:42

Holy Saturday: Job
14:1-14; 1 Peter 4:1-8;
Matthew 27:57-66

EASTER SUNDAY
(April 12)
Isaiah 65:17-25
Psalm 118:1-2, 14-24
1 Corinthians 15:19-26
John 20:1-18
   (or Luke 24:1-12)

April 13–19
Acts 5:27-32
Psalm 150
Revelation 1:4-8
John 20:19-31

April 20–26
Acts 9:1-6, (7-20)
Psalm 30
Revelation 5:11-14
John 21:1-19

April 27—May 3
Acts 9:36-43
Psalm 23
Revelation 7:9-17
John 10:22-30

May 4–10
Acts 11:1-18
Psalm 148
Revelation 21:1-6
John 13:31-35

May 11–17
Acts 16:9-15
Psalm 67
Revelation 21:10, 22–22:5
John 14:23-29
   (or John 5:1-9)

May 18–24
Acts 16:16-34
Psalm 97
Revelation 22:12-14,
   16-17, 20-21
John 17:20-26
   or ASCENSION DAY
   lections
      Acts 1:1-11
      Psalm 47
         (or Psalm 110)
      Ephesians 1:15-23
      Luke 24:44-53

May 25–31
PENTECOST
Acts 2:1-21
Psalm 104:24-34, 35b
Romans 8:14-17
John 14:8-17, (25-27)

June 1–7
TRINITY
Proverbs 8:1-4, 22-31
Psalm 8
Romans 5:1-5
John 16:12-15

June 8–14
1 Kings 21:1-21a
Psalm 5:1-8
Galatians 2:15-21
Luke 7:36–8:3

June 15–21
1 Kings 19:1-15a
Psalms 42 and 43
Galatians 3:23-39
Luke 8:26-39

June 22–28
2 Kings 2:1-2, 6-14
Psalm 77:1-2, 11-20
Galatians 5:1, 13-25
Luke 9:51-62

June 29—July 5
2 Kings 5:1-14
Psalm 30
Galatians 6:(1-6), 7-16
Luke 10:1-11, 16-20

July 6–12
Amos 7:7-17
Psalm 82
Colossians 1:1-14
Luke 10:25-37

July 13–19
Amos 8:1-12
Psalm 52
Colossians 1:15-28
Luke 10:38-42

July 20–26
Hosea 1:2-10
Psalm 85
Colossians 2:6-15, (16-19)
Luke 11:1-13

July 27—August 2
Hosea 11:1-11
Psalm 107:1-9, 43
Colossians 3:1-11
Luke 12:13-21

August 3–9
Isaiah 1:1, 10-20
Psalm 50:1-8, 22-23
Hebrews 11:1-3, 8-16
Luke 12:32-40

August 10–16
Isaiah 5:1-7
Psalm 80:1-2, 8-19
Hebrews 11:29–12:2
Luke 12:49-56

August 17–23
Jeremiah 1:4-10
Psalm 71:1-6
Hebrews 12:18-29
Luke 13:10-17

August 24–30
Jeremiah 2:4-13
Psalm 81:1, 10-16
Hebrews 13:1-8, 15-16
Luke 14:1, 7-14

August 31—September 6
Jeremiah 18:1-11
Psalm 139:1-6, 13-18
Philemon 1–21
Luke 14:25-33

September 7–13
Jeremiah 4:11-12, 22-28
Psalm 14
1 Timothy 1:12-17
Luke 15:1-10

September 14–20
Jeremiah 8:18–9:1
Psalm 79:1-9
1 Timothy 2:1-7
Luke 16:1-13

September 21–27
Jeremiah 32:1-3*a*, 6-15
Psalm 91:1-6, 14-16
1 Timothy 6:6-19
Luke 16:19-31

September 28—October 4
Lamentations 1:1-6
Psalm 137
2 Timothy 1:1-14
Luke 17:5-10

October 5–11
Jeremiah 29:1, 4-7
Psalm 66:1-12
2 Timothy 2:8-15
Luke 17:11-19

October 12–18
Jeremiah 31:27-34
Psalm 119:97-104
2 Timothy 3:14–4:5
Luke 18:1-8

October 19–25
Joel 2:23-32
Psalm 65
2 Timothy 4:6-8, 16-18
Luke 18:9-14

October 26—November 1
Habakkuk 1:1-4; 2:1-4
Psalm 119:137-144
2 Thessalonians 1:1-4,
    11-12
Luke 19:1-10
ALL SAINTS DAY
(NOVEMBER 1):
    Daniel 7:1-3, 15-18
    Psalm 149
    Ephesians 1:11-23
    Luke 6:20-31

Lectionary Readings

November 2–8
Haggai 1:15b–2:9
Psalm 145:1-5, 17-21
2 Thessalonians 2:1-5,
    13-17
Luke 20:27-38

November 9–15
Isaiah 65:17-25
Isaiah 12 (*or* Psalm 118)
2 Thessalonians 3:6-13
Luke 21:5-19

November 16–22
Jeremiah 23:1-6
Luke 1:68-79
    (*or* Psalm 46)
Colossians 1:11-20
Luke 23:33-43

November 23–29
**FIRST SUNDAY OF
ADVENT**
Isaiah 2:1-5
Psalm 122
Romans 13:11-14
Matthew 24:36-44

**November 30—
December 6**
**SECOND SUNDAY OF
ADVENT**
Isaiah 11:1-10
Psalm 72:1-7, 18-19
Romans 15:4-13
Matthew 3:1-12

December 7–13
**THIRD SUNDAY
OF ADVENT**
Isaiah 35:1-10
Psalm 146:5-10
    (*or* Luke 1:47-55)
James 5:7-10
Matthew 11:2-11

December 14–20
**FOURTH SUNDAY
OF ADVENT**
Isaiah 7:10-16
Psalm 80:1-7, 17-19
Romans 1:1-7
Matthew 1:18-25

December 21–27
Isaiah 63:7-9
Psalm 148
Hebrews 2:10-18
Matthew 2:13-23

CHRISTMAS EVE
    Isaiah 9:2-7
    Psalm 96
    Titus 2:11-14
    Luke 2:1-20

CHRISTMAS DAY
    Isaiah 52:7-10
    Psalm 98
    Hebrews 1:1-4 ,(5-12)
    John 1:1-14

December 28–31
Isaiah 60:1-6
Psalm 72:1-7, 10-14
Ephesians 3:1-12
Matthew 2:1-12

A Prayer for Ending

God of new creating,
who beckons us
to the dance of birthing
and sustains us
in our laboring,
hear this prayer:

From fear of the unknown
deliver me.
From doubts of my creativity
deliver me.
From ridicule by those around me
deliver me.
From my excuses about my abilities,
   my age, my education,
   my looks, my status
deliver me.

With your promise of companionship
comfort me.
With your creative spirit
bless me
With your pledge of sustenance
strengthen me.
With your embrace of all of me
heal me and set me to motion

You who called me to life
that you may be born again in me,
blessed be in this and all seasons!

—Jan L. Richardson

From *Sacred Journeys: A Woman's Book of Daily Prayer* (Nashville, TN: Upper Room Books, 1995). Used by permission.

ᛒ 1998 ᛒ

JANUARY

S	M	T	W	T	F	S
				1	2	3
4	5	6	7	8	9	10
11	12	13	14	15	16	17
18	19	20	21	22	23	24
25	26	27	28	29	30	31

FEBRUARY

S	M	T	W	T	F	S
1	2	3	4	5	6	7
8	9	10	11	12	13	14
15	16	17	18	19	20	21
22	23	24	25	26	27	28

MARCH

S	M	T	W	T	F	S
1	2	3	4	5	6	7
8	9	10	11	12	13	14
15	16	17	18	19	20	21
22	23	24	25	26	27	28
29	30	31				

APRIL

S	M	T	W	T	F	S
			1	2	3	4
5	6	7	8	9	10	11
12	13	14	15	16	17	18
19	20	21	22	23	24	25
26	27	28	29	30		

MAY

S	M	T	W	T	F	S
					1	2
3	4	5	6	7	8	9
10	11	12	13	14	15	16
17	18	19	20	21	22	23
24	25	26	27	28	29	30
31						

JUNE

S	M	T	W	T	F	S
	1	2	3	4	5	6
7	8	9	10	11	12	13
14	15	16	17	18	19	20
21	22	23	24	25	26	27
28	29	30				

JULY

S	M	T	W	T	F	S
			1	2	3	4
5	6	7	8	9	10	11
12	13	14	15	16	17	18
19	20	21	22	23	24	25
26	27	28	29	30	31	

AUGUST

S	M	T	W	T	F	S
						1
2	3	4	5	6	7	8
9	10	11	12	13	14	15
16	17	18	19	20	21	22
23	24	25	26	27	28	29
30	31					

SEPTEMBER

S	M	T	W	T	F	S
		1	2	3	4	5
6	7	8	9	10	11	12
13	14	15	16	17	18	19
20	21	22	23	24	25	26
27	28	29	30			

OCTOBER

S	M	T	W	T	F	S
				1	2	3
4	5	6	7	8	9	10
11	12	13	14	15	16	17
18	19	20	21	22	23	24
25	26	27	28	29	30	31

NOVEMBER

S	M	T	W	T	F	S
1	2	3	4	5	6	7
8	9	10	11	12	13	14
15	16	17	18	19	20	21
22	23	24	25	26	27	28
29	30					

DECEMBER

S	M	T	W	T	F	S
		1	2	3	4	5
6	7	8	9	10	11	12
13	14	15	16	17	18	19
20	21	22	23	24	25	26
27	28	29	30	31